ISBN 978-0-484-86287-5
PIBN 10525380

This book is a reproduction of an important historical work. Forgotten Books uses
state-of-the-art technology to digitally reconstruct the work, preserving the original format
whilst repairing imperfections present in the aged copy. In rare cases, an imperfection in
the original, such as a blemish or missing page, may be replicated in our edition. We do,
however, repair the vast majority of imperfections successfully; any imperfections that
remain are intentionally left to preserve the state of such historical works.

ATHCLICISM: Roman a
Anglican · By A. M. Fairbai
M.A. D.D. LL.D. Principal of Mansfie
College Oxford

SECOND EDITION

LONDON: HODDER AND
STOUGHTON 27
PATERNOSTER ROW 1899

Butler & Tanner, The Selwood Printing Works, Frome, and London.

TO

My Friends and Colleagues

THE TUTORS OF

MANSFIELD COLLEGE OXFORD

Contents

b

INTRODUCTION

THE Studies collected in this volume may fairly claim to be neither sporadic nor occasional essays, but chapters of a coherent and progressive work. While written at different times, they are yet products of continuous reading and reflexion on the problems they discuss. They have all been carefully revised, here abridged, there enlarged, but they have not been recast, nor have the notes of time and circumstance been erased.

The natural history of a book may have no great significance for any one except the man whose history it is. But there are cases where, apart from it, the true inwardness of the book may be hidden from the reader. Now what drew the author to the field which he seeks here in part to explore was a double interest—a religious and a philosophical, the one being the direct outcome of the other. On the religious side he was attracted by the men who had been the makers and leaders of the Catholic Revival, by what appeared their spirit of devotion, their sincerity, their simplicity of purpose and honesty of belief in an age of intellectual complexity, unrest, and change. They were picturesque figures, had

stood out from the prosaic commonplace of the
modern day ; they had loved the sound of the battle,
had known how to handle their weapons, and how to
smite and slay and not spare. They appealed to his
imagination, lived amid something of the glamour
which magnifies and adorns, and they illustrated the
heroism that can at once contend for victory and
live unvanquished amid and after defeat. He feels
as if reverence for the men who have striven and
suffered for the faith ran in his blood. The heroes of
his boyish dreams were saints, and the saints heroes
who had, by being faithful unto death, consecrated
the hills and moorlands he loves. And the Churchmen he had been taught to honour were not those
who walked in prosperous places and lived in comfort with well-trained and conformable consciences ;
but those who had been too rigorous and veracious
of soul to profess a belief they did not hold. And
when in comparative youth he came upon Newman's
Apologia, it seemed as if he had come upon a man
of the ancient heroic strain. He was blind to the
transcendent art of the book, to its apologetic purpose, to the imagination which had idealized its
author even to himself ; he only felt the passionate
conviction of the man, his obedience to the inexorable logic which through the intellect ruled his will.
Hence came the desire to know more intimately this
marvellous personality and the men who surrounded
him, who influenced him, whom he influenced, the ideas
and aims they had in common, the cause for which

they suffered, and the ends for which they strove.
But with the increase of knowledge came a discovery
that qualified the religious sympathy. Why did their
spirit express itself in the way it did, assume a form
and follow methods which were not only a protest
against all that the author's heroes, saints, and martyrs
had suffered for, but a denial of their heroism and
saintliness, and a reduction of themselves to vulgar
schismatics and of their beliefs to profane heresies?
The more the men were approached from this side,
the more the picturesque colour faded from their
faces ; and the more they appeared as victims of
sectarian spites, ill-informed, prejudiced, and violent,
darkened by qualities which neither literary genius,
nor spiritual passion, nor religious emotion and aims
could dispossess of their intrinsic meanness.

The consequence was the formulation of a most
interesting problem, though, unhappily, a problem of
an order too common in religious history :—How was
it that intellectual or even ecclesiastical differences
could so pervert the judgment as to make men unjust
to a piety so pure and noble as to be a reproof to
their own? Did not this signify a moral defect, a
blindness which could not but dim the clearness or
lessen the sureness of their spiritual vision? And this
vexing question became still more distressing when
it appeared that their own minds were not so simple
or so lucid and constant as had seemed. Some of
the " Tracts," and books like Froude's *Remains*, had
much in them to shock old-fashioned prejudices : and,

of course, there are occasions when such prejudices
ought to be shocked. But here was a moral per-
versity which would not be just to good causes and
better men. And in those early years, before the
imagination had idealized the Oxford men and movement, when the work was rough and the weapons
were even as the work, the persons who were thus
unjust showed themselves greatly in need of the
charity which thinks no evil, judges gently, and
hopes much. The man who looks back at them
through the serener atmosphere of to-day wonders
that they suffered so much; the man who comes
to them through the literature of the times may
well wonder that they suffered so little and prevailed
so completely. For they not only wrote with calculated vehemence, but they boldly practised " eco-
nomies," held back what they ought to have stated,
revealed their minds and purpose as those they
wished to lead were able to bear it; counselled
" reserve " and other things which men they inso-
lently assailed or despised would have scorned to
do. It was a point which touched the writer closely;
it moved him then and moves him now. Men
whose saintliness was to him a matter of experience,
of whom he could not think without, so to speak,
uncovering his soul as if in the presence of the
most Holy, were too near God and too like God
to be fit subjects of opprobrium by persons who
seemed so possessed of our commoner mortal frailties.

The religious interest thus passed naturally over

into the philosophical. Why should a mind open to truth be insensible to justice? Why should those zealous for religion judge so falsely those who were as religious as themselves, and who may have suffered infinitely more for conscience' sake? The question was more than a problem in casuistry; it involved principles that carried one down to the very roots of things—the attitude of the mind to religion as a whole, to God as truth and as righteousness. But though this determined the philosophical problem in its earliest form, it did not by any means fix its latest. On the contrary, it has never ceased to keep enlarging and growing in complexity. We are face to face with all the forces which make for differentiation in religion, tendencies which, by throwing the emphasis now on its intellectual and now on its ethical side, here on its social and political, there on its historical and traditional elements, create new parties and new sects. And we have seen in our own lifetime these tendencies produce their ancient and invariable results; and these Studies may be taken as a contribution to the discussion of this subject by the help of material which contemporary men and movements have supplied. The author is not so vain as to think that his contribution is more than a very partial handling of the questions he would fain have discussed; but he can say with perfect truth that he has honestly laboured to understand the men, and to render such an account of them, the tendencies amid which they lived, and the movement they helped to create and to guide, as need shame neither truth nor charity. He may also plead that while these Studies have everywhere had a very positive end in view, they have not been written with a controversial purpose. He has not attempted, indeed, to write with colourless neutrality, for it has not been granted to him on such questions to feel neutral or to be colourless. But it is a mistake to imagine that a man without convictions can comprehend convinced men : the men who are best radically disqualified for criticism being only of two sorts, (a) those who think there is no truth worth believing or contending for; and (β) those who so hold their own beliefs as to see no reason and recognize no truth in the beliefs of other men. From these disqualifications the writer would like, were he at all able, to keep himself tolerably free.

In preparing these Studies for the press the author has had frequent occasion to review his own earlier judgments. This is a process which it is good for a man to have now and then to undergo, especially as it is the most excellent, because the most effective, of all methods for teaching him humility. But in the present instance he feels that as regards his graver judgments on men, tendencies, and principles, which he can truthfully say were slowly, laboriously, and painfully reached, he has little to modify and nothing to cancel or recall. In particular he would specify—

(a) The conclusions reached on the part intellectual scepticism played in the development of Newman's mind and faith. There has been in our century no character more difficult of analysis, no intellect at once loftier and narrower, no greater adept at reasoning or thinker more arbitrary in selecting and defining the premisses from which he reasoned ; no one who was more transcendently and transparently sincere or so acutely sophistical, or who had in such a degree the faculty for both logical and moral analysis and the incapacity or distaste for the higher speculation. His passion for certitude was equalled only by his inability to find it in any way save by the sacrifice of his intellectual pride; and there was nothing in which he gloried more than the invincible logic which drove him to what was at once the surrender and the realization of self.

(β) The analysis of the course and tendency of the Catholic movement, especially in its effects on the mind and status of the Anglican clergy. It has been nothing short of a calamity to the English Church that her claims to be Catholic have been made to turn so much on the question of orders : for it has disturbed the whole balance of the Anglican system, and changed the ministry from being its means of service into being its pillar and ground of truth. The immense emphasis which has been laid upon the apostolic descent of the priesthood, has created a body which can only live by every priest feeling as if he were himself invested with apostolic authority. They have pleaded that they were a Catholic Church because they had an apostolic ministry; but it was easier to argue that their ministry was apostolic than to organize Catholic unity and order. The Anglican Church is here almost the exact opposite of the Roman. There is no one the Church of Rome more profoundly distrusts than the independent priest, no one whose existence it has contrived to make so impossible within its ample but clearly drawn borders. From the humblest parish priest right up through bishop and archbishop to the Pope himself, the dependence of the lower on the higher office is consistent and complete. Rome is specially careful of the priest in the act and article of absolution; it fears the confessional even while it lives to a large extent by the powers it gives. And so it has jealously surrounded the penitent with a means of protection against the confessor, and it has with equal jealousy imposed upon the confessor limitations he may not overstep, and responsibilities he must not forget. But the Anglican priest is free from the canonical laws which bind the Roman, and he can work his inexperienced will, and often does work it, not simply within the parish or congregation, but even within the more sacred sanctuary formed by the souls of its most pious members. For the Anglican episcopate, even more than the priesthood, is not as the Roman. It is in a cardinal degree civil both as to its origin and as to the terms on which it exercises jurisdiction and discipline. The Bishop has to think not simply of administering a canon law, but much more of those secular courts, juridical in mind, legal in spirit and in method, civil in sanction and in source, that may be called upon to review, modify, or even disallow his judgment. And as he knows he can never act as if he were a purely ecclesiastical authority, he has become a master in the art of inaction, which tempts the more convinced or daring of his clergy to become masters in the art of doing as they list. The result is an episcopate burdened with administrative functions, but almost void of authority, judicial and disciplinary. And as if out of sheer love of an ironical situation, those of the clergy who have most pleaded for an apostolical episcopate as the condition of Catholic unity, defer least to the episcopal voice. Thus after the Primate had spoken out with remarkable courage on the questions most keenly debated in the Anglican Church, an Anglo-Catholic priest, typical in his devotion, in his piety, in his self-denial and self-assertion, wrote to the public prints to say that it was of vital importance to realize that these primatial charges were "merely the words of a single Anglican, however learned, however exalted, however revered, and cannot in any sense bind the conscience of any other Anglican." And he adds, "One can hardly imagine what the Church of England would have been to-day, if at any other period of her existence the *ipse dixit* of the Primate, or indeed of the whole Episcopate," had been regarded as more than "the mind of individual prelates." It would be hard to discover a more extreme form of Protestantism. It is individualism so pronounced as to be a personal rather than congregational independency. For this independence of the bishop finds its parallel in the independence of the parish ; the writers who have most exhaustively proved the ministry apostolic are least able to discover who or what the laity are, whether they are only " communicants," or " all baptized and confirmed persons." And so the one clear and certain divine order in the Church is the priesthood ; and they, emancipated from the rule of the bishops on the one hand, and the control of the laity on the other, are free to follow the authority which belongs to their descent. And this is the high Catholicism which the Anglican has realized.

(γ) Since the criticism of Mr. Balfour's *Foundations of Belief* was written, Professor Seth Pringle-Patteson has published his genial and kindly interpretation of that ingenious book. He has said the most and best that can be said in its defence. But he will not misunderstand me if I claim the right of a criticized critic to say that his essay seems to me an excellent example of *hineinerklärung*, and saves Mr. Balfour's argument by sacrificing much of his competence as a philosophical writer. And this appears a rather harder measure than ought to be dealt out to so very capable a student in the field of philosophy.

The scope of the book is not so large as the title

may seem to suggest. Catholicism, even as qualified by Roman, does not here denote the Church of Rome. Its system is not here in dispute. Were it so, the work would have been quite other than it is, both as regards matter and form. What is meant is the Catholicism which grew out of the Anglican Revival—the movement, with its Roman affinities and ideals, which began in Oxford, and has so profoundly modified the religious temper and practices of the English Church and people.

It only remains to add a single word of gratitude to the editor of the *Contemporary Review*, where these chapters originally appeared, for his kind consent to their republication.

I

THE CHURCHES AND THE IDEAL OF RELIGION

§ I. *The Distinction between Religion and Church*

1. THE people of England seem to be at last awakening to the truth that to have a church or churches is not the same thing as to have a religion. Churches are, that religion may be realized: but it does not follow that to multiply or enlarge churches is to realize religion. On the contrary, it is possible by having too much church to have too little religion; the most perfectly organized and administered ecclesiasticism may but effectually imprison the living Spirit of God. The churches are the means, but religion is the end; and if they, instead of being well content to be and to be held means, good in the degree of their fitness and efficiency, regard and give themselves out as ends, then they become simply the most irreligious of institutions, mischievous exactly in proportion to their strength. Religion is too rich and varied a thing to be capable of incorporation in any one church, or even in all the churches ; and the church that claims to be able to embody it, whether for a people

or for humanity, simply shows the poverty and impotence of its own religious ideal. It is a small thing, nay more an easy thing, for a church to make out its historical continuity and catholicity—that is only a matter of deft criticism and courageous argument; but it is a great thing for any church to have created or to be creating a society correspondent to the ideal of Christ.

Now, the truth that seems to be breaking upon the English people is this—that they have still to set about the realization of this ideal, and that to accomplish it they must take some higher and nobler way than the ancient method of founding and maintaining churches. What makes us feel so distant from the religion of Christ, is not the amount of belligerent and most audible unbelief, both of the critical and uncritical order; nor the relatively, and to many good people dishearteningly, small number of church-goers; nor the failure of missionary zeal to keep pace with the increase of the population and its aggregation in large towns; nor the number and quality of the bodies that describe themselves as churches, but other no less honourable bodies as sects; nor the decline in the churches of the love that seeks to emulate, and the growth of the envy that loves to disparage; but something more radical than any one of these, or even than all of them—the small degree in which the Christian ideal has been and is the constitutive and regulative idea of the State and society in England. We have suddenly

become conscious that our legislation and civilization have been too little penetrated by the spirit of
Christ, while so pervaded and dominated by the
spirit of selfishness, that they have been making heathens faster and more effectually than the churches
have been able to make Christians. The people feel
that the Church, satisfied with what the State has
done for *it*, has failed to stand by them in their dumb
quest after a fuller justice and a fairer freedom; and
that they but do as they have been done by, when
they forsake the society which forsook them in their
sorest need. It is easy to be indiscriminate, to
speak without measure as to the rights of property
being the wrongs of man; but evidences, too many
to be enumerated, prove that property and privilege
have been so conceived and guarded as to help in
the production of certain great social disasters and
dangers. The idea that the men who could best
assert their rights had the most rights to assert, has
been too potent a factor in the creation of our social
order, and may yet beget a reaction of the sort men
call revolution. The converse, indeed, were more of
a Christian principle—those least able to assert their
rights have, if not most rights to be asserted, most
need for their assertion; for the things they claim in
weakness are the duties of those in power. And as
the religion which Christ revealed and embodied is
most jealous about the performance of these duties,
the church that neglects their enforcement abdicates
its truest social function. And it is because there has

been such neglect in England that we are face to face with so many grave problems—political, social, religious. We have in our midst outcast masses, multitudes who have lapsed into something worse than heathenism, into merest savagery; and have done so, not through lack of religious agencies, but simply through lack of religion, the absence or inaction of the higher Christian ideals in the mind, heart, and conscience of the body politic. The worst depravity, because the least open to reproof or change, is not the depravity of the individual, but of the class or State; and the churches, while doing zealous battle against the less, have too much forgotten the greater. And now it is seen that neglect brings the inevitable retribution. Our outcast are our lapsed classes; and it is easier to teach religion to the heathen than to restore the lapsed. There is less hope of a debased civilization than of the rudest and frankest naturalism.

The judgment expressed in these sentences may be thought too sweeping ; yet, however much he may be inclined to qualify it, no thoughtful Christian man can regard the religious condition of the English people with a light or satisfied heart. Of course, a determined optimism can find much to say in its own behalf. It can reckon up the sums spent on building churches, supplementing stipends, founding and maintaining religious houses and institutions, prosecuting missionary enterprises at home and abroad ; and may victoriously argue that these sums are so immense as to prove the spirit of faith to be a living and zealous spirit, devoted and self-sacrificing. It can also appeal to the multitude of beneficent agencies and benevolent institutions worked by the churches ; and may veraciously enough affirm that without them the hand of charity and generous helpfulness would be almost, if not altogether, paralyzed. I am far from wishing either to question these facts or to deny the inference which may be most fairly drawn from them ; but the point lies here : Grant the facts and the inference to be alike true, ought they to satisfy the Christian conscience? or ought not that conscience—in the face of the destitution, depravity, utter and shameless godlessness, which exist in spite of all the expenditure and efforts of the churches— to be filled with deep dissatisfaction? For what do these evils mean? That our society is to the degree that they exist not only imperfectly Christian, but really un-Christian ; that, so far as they were pre- ventable, Church and State have alike been forgetful of their highest obligations, or unequal to their performance. To cure an evil is a less excellent thing than to prevent it ; and few things fill the heart with deeper pity than the thought that there are evils which ought not to have been, and would not have been, if the Christian religion had so reigned as to be sovereign in this realm. This is a sad and humiliating reflection to men who believe that Christianity is of God, instituted by Him that His will might be done on earth as it is done in heaven.

Centuries indeed are little to God; but they are
much to man. The thousand years that are but a
moment in the presence of His Eternal Being, are a
large fraction of the period allotted to humanity.
Loss of good is to it an irretrievable loss; and the
happiness of ages to come can never bless hapless
ages that have passed and perished. And if Christianity has, in the course of its history, not done all
the good it was intended to do, and therefore ought
to have done, then the result has been an absolute
loss to man; the possible best has not been reached
by him, the best possible has not been done by it.

2. Now, one main reason why our religion meets
with so much neglect and opposition is that it has
not prevented, or remedied in the measure man had
a right to expect of it, the evils from which he suffers.
Our modern Socialisms, Nihilisms, Secularisms, and
such-like, have not lived without a cause. In the
polemical method and by the polemical spirit they
can be easily dealt with; in the supple and dexterous
hands of an apologetical protagonist they can be made
to look void of intellectual strength, full of political
and economical immoralities. But it is a small thing
to expose their mental or moral crudities—that in no
way ends their being or prevents their rise; it is a
greater thing to inquire, Why are they?—what are
the causes and conditions of their existence?—for to
ask this, may be to find a way to prevent their
formation and growth. They are but symptoms of
a disease; cure the disease, and the symptoms will

cease. Now, these Nihilisms and Secularisms of ours have been born of the sense of evils religion ought to have mitigated or remedied, but has not. In despair of help from their natural helper, men have taken counsel with despair. In our anti-religious movements there is a dangerous fanaticism, the child of passion, not of thought. The unbelief the churches have to fear is not a thing of the critical or rebellious reason, but of the hate begotten of disappointed hopes. And because the hopes were legitimate, the disappointment is natural. The poor were right in expecting help from religion, in believing that its mission was to lift them out of their poverty, to make an end of the charities that are the luxuries of the rich and the miseries of the poor, and to create a society where freedom, justice, and plenty were to reign. But the people are wrong in making their revolt against religion, rather than against the causes and conditions which have hindered its realization. What they need is, not its destruction, but its emancipation; to destroy it were to destroy the only foundation on which a society, which shall be a free and ordered brotherhood, can be built; to emancipate it were to set all its ideal principles free for creative and incorporative action in society and the State. An order that is not moral can only be one based on force and maintained by despotism; an order that is moral must be based on religion and maintained by the principles that create and work through free men.

Here, then, there is raised a question of the deepest
interest: How, or under what conditions, can religion
be made most active and authoritative among a
people? What agencies or forms do its ideals need
that they may work most creatively and towards
completest embodiment? This is a question not concerned with the relations of Church and State, but
with the far more radical and determinative relations
of Church and Religion. There are no controversies
so wearisome and infructuous as our ecclesiastical,
but no problems of so vital and universal interest
as our religious; and here we so touch the heart
of the matter that our ecclesiastical is sublimed
into our most living religious question. In seeking
the reasons why the State, the civilization, and the
society of England are not so Christian as they
ought to be, we cannot escape asking whether
blame attaches to the churches? Proofs of historical
continuity and catholicity are but sad playthings
for the ingenious intellect, when urged in behalf
of churches confronted by such invincible evidences
of failure as are the miseries, the sins, the poverty
and want, the heathenisms and civilized savageries
of to-day. To find the causes of this failure in
the wickedness of man, were to make it stronger
than the religion ; to find them in the religion, were
to charge it with inherent weakness. But to seek
these causes in the churches, is to ask whether they
have fulfilled their mission, and whether they have
understood the mission they were meant to fulfil :

in other words, whether they have been so possessed with the ideal of religion as to live for it and it only, as to interpret it in the fittest forms and speech, and work for its realization in the best possible ways. In these questions we have our more immediate problem stated.

§ II. *The Relation between Theology and Polity*

1. Our problem raises indeed the question as to the polity of the Church, but not in a form that requires here detailed discussion. We postpone to a later chapter any attempt at historical criticism or adjudication between the claims of the rival systems. All that is here necessary, is to determine the relation between the religious ideal and the political form, which is the vehicle or medium through which the ideal is translated into reality. The vital questions in religion relate either to theology or polity; and these form so real and living a unity that the latter may be regarded as the organism or body through which the life or spirit of the former is expressed and realized in the field of personal and collective history. In theology the main matter is, how are we to conceive the truth? But in polity, how can we best translate it into concrete and living forms? In theology we are concerned with the ideal contents and aims of religion; but in polity with the means and methods for their realization. If the place and relation of ecclesiastical polity be so conceived, then its funda-

mental questions will touch the ideal on the one
hand, and the actual on the other; will bring us
face to face on the one side with the idea of religion,
and on the other with the forms in which it can
best be embodied, the institutions through which
it can be most completely realized. For a polity
to fail to understand the spirit and purpose of
religion, is to fail throughout; to succeed anywhere
it must succeed here. To express a true theology in
a living polity is, as it were, to charge a system with
the quickening and plastic potencies that can make
man live after the mind and as the image of God.

But if theology and polity be so related, then
the one must be studied and interpreted through
the other; because it is necessary that they in
character and quality correspond throughout. Out
of the idea of the religion the notion of the polity
ought to grow; to find the idea is to determine the
notion. This point of view will enable us the better
either to appraise or comprehend the more familiar
methods followed in discussions on this field. These
methods, which, though distinct, do not necessarily
exclude each other, may be described as the Biblical,
the Philosophical, the Political, and the Historical;
but each of them assumes or implies some underlying and determinative conception which gives to
its arguments all their relevance or cogency. This
deeper conception indeed determines the method to
be used, whether one or more is to be followed, and
on which the stress is to lie. Thus the Biblical

method, building on a large doctrine as to the Bible and the significance of the institutions it describes, either makes the Mosaic state the ideal which religious men ought to seek resolutely to realize in a hagiocracy or hierocracy ; or it erects the apostolic churches into the perfect and permanent model which all future Christian societies ought to copy and reproduce. By this method the polities of Rome and Geneva, of the Anglican and the Independent communities, have alike been defended. The Philosophical method, implying an exactly antithetical Biblical doctrine, works constructively from a given principle or series of premises, say the idea of law or order, which may be made to vindicate a papal, episcopal, or presbyterian polity, according as the thinker conceives the monarchical, the aristocratical, or the republican to be the most perfect form of government, most able to create order, to exercise and develop the noblest life. The Political method is indifferent or even hostile to all arguments that assume an absolute standard or permanent divine rule, and builds on expediency and prescriptive right. It was the characteristic creation of the eighteenth century, which, as became an age that had lost all faith in the Ideal, cultivated the happy optimism that identified the actual with the rational ; and, as a consequence, resisted all change as bad, standing strong in the conviction that there was no proof of right like the fact of possession. But there are many lofty and proud spirits who hate expediency, and believe that in matters of religion the only valid rights are divine ; and to them the historical method has offered a more excellent and agreeable way. They have formulated to themselves, on the one side, a narrow theory of history ; and, on the other, as the mental basis of all their work, a large supernaturalism, which made light of impossibilities and turned so much of the religious society as was constituted on given political lines, and stood in a given succession, into the one church of Christ. And they have then, by the help of a minute and curious, though not scientific or open-minded scholarship, laboured to represent this church of theirs as instituted of God, governed and inspired by Him, secured from the moment of creation till now in continuous being and activity by the orders and instruments, symbols and sacraments that were the conditions of His presence and the media of His grace.

2. Now these differences of method are not arbitrary or accidental ; they are the result of the underlying differences of thought or belief, of theology and the religious ideal. As this is, so must the polity be ; it is the men who have no religious ideal that have no ideal of polity, who, without any preference for what ought to be, accept what is and defend it as altogether of man—which is to them quite as good as being altogether of God. The men, indeed, who have most differed in method have often seemed to agree in end ; those who have used, and those who have

most deeply despised, the argument from expediency have stood often together within the pale of the same church, exponents and defenders of the same polity. But the association was accidental, the agreement only apparent, masking the utmost distance and dissonance of spirit. The church defended by arguments from expediency is no city of God, no ideal of the Eternal realized in time ; the church defended by the claims of divine right and authority must be of divine institution and guidance, to be a church at all. The man who sees in the church a department of the State, and the man who regards it as a direct and miraculous creation of God, miraculously governed, may by the irony of circumstances be ecclesiastical brethren ; but in the region of fundamental belief they are absolutely opposed, their only possible attitude to each other being one of radical disagreement and contradiction.

This, then, brings out the point to be here emphasized: in all such discussions the really cardinal matter is the underlying conception, the determinative principle or idea, the idea of religion. The ultimate questions in ecclesiastical polity are religious. What have to be dealt with are not so much opposed political systems as religious conceptions fundamentally different and distinct. But this position involves another: the fundamental is the creative and regulative, or constitutive idea. And this means that the church must be construed through the religion, not the religion through the church. The one must harmonize with the other; but the creative and normative idea is the religion, the church the created and accordant. And the latter must agree with the former, in order that it may be its interpreter, the agent or medium for its realization. But this again determines the order of our subsequent discussions: we must discover and define the idea of religion that we may find the ideal which has to be realized. And once we have found it, we shall be in a position to discuss and, if possible, determine what kind or order of polity or institution will best work its realization.

§ III. *The Idea of Religion*

1. Of the idea or nature of religion an exhaustive discussion is not here possible; the doctrine and its implicates must simply be stated in the most general way. Well, then, religion is here conceived neither as knowledge, whether described with Jacobi as faith, or with Schelling as intuition, or with Hegel as thought; nor as feeling, whether it be, as with Schleiermacher, the feeling of dependence, or, as with the author of *Natural Religion*, of admiration, or, as with Mr. Herbert Spencer, of wonder; nor as a sort of transfigured morality, whether it be represented with Lessing, as a species of objective conscience, meant to hasten the birth and action of the subjective, or with Kant, as duty apprehended as a divine command, or with Matthew Arnold, as "morality touched by emotion." Religion is no one of these, yet it is all of these—and something more. Each of

these definitions is simple only so long as there is no analysis ; but under analysis they one and all become as complex as the very notion they seek to define. Religion, indeed, is too large and rich a thing to be defined by any single term or reduced to any single element, whether intellectual, emotional, or moral ; it too completely covers and comprehends the whole nature of man to be denoted by a name borrowed from a section of his experience, or from one department of his rational activity. And so one may say that these definitions, taken together, would give a better idea of religion than taken singly or in isolation. There can be no religion without thought, for a man must conceive an object before he can sustain any rational relation to it; not to think, is to be without reason, and where no reason is, no religion can be. Nor can it be without feeling, for feeling, though distinguishable, is inseparable from thought. If we think, we must feel ; if we feel, we are conscious first of ourselves as subject, and next of a not-ourselves or object : and it depends on how we conceive the object whether our feeling be one of dependence, admiration, or wonder, or an emotion higher and comprehensive of all the three. Nor can religion exist apart from conduct or con-science ; for man cannot conceive himself standing in relation to a supernatural or a supreme power, without feeling himself constrained to act either in harmony with it or in opposition to it, and as subject to its judgment either of approval or the reverse.

And this involves the direct discipline of the moral nature and the exercise of the moral judgment.

Where the product includes in an equal degree intellectual, emotional, and moral elements, it cannot be traced to the sole causation of either the intellect, or the heart, or the conscience. We must find, then, a notion of religion large enough to comprehend these varied elements, able also to bind them into organic and living unity. Now, if we look out for the most general characteristic common to all faiths, we would say that in religion man conceives and realizes himself not as a mere sensuous and mortal individual, but as spirit, and conscious spirit, who has overcome, or who is endeavouring to overcome, the contradictions within his own nature, and between it and the order or system under and within which he lives. But so to conceive himself is to be for himself not simply a transitory detached or isolated individual, but a unit who is a member of an organic whole, a being with universal affinities, and relations both to the seen and the unseen—whether the unseen be conceived as the magic present in a fetish, or as collective humanity in its past, present, and future, or as an unknown force, or as a known and living God. It is hence not necessary that religion be theistic, to be so conceived ; it is meanwhile only necessary to see that man so conceiving himself and his relations is religious. But so conceived, religion becomes the conscious relation of man as spirit to the creative and universal and regnant Spirit, under whatever form he

may conceive Him ; in other and homelier and more
perfect words, religion is the relation realized by the
man who knows the love of God, loves God, and
feels bound to express his love in the fittest and
surest ways. Here thought, feeling, and conduct are
all contained, and stand in living and inseparable
unity. He who loves God knows God, lives in
harmony with the will he loves, and for its ends.

2. But it is necessary that some of the more significant principles implied in this position be made
explicit.

i. The determinative idea in religion is the idea of
God. A religion always is as its deity is—indeed,
the former is but the latter become explicit, as it were
the explicated idea of Him. As the one is conceived,
the other must be through and through. A religion
is perfect in the degree that its conception of God is
perfect ; it is the way in which a church thinks of
God that determines its religious place and power,
whether it be a standing or a falling church. And
so where God is conceived as the Absolutely Good,
as if He were the personalized moral energy of the
universe working beneficently on behalf of each and
of all, there the religion ought to be as if it were the
organized beneficence of humanity, the power that
works by divine inspiration for human good. For a
religion not to be as its God is, is to be a thing of
falsest nature, a satire on sincerity, a contradiction to
the very idea of the truth.

ii. The primary and causal relation in religion is

2

not man's to God, but God's to man. His action precedes and underlies ours. For Him to be is to act; wherever He is He is active, and His action may be silent, but is never stayed or inoperative. Hence God's relation to man is the basis of man's relation to God; and religion is but man become so conscious of this prior relation as to live in harmony with it, as to attempt to realize the life and ideals and ends that come through it. But this involves the counterpart and complement of the first principle— viz., that a religious man always is as his God is, an image or miniature of Him, a form realizing in time the thought of the Eternal. But so construed he becomes not simply a person related to God, but a vehicle of the divine ideas, an organ or agent of the divine purposes. A nature that touches the divine, and exists through it, must be penetrated and moved by it; but to be so penetrated and moved is to exist and to work for ends that are God's, though they may be ends that can only be realized through man. The religious individual is really the minister of a universal purpose, a temporal agent of the Eternal will.

iii. The function or end of the religious man is to be a minister or vehicle of the divine purposes: and so the function or office of religion is to qualify man for this work. To perform it he must have a nature more or less open to God, and stand, so to speak, in a relation of reciprocity with Him. The worst atheism is that which reduces all God's action in the world to interference or miracle. The supernaturalism which limits His grace and truth to a single church, however universal it may claim to be, profanely expels Him from nature and humanity. There is a sense in which the highest ecclesiasticism is the worst theism ; it lives largely by its denial or limitation of Deity. Nature is, because God everywhere acts ; religion is, because He is the everworking Spirit. In the field of nature He acts through forces ; in the field of history He acts through persons, and the persons who best serve Him are religious men, *i.e.*, the men who so love the divine will as to labour to bring everything in themselves and in society into harmony with it. Such men know that they are not saved for their own sakes merely, but for man's ; that to be religious is simply to become a means for the ends of God. For God governs man through men ; great and good personalities are the chiefest works of Providence, the agencies through which it accomplishes its noblest moral results. There is no contribution to the common good like a good man ; through him the mind of the race is lifted, its progress effected, something done towards the embodiment of the divine ideas, the realization of the divine order. It is in religion as in music. Nature is full of musical voices, of simple notes that sound melodiously in every ear ; but out of these the cultured and quickened imagination of the master can create harmonies such as Nature never has created or can create—can in his *Oratorio* weave sounds into symphonies so wondrous that they seem like the speech of the gods suddenly breaking articulate upon the ear of man, speaking of passions, hopes, fears, joys too tumultuous and vast for the human tongue to utter ; or opening and interpreting for mortals a world where, remote from discord or dissonance, thought and being move as to the stateliest music. So in the spiritual sphere the real and holy religious person is the master spirit, making audible to others the harmonies his imagination is the first to hear. In him the truths and ideas of God, as yet indistinctly seen or partially heard by the multitude, are embodied, become as it were incarnate and articulate, assume a visible and strenuous form that they may inspire men to nobler deeds, and show them how to create a higher manhood and purer society. For these two stand indissolubly together ; the most distinctly personal is still a collective good, reduces the amount of evil in the world, augments the forces that contend against it. The better a man is, the more he feels the burden and the pain of sorrow, the mightier his ambition to help in the creation of a happier and a more perfect state. And as his most individual are still universal ends, he must seek the help of the like-minded, attempt to organize the good against the evil in the world. Thus, as religious men multiply, the enthusiasm of pity is sure to increase, the energies directed against sin and suffering are certain to grow more victorious. Every man possessed of the Spirit of God feels the divine passion in the presence of sin : and so in him and his society, to the degree of their capacity, the redeeming energies of God may be said to work. The end of the Church is the salvation of the world, its redemption from the pain under which it has travailed from creation until now.

3. Let us see, then, whither our analysis of the idea of religion has conducted us :—Religion is essentially a relation of harmonious activity with the will of God ; the man who realizes this relation is a religious man, the society which exists through and for its realization is a religious society. So understood, religion may be regarded, on the one side, as God's method or way of working out His beneficent purposes ; on the other, as man's following the way that he may fulfil the ends of God. Through religion God creates the order, works the progress, and achieves the good of mankind ; and His agent or organ throughout is the religious man and society. From this point of view, everything that makes for human happiness and wholeness is of religion ; whatever fears man's growth in freedom, in culture, in science, in everything meant by progress and civilization, may be ecclesiastical, but is not religious. The organized society that seeks to enforce respect for its orders, observance of its ritual, participation in its worship, submission to its authority by invoking the terrors of the world to come, may be a church, but is not a religion. The distinctive note of the latter is that it looks at the duties of the moment in the light of eternity, the character and needs of the

individual as in the presence of the universal and in
relation to the imperishable ; and it does this not
that it may despise time and the individual, but that
it may magnify both ; not that it may enfeeble, but
that it may enlarge and strengthen duty ; not that it
may weaken the worth of character or make light of
human need, but that it may lend a mightier import
to the one, and give a vaster reach to the other.
The men who live as for eternity, believing that the
problem of their being is, in harmony with the will
of their Creator, to work out the ultimate order and
good of the universe, live under the noblest and
humanest inspiration possible to man. And this is
the inspiration given by religion ; to have it is to
breathe the thoughtful breath that comes of a living
faith. But this idea of religion requires, as a clear
necessity, that the polity which seeks to articulate
and incorporate and realize it be a polity that allows
the religious society to live under the inspiration of
its own ideals, under the control of its own truths,
obedient to its own laws, altogether as a society
whose energies and ends are all religious and all of
God.

§ IV. *The Ideal of Religion Embodied in Jesus Christ*

But so far the discussion has been almost purely
deductive ; and so it may be as well to confirm and
illustrate the conclusion from the inductive or historical side. To discuss the abstract idea of religion is

a small thing ; it is a greater to look at it as embodied and expressed in the supreme religious
personality of the race. In Jesus Christ what we
term the ideal was realized, perfect religion became
a living and articulate reality. Through His only-
begotten Son, God declared what He meant and
what He means man to be.

1. We must interpret Christ's idea of religion
through His life. That life was one of remarkable
simplicity, but still more remarkable significance.
There were in His day two traditional ideals of the
religious life, the priest's and the scribe's ; but His did
not conform to either. The priest's made the temple,
with its worship and priesthood, the great factor of
religion ; in the temple God was to be found, the
way into His presence was through His priests, the
method of winning His favour or obtaining pardon
was by their sacrifices. The holy man was the man
who came often to the temple and made generous use
of its priesthood, places, articles and modes of worship.
Worship conducted by authorized persons within the
sacred place and in the established way, became the
very essence of religion ; and the priesthood themselves are our witnesses as to how completely their
ceremonial had swallowed up God's moral law. The
ideal of the scribes was different, yet akin ; it was
made up of rules, constituted by regulations as to the
doing and ordering of the sensuous things of life. It
observed days and months and seasons, was great
in fasts and alms, in times and modes of prayer. It

found great merit in phylacteries and in the reading
of the Scriptures ; it was devotedly loyal to the
unwritten law, which was formed of ancient custom,
the decisions of the great synagogue or council of
their church, and the wisdom of the fathers. Knowledge of this law was the most esteemed learning, and
the esteem was expressed in a notable way ; the man
wise enough to interpret the law made laws by his
interpretations. And so the holy man of the scribe
forgot no sacred day or solemn time, neglected no
fast, gave alms of all he had, prayed by book, wor-
shipped according to rule, and otherwise toiled and
comported himself as became a man who lived by a
written and traditional code. Excellent men they
were—honest, scrupulous, faithful in the minutest
things, only forgetful that the kingdom and truth of
God were infinitely wider than their law. And here
the kinship of the ideals appears ; both could make
scrupulous, neither could make magnanimous, men.
Each had had its heroes, who had suffered, and even
died, in defence of altar and ritual, or through fidelity
to all the ordinances of the law ; but neither had
produced a man possessed of the enthusiasm of
humanity, full of holy passion for the universal or
humane moral ends of God. The man who has the
strength of fanaticism in things sacerdotal is by this
very fact made a stranger to the spirit and inspiration
of true religion.

For let us look at Jesus in relation to the priest
and the scribe. His ideal stood in so sharp an

antithesis to theirs that He was unintelligible to both, was regarded and treated by both as an absolute enemy. In the eye of the scribe He was a religious alien, standing outside the continuity and catholicity of Jewish tradition and doctrine ; in the eye of the priest He broke the unity of the order and worship established of old by God, consecrated by law and custom, possessed of divine authority, the very symbol of the national life and condition of the people's well-being. His home was in Galilee, remote from the city of the religion where the priest was the ruler and the sacerdotal was also the civil law. When He visited their city the priests could not understand Him, for His temple and worship were spiritual, His God was a Father who made sacrifices to save men, and did not need incense and sacrifices and burnt-offerings to become propitious towards them. And so they knew not what to do with Him, knew only how to hate Him, and how to glut their hate in the infamy and death of the cross. In the province where He familiarly lived, the distance of the priest and the presence of the Gentile made the atmosphere clearer, ritual law and custom less rigid ; and so it was more favourable to a religious development regulated throughout by the spontaneous and normal action of His own ideal. But here He met the Pharisee and the scribe, and their relation to Him was one of radical contradiction and fretful collision, proceeding from their fanatical devotion to the traditions of the fathers and their consequent inability

to understand His spirit and His truth. In His
daily and familiar life they found none of the customary signs of religion—fasting, alms, the phylactery,
stated forms and times and places for prayer, ceremonial cleanliness, punctilious observance of the
Sabbath law and customs; nay, they found not only
these absent, but a conduct that seemed studiously to
offend—kindly speech to Gentiles, association with
publicans and sinners, unheard-of liberty allowed to
His disciples and claimed for Himself on the Sabbath; and the right to do all this vindicated by the
denial of the authority of tradition and the elders,
and by the assertion of His own. It was to these
scrupulous and conscientious men all very sad, even
awful; and so they judged Him a profane person,
acting from no other purpose or motive than to
destroy the law and the prophets. As later the
Christians, too religious to be understood of the
heathen, were judged to be men without religion, and
condemned as atheists; so Christ, without any of the
notes distinctive of sacerdotal and legal piety, was
deemed altogether impious and declared worthy of
death.

2. But to the men He called and made clear of
eye and open of vision, the real secret of His spirit
stood disclosed. They saw that the denials were the
accidents of His life; but the affirmation of a new
religious ideal was its essence. Of this ideal the
prophets had dreamed, but He made it an articulate
reality. God was to Him what He had never yet

been to man—a living Father, loving, loved, in whom He was embosomed, through whom and to whom He lived. He knew no moment without His presence; suffered no grief the Father did not share; tasted no joy He did not send; spoke no word that was not of Him; did no act that was not obedience to His will. Where the relation was so immediately filial and beautiful, the mediation of a priest would have been an impertinence, the use of his sacrifices and forms an estrangement—the coming of a cold, dark cloud between the radiant soul of the Son and the gracious face of the Father. Where true love lives it must use its own speech, speak in its own name, and feel that it must touch and, as it were, hold with its own hands the higher love that loved it into being. And because He stood so related to the Father, He and the Father had one love, one work, one will, one end. To see Him was to see the Father; His working was the Father's. Through Him God lived among men; the glory men beheld in Him was the glory of the Only Begotten, the incarnated grace and truth. And so this love of God was love of man; in the Son of Man the Father of men served His children, and humanity came to know its God and the things in which He delighted. The best service of God was a ministry that redeemed from sin, a sacrifice that saved from death. The wonderful thing in religion was not what man gave to God, but what God gave to man—the good, the truth, the love—the way in which He bore his sins and

carried his sorrows, made human guilt an occasion
for divine pity, and the cure of hate the work of love.
What God is among His worlds Jesus was among
men. He is the mind and heart of God personalized
for humanity ; His universal ideal realized. And after
what manner did this realized ideal live? As embodied compassion, beneficence, truth, love, working
for the complete redemption of men. Every kind of
evil was to Him a misery from which He could not but
seek to save. Disease He loved to cure; poverty He
pitied, doing His utmost to create the temper before
which it should cease; the common afflictions of man
touched Him with sympathy, subdued Him to tears.
But what moved Him most was moral evil—the sight
of man in the hands of sin ; and in order to save him
from it, He took an altogether new way. He dismissed the venerable methods and impotent formal-
isms of the priest and the scribe ; and went in among
the guilty, that He might in the very heart of their
guilt awaken the love of good and of God. He did
not feel that He condescended, only that His love
was a sweet compulsion to save; they did not feel
His condescension, only the goodness that was too
pure for their sin to sully, that so thought of their
good as to win their souls for God. And the result
was altogether wonderful. The laws of the scribe and
the religion of the priest had only divided men—had
made good and evil accidents of custom, not qualities
and states of the living person, had cured no sinner,
had only created fictitious sins, the more damning

that they were so false. But the new spirit and way of Christ found the common manhood of men, united them, made sin moral, change from it possible, even a duty; made religion seem like the concentrated and organized moral energy of God working redemptively through men on behalf of man. There never was a grander or more fruitful revolution of thought, more needed on earth, more manifestly of heaven. He who accomplished it was indeed a Redeemer; through Him religion ceased to be an affair of.the priest or the magistrate, transacted in the temple and conducted by a ceremonial which was prescribed by law; and became the supreme concern of man, covering his whole life, working in every way for his amelioration, satisfied with nothing less than the perfect virtue and happiness alike of the individual and the race—in simple truth, God's own method for realizing in man His ideal of humanity.

3. As Jesus lived He taught; His teaching but articulated the ideal He embodied in His character and life. One thing in that teaching is most remarkable—the complete absence of sacerdotal ideas, the non-recognition of those customs and elements men had been wont to think essential to religion. He spoke of Himself as a teacher, never as a priest; assumed no priestly office, performed no priestly function, breathed an atmosphere that had no sacerdotal odour, that was full only of the largest and most fragrant humanity. He instituted no sacerdotal office or rite, appointed no man to any sacerdotal duty,

sent His disciples forth to be teachers or preachers,
made no man of them a priest, created no order of
priesthood to which any man could belong. Worship
to Him was a matter of the Spirit; it needed no
consecrated place or person—needed only the heart
of the son to be real before the Father. The best
worship was obedience; the man perfect as God is
perfect was the man who pleased God. His beati-
tudes were all reserved for ethical qualities of mind,
were never promised on any ceremonial or sacerdotal
condition. His good man was " poor in spirit,"
" meek," " merciful," " pure in heart," "hungering after
righteousness," " a peacemaker." In describing His
ideal of goodness He found its antitheses in the
ideals of the temple and tradition. His example of
universal benevolence was "the good Samaritan"; its
contradiction the priest and the Levite. True prayer
was illustrated by the penitent publican, false by the
formal Pharisee. The parables that vindicated His
treatment of sinners enforced the high doctrine that
nothing was so agreeable to God as their salvation,
that the mission of the godlike was to seek and save
them. The duty that summarized all others was love
to God; the man that loved most obeyed best—for he
could not but obey. To love God was to love man,
to love the Divine Spirit was to do a divine part, to
be pitiful, to forgive as God forgives, to bear ill and
do good, to act unto others in a godlike way that
they might be won to godlike conduct. And He did
not conceive good men as isolated—they formed a

society, a kingdom. The citizens of His kingdom were the men who heard His voice and followed His way. God reigned in and over them, and they existed for His ends, to create good and overcome evil. The kingdom they constituted was "of heaven," opposed in source and nature to those founded in the despotisms and iniquities of earth; and also "of God," proceeded from the Creator and Sovereign of man, that His own high order might be realized. Such being its nature, it could be incorporated in no polity, organized under no local forms, into no national or temporal system; it was a "kingdom of the truth," and all who were of the truth belonged to it. It was a sublime idea; the good and holy of every land and race were gathered into a glorious fellowship, dwelt together, however far apart or mutually unknown, as citizens of the same Eternal City, with all their scattered energies so unified by the will of God as to be co-ordinated and co-operant factors of human progress and happiness. Men have not yet risen to the clear and full comprehension of this ideal; and the tardiest in reaching it are those organized polities or institutions which boast themselves sole possessors of Christ's truth and life.

The meaning of Christ's person and teaching for our thesis is too evident to need detailed discussion. To Christian men He is the normal and normative religious person—*i.e.*, the person whose living is their law, who made the standard to which they ought to conform, and who distributes the influences creative of conformity. Now, in Him religion was a perfect relation to God expressed in speech and action creative of a perfect humanity, a humanity made through knowledge of God obedient to Him. As embodied in Him, religion was in the presence of sin and sorrow a holy passion, a suffering unto sacrifice due to a love that identified the sinless Seeker with the sinner He sought; but in the presence of the salvability of man, it was an enthusiasm of redemption, the victorious working of the Spirit that can spare no evil and can be pleased with no good that falls short of the perfection which can alone satisfy God. So understood, religion is man's living in loving and holy harmony with the will of God; and its work, the creation of a humanity that shall in all its persons, relations, and institutions, express and realize this harmony.

§ V. *The Ideal of Christ and the Christian Churches*

Such then is the ideal of the religion of Christ; we have now to discuss briefly the relation of the churches to it.

I. Our fundamental principle here is this: The churches exist by the religion, and for it; the religion does not exist because of the churches, or for them. The religion is the creative, the church the created idea; and here, as everywhere, the law ought to be valid, that the measure of truth for the created idea is that it shall harmonize with and truly express the creative. The churches must be construed through the religion, not the religion through the churches. It is true independently of them, but they are right only as they are in nature and character throughout accordant with it. Now this accordancy may be tested in two ways: either by comparing the two ideals, that of the church and that of the religion, or by the simple historical inquiry, Has the church made the people among whom it has lived fulfil, individually and collectively, Christ's ideal, or approximate to the fulfilment of it? The latter is a grave question for all the churches. The degree in which they have worked this realization is the measure of their success; the degree in which they have not, is the measure of their failure.

It would lead into a region I am most anxious to avoid, were any attempt here made at detailed comparative criticism of the ecclesiastical and the religious ideal. Our purpose is more positive, by discussing the religious to show what the ecclesiastical ought to be. Yet it may emphasize this purpose and illustrate the idea which underlies it, if we look in the light of our previous discussions at the spirit and motives which produced the Anglican revival of sixty years ago. That revival was at its birth distinctly doctrinal or ideal, and though it used history to support and commend its idea, it did so at first in faith rather than with knowledge. The success that attended this use was more due to a courage that walked fearlessly into

the unknown than to any clear light of science.
When one turns to the tracts and treatises of the
period, one wonders, when regard is had to the
historical material and the method of handling it,
at the extraordinary effects they produced. Keble,
Newman, and Pusey are indeed illustrious names;
at no time has the church of England or the
University of Oxford had names more venerated
or worthier of honour. But the work they did was
accomplished through what they brought to history,
not through what they found in it; at least, through
what they found only so far as it was the vehicle
of what they brought. The movement they inaugurated may be described as a movement for the
recovery of the lost or forgotten ideal of the Anglican
church. They, at the bidding of conscience, worked
out the ideal from their own consciousnesses, and
then they made inroads into history, in search
of the means of realization, though their researches
and labours were, in the case of many, to have a
tragic effect upon the ideal. Still the motive or
spring of their endeavour was the wish to call into
being a nobler faith, the belief that their church
was one of apostolic descent, of continuous life,
supernatural endowment and divine authority.

In order that they might evoke and vivify this
faith, they tried to enrich the church of to-day
with the wealth of all her yesterdays, to adorn her
age with the grace of her youth and the fruitful
strength of her maturity. And so they recalled the

memories of her illustrious saints and fathers, woke into speech the long silent wisdom of her divines and teachers, searched out and restored her ancient treasuries of devotion, her richest and sweetest forms for the service of God. They studied how to make again significant and symbolical, or, as they loved to think, beautiful with holiness, her homes and temples of worship; how to deepen the mystery and enhance the efficacy of her sacraments; how to invest with all needed virtue and authority her orders and her offices—in a word, how to make her live to the eye of the imagination as to the eye of faith arrayed in all the grace of her Lord, clothed in all the dignity and loveliness of the historical "Holy Catholic and Apostolic Church." The ideal was at once winsome and majestic, well fitted to awe into reverence and inspire with the enthusiasm of devotion. It came like a revelation to an age weary of a hard and pragmatic evangelicalism, with its prosaic spirit, narrow interests and formal methods of reconciling God and man. It appealed to the imagination which Romanticism had touched and quickened, doing for the church what the poetry of Wordsworth had done for nature, and the novels of Scott for the national history. A new notion of religion came through the new idea, and the men it penetrated and held were like men possessed of a new spirit of worship, a seemlier, a more reverent and holy sense of God. We need not wonder at its victories; man would have been more ignoble than he is if he had remained insensible to its charm. Happily, for human nature and progress, there is no law more sure in its operation than this—that a belief ennobles in proportion to its own nobility; what has no intrinsic goodness can never evoke enthusiasm for good.

2. But it is not enough to construe the Anglican ideal through the notion of the church; it is necessary to study and criticise it through the idea of the religion. This is not only to change the point of view, but it is to assume a much higher one; for religion being greater than the church, a rich and sublime ecclesiastical may be a poor and mean religious ideal. The question here, then, is—whether the Anglican ideal did really articulate and faithfully interpret the religion of Christ: whether it translated into visible speech and living form for the people and state of England His mind as to His society or kingdom. Here the main point of the problem does not relate to a great clerical and sacerdotal corporation, instituted for the maintenance and realization of worship; but to a society that claims to embody and to work for the completer embodiment in everything and in every one of the order and ideas of God, of the spirit and truth of Christ. This is a larger, grander, and harder matter than the creation of a clerical corporation, and implies two things: on the one side, a clear and complete comprehension of the idea of the religion, and on the other, a full and sufficient articulation of the same in

the institutions and agencies needed to its realization. Now when we analyze the principles or
elements that underlie the Anglican ideal, what do
we find? A singularly imperfect and narrow idea of
religion, supported by an equally narrow and one-
sided theory as to human nature, as to history and
providence, as to God and man in themselves and in
their mutual relations. On the one side, the ideal
rested on the twin pillars of a great doubt and a
great fear. It doubted the presence of God in
humanity, the activity and reality of His grace
outside the limits of a constituted church, and apart
from sacramental persons, instruments and symbols.
It doubted the sanity of the reason He had given,
thought that this reason had so little affinity with its
Maker as to be ever tending away from Him, its
bent by nature being from God rather than to God.
And so it was possessed of the great fear that the
reason, freed from the authority and guardian care of
an organized and apostolic church, *i.e.* clergy, would
infallibly break from the control of His law and His
truth. It thus made man an atheist by nature,
and so confined divine influence to artificial and
ordained channels as to make the common life, which
most needs to be illumined and ennobled by the
divine, either vacant of God or alien from Him.
And so it enriched the church by impoverishing
humanity, what it took from the one being its loftiest
ideals, what it gave to the other being but their
sensuous and baser counterfeits. On the other and

more positive side, this ideal implied principles that had no place in the mind of Christ, or any real affinity to His free and gracious spirit. Its most beautiful quality was its reverence ; it was possessed by the enthusiasm of devotion ; but even here it knew too little of His joyous and sweet spontaneity, the glad and trustful filial spirit that loved immediate speech and fellowship with the Father. Then its ideal of duty was too ecclesiastical to be His, was without His large beneficence and healthful humanity. Its knowledge of Him was mediæval, not primitive ; the Christ it knew was the Christ of mystery and sacraments, not the Christ of Nature and of God. He did not love tradition, did not believe in the sanctity of formularies, in the holiness of fasts, the sin and apostasy of all who refused to conform to the priestly law or order. And what He did not love for Himself, He could not love for His people ; what displeased Him in Judaism, He could not be pleased to see crystallized round Himself. The living man, the conscious home and son of God, with love breaking into spontaneous speech and filial act, was more to Him than the orderly observance of ritual, or than the stateliest worship of the temple. His ideal of worship was filial love expressed in filial speech and conduct; and this love made all places sacred, all times holy, all service religious, all actions duties done to the Father in heaven. There never was a humaner or saner ideal, one that so consecrated and elevated the whole man, so penetrated and transfigured his whole life. Its essential elements were all natural, and in no degree sacerdotal, traditional, or ecclesiastical; where man knew God as the Father and himself as a son, worship could not but be; not elsewhere or in other sort was worship possible.

3. Now, it is by this vaster and grander yet simpler ideal that the Anglican must be measured; it must fulfil the idea of Christ to be a true ideal for a Christian church. We may not draw conclusions that only a detailed comparison, running along many lines, would warrant; but two sayings, an Anglican and a Christian, may be compared. Here is the Anglican : " There is a well-known sect, which denies both Baptism and the Lord's Supper. A churchman must believe its members to be altogether external to the fold of Christ. Whatever benevolent work they may be able to show, still, if we receive the church doctrine concerning the means generally necessary to salvation, we must consider such persons to be mere heathens, except in knowledge."[1] That is the church's doctrine. Here is Christ's:[2] " Whosoever shall do the will of My Father which is in heaven, the same is My brother, and sister, and mother." In the light of Christ's doctrine the church's looks hard, and mean, and false enough. A theory that has to make mere heathens of some of the most beautiful and devoted spirits that have adorned the religion

---

[1] J. H. Newman, *Via Media*, vol. ii., pp. 29-30 (1877).
[2] Matt. xii. 50.

and promoted the philanthropies of modern times, may be good ecclesiasticism, but it is bad Christianity. The difference between the doctrines is the difference between two ideals, that of the Son of Man and that of the Son of the church. If the Anglican revival has sublimed and softened and enriched our worship, it has also narrowed and hardened and impoverished our religion. Sensuous excellence may be the most serious of spiritual defects; and a political system which suppresses or misconceives essential elements in the religious ideal wants the most distinctive note of truth.

§ VI. *How the Ideal is to be Realized*

1. We return then to our fundamental principle: The churches exist for the religion, and ought to be as it is, agencies and institutions for its realization, good only as adapted to this end. The character of a religion is determined by its idea of God; the constitution, action, and ambitions of a church are determined by its ideal of religion. To be unfaithful to any element in the latter is to be without the highest kind of catholicity, catholicity as regards the truth. The glory of the Christian religion is its conception of God. He is the common Father and Sovereign, benevolent and beneficent, gracious yet righteous. He loves all men, and wills their good; hates sin and contends against it with all His energies. He finds His highest beatitude in the happiness of the creature, but makes holiness the

condition of happiness. To create holiness that happiness may be realized, is the aim of the divine moral government; in making for righteousness it makes for the highest good of the universe. But the religion that articulates this conception must be as if it were the moral forces of mankind organized and inspired of God, for the creation of holy happiness and happy holiness. And the churches that interpret the religion must have this as their supreme end, the regnant idea that determines the range and modes of their activities. No element or province of good can be alien to them; whatever tends to bring in a more perfect order is their proper work, whatever tends to delay or defeat its coming is their proper enemy. They are associations for worship: for the societies that are to carry out God's purposes must depend on Him and stand with Him in living fellowship and sympathy. But their worship is only a means, not an end; it is meant to create a gentler and more reverent spirit, a holier passion of benevolence, a more exalted moral enthusiasm, not simply to soothe and satisfy the soul. They are homes of instruction: for men must be informed of the truth if they are to be formed by it. But the instruction is in order to better living, to nobler and more efficient action in the way of Christ and for the ends of His kingdom. In Him all the churches find their ideal religious person; to create Christlike men and to realize in society an order and law worthy of Him, is their mission. To fulfil it they must work as He worked, by love, by gentleness, by speaking the truth, by creating a manhood that praises God and a brotherhood that rejoices man ; by bearing the sins and carrying the sorrows of men till the life of sorrow and the being of sin shall cease ; by unweariedness in well-doing increasing the number of good men and the quality of their goodness, so making earth in an ever brighter degree the home of a redeemed humanity. Churches that do not work for these ends are not churches of Christ's religion ; those that work for them by fittest means, and so to best issues, are the most Christian of churches.

The range thus opened up to the activity of the churches is immense; it is co-extensive with the needs of society and man. Their primary duty is to the individual ; with him they must begin. Good persons are the most efficient factors of good ; what makes the most good men does the most good to man. Now, religion has in a unique degree the power of conversion ; we may say, indeed, it is the sole possessor of this power. Any great ambition or affection may exalt, or even in a sense purify, a man ; but a man must have a certain largeness and elevation of nature before he can feel it. Love of art or science, literary, political and other ambition, may persuade a man to live both purely and laboriously; but the nature to which they appeal must be already a noble nature. The arts and sciences do not so much elevate man as witness to his elevation. But religion has an altogether peculiar power : it can touch the bad man, find the good in him, so possess as to transform his nature, making him in all things the servant of righteousness. Now, this power the churches ought to labour to exercise in the highest possible degree. They ought to burn with a passion for souls, be consumed with the desire to save. This does not mean the ambition for numbers, but the enthusiasm for the religious change which is a moral regeneration. To the extent that a profession of religion does not carry with it purity, chastity, truth —in a word, integrity of moral nature—it is an evil and not a good. The churches must bring together faith and conduct, translate the ideal of their Master into the living of their disciples, if they are to live to purpose and grow in power.

2. This, then, is their primary duty—to save men ; but their first is not their last. Saved men are means, not ends ; they are saved that they may save, *i.e.* work out the moral regeneration of the race. The churches that convert most men, and best use the men they have converted, realize religion in the most efficient way. It is the work of these men, instructed and inspired by their churches, to carry their high principles everywhere and into everything. They are not to conserve the actual, but to create the ideal, to labour along all lines that promise the amelioration of the human lot. They may think the world bad, but it is capable of being mended, and to mend it is the very reason of their being. The

churches ought to be the mothers of strenuous
philanthropists, encouraging their sons to labour
among the men who make crime, and against the
conditions that make criminals; in the hospitals
where the diseased are tended, and against the slums
where they are bred; in the charities where the poor
are helped, and against the poverty and the causes of
the poverty that make the charities necessary. They
ought to be the teachers of statesmen, and demand
that the nation, in all its legislation and in all its
conduct, home or foreign, shall follow the righteousness that alone exalteth, recognizing no law as good,
no action as honourable, that denies or offends
Christian principle. They ought to be the weightiest
preachers of economic doctrine, building on the
principles of Christian brotherhood and equity an
ideal industrial society, where all should work and
all work be honoured; where wealth, without any
schemes of violent and wrongful division, should by
the action of moral laws through moral men be so
distributed as to create a State where poverty was
unknown and charity was unneeded. They ought,
too, to be the great mothers and guardians of social
purity, fearing not to rebuke the sins of class and
caste, of idleness and luxury, bending their energies
to the creation of a loftier ideal of manhood and
womanhood, a chivalrous chastity of thought and
conduct that should, were it only by the courage of
innocence, rebuke or shame into silence the lower
passions and lusts. Were the churches to forget all

their sectional jealousies in the grand remembrance of their high mission to further the common good, were they to lose the mean political and sacerdotal ambitions that have narrowed and materialized the prouder and more historic of them, in a sublime moral enthusiasm for the realization of the religious ideal, they would become possessed of a power which could be described only as a baptism of the Holy Ghost and of fire. The paralysis of the churches in the religious sphere is due to the narrowness of their spirit and aims. They have been contented with too little ; they need to make a reality of their faith and its laws for the whole life of society and man.

It need not be said that this is not meant to be a plea for an extension of ecclesiastical jurisdiction ; on the contrary, that would seem to me a simple calamity. Nor is there any argument on behalf of the supremacy of the church over the civil courts in matters ecclesiastical ; on the contrary, these judicial conflicts but show to me the disastrous depravation of our idea of religion. There is nothing that has so hindered the supremacy of religion as the struggle for ecclesiastical supremacy. The ecclesiastic is not made by his function a religious man ; his position rather makes him but a statesman of narrower interests, with ambitions circumscribed by the limits of his society. To allow ecclesiastics to rule the nation is, as history has so often calamitously proved, but to sacrifice the people to a class. That is the best civil polity which secures at once perfect order and perfect freedom, the highest happiness and the most happiness to its people ; and that is the best ecclesiastical polity which develops, exercises and organizes to the highest degree, in the wisest ways, and for most beneficent ends, the moral and spiritual energies of the religion and of the religious. And so what is here pleaded for is the sovereignty of religion, the reign through the reason over the conscience of the beliefs, truths, ideas that constitute it. What is needed to this reign is a teacher who can interpret the meaning of a God who is a moral Sovereign, for the whole nature, the whole life, and the whole duty of man. Such a teacher the churches ought to be : but to be it they must be in Novalis' phrase, here used in all reverence, *Gottgetrunkene*, possessed by an unresting and inextinguishable passion for His moral ends, for the creation of an order that shall in its measure fitly express or reflect His eternal ideal. Within the Christian conception of God there lies for the Christian religion a world of unexhausted possibilities. Only when it has been fully construed will theology be perfected, only when it has been so applied as to order and regulate the life, individual and collective, will religion be realized. Once this idea has become the inspiration of the church, it will look back with shame on the days of the old ecclesiasticism when it lived in bondage to the letter; and it will contrast, in large joyfulness, the freedom that allows its people to build by spiritual methods and through moral agencies " the City of the living God," with the liberty they knew and loved of old, the liberty of so manipulating the past as to make it approve the present. Then working, not under the belittling burden of an exhausted yet authoritative past, but for the future and under the inspiration of the sublimest of all ideals, they will become fit vehicles for the religion that alone possesses the secret for promoting without cessation human progress and human good. The abstractions of Positivism are potent and significant only to the studious enthusiast; but the moral energies of religion are for all men engines of mightiest dynamic power. They enlarge the individual life with universal ideals; they lift time into the stream of an eternal purpose and fill it with eternal issues; and they make the simplest moral act great as a real factor in the evolution of a higher order and an immortal character. To the imagination that has been touched by the real ideal of religion, the fervid prophesyings of our modern Agnostics and Positivists are but the tamest and earthliest of dreams.

March, 1884.

II

CATHOLICISM AND THE APOLOGY FOR THE FAITH

§ I. *The Question to be Discussed*

IF the highest function of the Christian church
be so to interpret the Christian faith as to
secure the progressive realization of the Christian
religion, then it becomes a question of the most
vital interest:—Has any one of the many bodies
claiming the name of church proved itself to be
supremely efficient in the exposition and vindication
of the faith?   On this point there may be many
differences of opinion, but as to one thing there
can be no doubt ; of all the churches in Christendom
the Roman Catholic is, in all matters or questions
affecting the faith, the most conscious of her own
sufficiency.   She has proclaimed it in every possible
form, has decreed herself infallible, had tried to live
up to her decree even before she had formally
passed it, and has proudly moved among the churches,
challenging them to submit to claims they cannot
surpass and dare not attempt to rival.   We assume,
of course, the sincerity of the Roman Catholic
church, and her honest belief in this the most

stupendous of all claims ever made by any society, especially a society which at once addresses the reason and stands at the judgment seat of history : and we proceed to inquire whether her behaviour as she lives in our midst at all corresponds to her claims. In other words, our question is, To what extent has the Catholic movement in England helped the English mind to a higher and more satisfactory doctrine of religion than could have been found outside or apart from it ? To what degree has it, in an age, if not of denial, yet of transition and the inquiry which leans to doubt, contributed at once to conserve and quicken the Christian faith ; to make it credible to living minds, real to the men who feel that their religious beliefs are the dearest to the heart, but the hardest to the intellect, and the least practical or relevant to the life ? These are questions it is easy to ask, but very difficult to discuss judicially or even judiciously ; while the most difficult thing of all is to find a just and sufficient answer. Underneath all such questions others still more fundamental lie, and the principles implied in the deeper must always regulate the criticism and determination of the more superficial. The writer is clearly conscious that his attitude to religion and our religious problems is one, and the attitude of the Roman Catholic another and very different ; and it would be simple impertinence in him to ignore the difference, or enforce his own canons of criticism on the Catholic mind. He does not mean to

judge those who have found refuge and peace in
Catholicism—indeed, he would not do so if he could.
If it has made its converts happier and better men,
it has done a work for which all good men ought
to be grateful. But the question that now concerns
us in no way relates to the sufficiency of Catholicism
for Catholics, but to the adequacy and relevance
of what may be termed its special apologetic to
the spirits possessed and oppressed by the problems
of the time. The power of Catholicism to satisfy
convinced religious men in search of the best
organized and most authoritative Christianity, is one
thing ; and its ability to answer the questions and
win the faith of the perplexed and critical mind,
is another thing altogether. This is a matter we
are all free to discuss, nay, every man concerned
for the future of faith is bound to discuss it ; and
the frankest will always be the fairest discussion.

Of course, it may be said, and said quite truly,
that the infallibility of the Roman church does not
guarantee the infallibility of her ministers, doctors,
or divines, or even the moral integrity and intellectual sufficiency of every movement that may be
described as Catholic. This may at once be granted,
but it only reduces the significance and impairs the
competence of the infallibility which can render so
little service to those who most need it. We shall
meet this question again, and for the present confine
ourselves to the problem:—How far have thinkers
and teachers who have been either the ordained and

recognized ministers of an infallible church, or the unauthorized exponents of her faith, supplied living thought with a cogent and relevant apologetic for religion?

§ II. *The Need of a Relevant Apology for the Faith*

.1. In order to an intelligent discussion of this question, it may be as well to explain what is here meant by a relevant apologetic. It means not a mere defence of the faith, a marshalling of evidences, a method or process of proof, but such a constructive interpretation and presentation of Religion as shall make it stand before the living reason as a coherent and intelligible thing. Evidences may admit of no answer, and yet produce no conviction: if the things they are meant to prove have no reality or adequate meaning to thought, no concrete rationality for reason, they may be multiplied to almost any extent without gathering weight or begetting belief. Men lose faith in religious truth not so much through a failure in its evidences as through a failure in its relevance; in other words, the terms in which it has been interpreted cease to be credible either by ceasing to be intelligible or by falling out of harmony with the logical basis and methods of living mind. Of course it may not seem fair to illustrate a point by the words of one who is but an echo of other minds; but the reflection in a mirror often reveals more of the original than may be discovered by the searching scrutiny of the naked eye.　Well, Mr. Lilly—and the remark summarizes a wonderful deal of Catholic argumentation—meets some very grave objections to Christianity by saying, "in the light of reason, man has in strictness no rights against God."[1]　Now that is not an answer, but a confession that no answer can be given.　It means that if there were a sovereign being against whom man had rights, that being would, in the given circumstances, be in the wrong.　And such a defence is the worst indictment of Providence.　Looked at in the clear light of reason, man has rights against God.　To be made, is to be invested with rights ; to create, is for the creator to assume duties.　I do not like such modes of speech, but an argument like Mr. Lilly's compels their use. I prefer to say that God's ways towards men are regulated, not by what He owes to men, but by what He owes to Himself.　But so to conceive the matter is to affirm, if not " man's rights against God," yet God's high duties towards man—which means here, that the justification of God's ways must proceed on a far loftier and truer principle than either the denial or the affirmation of the creature's rights, viz., on the principle that the Divine nature is a law to the Divine will, and　that that nature is perfect reason, righteousness and love.

A relevant apologetic, then, may be described as one which, by the use of rational principles and methods, satisfies　the　reason　as　to　the　truth

---

[1] *Ancient Religion and Modern Thought,* p. 261.

of things it had doubted or even denied, and which addresses it as if it were honest and reasoned honestly concerning their truth and were constantly in search of it. Now every age has its own mental habits, which imply common principles, fixed processes of inquiry and proof, and modes of apprehending and handling questions; and these affect man's attitude to every matter of thought and belief. An idea like evolution, for example, changes, not only our notion of the mode in which nature does her work, but also the way in which we study alike her works and her manner of working, the methods by which we inquire into the phenomena of life, the order and facts of history, the appearance and meaning of man. It causes, in a word, such a revolution in our basal conceptions as to demand, in order to mental wholeness and harmony, that they and their related beliefs be re-stated or reformulated. In a period of transition faith is difficult, because religious ideas at once resist formal change and seem to suffer more from it than empirical or scientific; and men hastily or fearfully conclude that the change which is glorifying science will abolish religion. On the one side it stands, by its theistic idea, so related to nature as to feel every variation in men's notions concerning the creative cause, method, purpose or tendency; and on the other side, it is by its beliefs, institutions and life, so related to history as to be sensitive to every new historical doctrine, discovery, or process of inquiry. Hence, when the cosmic idea has

changed its form, while the religious has not, when
a new conception reigns in every department of
history save the religious, the chronic difficulties
between Science and Religion become to many
minds insurmountable, and they cease to believe
simply because Religion has ceased to be intellectually relevant—*i.e.*, to belong to the living and growing body of truth, which at once possesses and
inspires living mind. Men so situated are men
whom no mustering of conventional evidences can
convince ; to reach or even touch them, apologetic
thought must seek to construe Religion as scientific
thought has construed nature and history. What
can make men feel at harmony with themselves and
their universe, will always be the system most open
to successful proof; what cannot accomplish this,
no mass of probable or other evidence will save
from ultimate disbelief.

It would lead us much too far to illustrate, with
all the needed detail, the principles now stated ;
but two works will show what is meant. The *De
Civitate Dei* is perhaps the greatest work in the
whole region of Christian apologetics. Yet its form
and argument were determined by the conditions
and questions of Augustine's own day ; these must
be understood before its significance and force can
be felt. The ideas of the time, heathen and
Christian, political, social, philosophical, religious,
its conflicts, fears, hopes, despairs, must be recalled.
The student must fill his imagination with the Roman

ideal of the Eternal City; he must realize what
may be described as its apotheosis by the Latin
peoples, the degree in which it was a city at once
sacred and imperial, venerable, august, invincible,
queen for centuries of civilized man, sole mother of
the law that ruled him and the order he loved,
invested with a more awful sanctity than any religious city; nay, as the embodiment of the Roman,
the symbol of a universal, religion, and of one that
out of ceaseless war had called universal peace.
Once he has made this worship of Rome live in his
consciousness, he must conceive the consternation,
the horror and shame, that must have seized the
Romans when they saw their city stormed and
plundered by the barbarians, and the consequent
indignation and hate which broke out in the Pagan
charge:—"This ruin is but the last and highest
achievement of the new religion!" Augustine's
apology was the answer to this passion, and to the
belief by which it lived; and the answer was as
splendid as complete. The new religion was conceived and represented as a new city, a diviner and
more eternal Rome, which transcended the old as
heaven transcends the earth; which came not from
a people, but from God; which was created not of
human ambition and hate, but of divine grace and
love; which comprehended not a few nations, but the
race; which produced no evil, and fostered no wrong,
but formed all the virtues and embraced all truth,—a
city destined to growth, but not to decay, whose

building might indeed proceed in time, but whose continuance was to be unto eternity.　Beside the *Civitas
Dei* the *Civitas Romana* was made to seem a feverish
and shadowy and inglorious dream ; the ideal of the
celestial rebuked by its very divineness the poor
reality of the earthly city.　The power of the apology
lay in its being a constructive presentation of the
Christian religion in a form relevant to the men
and the moment ; their knowledge of the city that
was perishing constituted the very capability to
which Augustine appealed.　And so accurately does
his work in its method and argument reflect the
spirit and ideals, the disillusionment and alarms of
the times, that the man who does not live through
them and in them will never see its meaning or
feel its power.

Take, again, Butler's *Analogy.*　It was a most
relevant book ; its relevance was the secret of its
strength, and is the secret of its weakness.　On its
every page, in its every paragraph, we hear the
controversies of the time ; the freethinker, the deist,
the airy rationalist, who will have a religion without
mystery and without miracle, appear and deploy
their arguments ; but only that they may be judicially
analyzed, reduced to their true insignificance, and
finally translated into proofs tending to justify faith
in the revealed religion they had been used to
condemn.　Some things Butler did once for all.
His method ; his doctrine of nature and man ; his
proof of the religious worth and work of conscience ;

his demonstration that religion when most accommodated to the standard of a conventional and unimaginative rationalism, becomes only the less reasonable, beset with graver and more insoluble difficulties; the way he used the facts of life to illustrate and verify certain truths of faith, like the doctrines of substitution and atonement,—are now inalienable possessions of constructive Christian thought. Yet the strength of his argument, taken as a whole, was due to the use of principles common to the belief and unbelief of the day. Grant those principles, and the *Analogy* is one of the most marvellous structures of solid, cumulative, convincing argumentation ever built by the mind of man; deny those principles, and while the work remains a monument of dialectical genius, it has lost its power to convince. And they are explicitly denied by systems that now confront us; the unbelief of our day is more radical than the unbelief of Butler's; and, in some degree, we have to thank him for its being so. He showed it the necessity of increasing its negations if it was to remain negative at all. Hence our living apologetic must begin without any help from those common principles which were the basis of Butler's work; it must get even nearer the rock, seek a stronger and broader foundation, if it would construct an argument as relevant to our day as the *Analogy* was to his. And whatever it does, it must not seek to relieve the difficulties of revealed religion by deepening those that sit upon the

face of nature; rather it must illumine and transfigure the darkness of nature by the light of
revelation. Religion has need to penetrate and
exalt both nature and man with her own transcendental ideals, that men may have a new sense
of the value of life, and win a new heart for braver
and nobler living.

2. But now there is another point that must
be emphasized :—the need for constructive religious
thought does not so much arise from the speculations and criticisms of a few active intellects
without the churches, as from a common intellectual
tendency or drift which causes a shaking and
unrest, a sense of insecurity and change, within
them. This is what tempts men either to break
with the old beliefs, or to doubt them, or to demand
that they shall be clothed in new forms or that
from the old forms a new spirit shall come forth.
The churches are now face to face with the gravest
questions that have confronted Christianity since her
life began ; questions not simply doctrinal, political,
or social, but fundamental and final,—whether men
are to be Christians any more, or even in any
tolerable sense theists. These questions exhale, as
it were, the intellectual difficulties which diffuse
themselves everywhere, stealing into the best disciplined homes, penetrating the most rigorously
organized and jealously guarded churches, pervading
the atmosphere in which thought lives and breathes,
touching our finest spirits with the slow paralysis

of doubt, or the hesitancy which is the death of all enthusiasm. The men have not created the difficulties or raised the doubts; on the contrary, the doubts and difficulties have sought and found the men; they are creations of the time, and spring from the characteristics and achievements of its thought, its wider knowledge, its vaster outlook, its new methods of interpreting nature and history, its deeper insight into the way of nature's working, and into the affinities of man and his universe. They are utterly misunderstood when traced to an evil heart of unbelief, or to some taint or sin of will, or to any other source than honesty and integrity of intellect,—the determination to be as clear and scrupulous in the realm of spirit and faith as in the region of experience and experiment. Scientists who have studied nature and become so possessed by the ideas of law and energy, continuity and development, as to feel unable to reconcile them with their older ideas of God and His creative method, are men whom the churches are bound to help to a solution. Scholars trained in the newest critical methods, literary and historical, cannot forget them when they turn to the study of the Bible, and of Hebrew and Christian history; and cannot pursue them in these fields without raising questions they have a right to submit to the churches, and to require the churches frankly and honestly to answer. Mr. Lilly's vindication of the attitude of his church to the "higher criticism" seems to me her severest condemnation. She is to "wait until the higher criticism" has really established something certain, and then she will consider how far the "traditional thesis" taught in her schools should be modified in consequence.[1] There is here the abdication of the highest functions of the church; she ceases to be the teacher of truth, and leaves it to men, whom she bans the while, to be its discoverers; and then the truths they have with pain discovered and with loss established she will reconcile to her tradition. In harmony with this, he—with special reference to the question, what would happen to a Catholic priest who should teach his people certain critical conclusions, some of them conclusions certain enough—says, such a one "would richly deserve suspension," for "his business is to watch for men's souls, not to unsettle their faith."[2] But his business ought to be to teach the truth; and if in the process faith is unsettled, it will only be to the greater saving of the soul. The primary right of every man is to the truth, and the best truth his teachers can give him; the primary duty of the teacher, especially of the collective teacher called the church, is to communicate the truth, not speaking with authority or certainty where certainty is not. A church that is true and the infallible teacher of truth and guardian of souls, can in no way so well justify its claim and its being as by teaching

[1] *Ancient Religion and Modern Thought*, p. 279. [2] *Ib.*, p. 278.

the truth to souls perplexed. These souls are seeking the truth, and would be saved by it; but they are simply mocked if a church says to them, "Find out for yourself without any help from me the truth on those critical and historical questions which are matters of life and death for you, and, to speak honestly, for myself also; and then I will tell you how this truth is to be reconciled with my 'traditional thesis.'" It would hardly be possible to conceive a more helpless or ignoble attitude on the part of man or church. For the men whose doubts come from brave thought and honest inquiry have the highest claim on the best consideration and clearest light of all the churches and all their thinkers. Doubt never appears without reason; and the removal of the reason is the only real way to the removal of the doubt. The churches that do nothing to reach and purify the source only help to muddle the stream.

§ III. *Deism and Apologetics in Catholic France and in Protestant England*

1. Constructive apologetic is thus at once the highest work of living religious thought, and the common duty of all the churches. In it the Roman Catholic must bear its part. It is too wise to trust here to its infallible authority, matchless organization, rigorous discipline, and jealously guarded education; indeed, experience has thoroughly well taught it how little these are able to keep down the critical

and sceptical spirit among its laity, or even, as
certain cases have flagrantly proved, to keep it
out from the ranks of its clergy. It is but natural
that the church which most taxes faith should
most provoke unbelief; but it ought not to follow
that the claims that most challenge criticism are
claims that can as little recognize as bear the
criticism they challenge. It is the simple and
sober truth to say that no church has begotten
so much doubt and disbelief as the church of
Rome. And she has begotten it, not by the
demand she makes on faith, but by her inability
to justify the demand. History bears here an indubitable and incorruptible witness. Of the Middle
Ages we need not speak ; or of the Renaissance,
when the educated intellect of Italy almost ceased
to be Christian, and became at once sceptical
and pagan ; or of the sixteenth and seventeenth
centuries, with such notable figures as Giordano
Bruno and Vanini, and tendencies so significant
as those impersonated in Montaigne, Bodin, and
Charron. But we may glance at our own and the
previous century. The eighteenth was the century
of Rationalism : and it is customary to credit England
with being its nursery and home, where, as Deism,
it assumed its most anti-Christian and aggressive
form. But English Deism was, from a literary
point of view, a poor and vapid thing compared
with the Free Thought of the France whence Protestantism and Jansenism had been expelled that

the Catholicism of Rome might have it all its
own way. In England Deism had a host of obscure
writers, now well-nigh forgotten, irrepressible men
like Toland, men of mediocre ability and culture
like Anthony Collins, vulgar men like Chubb,
irritated and disagreeable men like Matthew Tindal
who conformed that he might enjoy his Oxford
fellowship and wrote anonymously that he might
relieve his conscience. But it can reckon only two
names illustrious in literature, Hume and Gibbon;
the one embodying his scepticism in the subtlest
of English philosophies, the other distilling his into
the stateliest history in the English tongue. But
the active intellects of France, the men who give
name and character to the century, were either
sceptical or infidel. It opens with Bayle, once a
Jesuit convert, the father of critical Rationalism.
The man who stands above all others, and shadows
all beneath, is Voltaire, a Jesuit pupil. The men
who form and express the mind of Paris, then the
head and heart of France, are Diderot, D'Alembert,
and the other Encyclopædists; the lion of its *salons*
is Rousseau. And while the literature of France
was vehemently anti-Christian, the church of France
was not strenuously apologetic, as was the English
church. Here, men like Addison, most classical
and pure and elegant of English essayists; Clarke,
most metaphysical and in logic adventurous of
English divines; Butler, Anglican Bishop and Christian Apologist, who had the utmost curiosity to

know what was said, in order that he might ascertain whether it was true ; Berkeley, a philosopher as lucid and graceful in style as he was subtle in argument; Law, a man whose apologetic power was only surpassed by his passion for the holier mysticism; Bentley, greatest of English scholars, yet master of a pen that could bite as if it were a living creature ; and many names hardly less great, like Warburton, Lardner, Paley—made Christian thought, even as a mere matter of literature, distinguished beside Deism. But in France the power of resistance was so feeble that no one would think of naming the churchmen alongside the men of letters, their most illustrious name, Malebranche, belonging, so far as philosophical and literary activity is concerned, rather to the seventeenth than the eighteenth century.

2. But it were a grave mistake to conceive the defence of the Christian Faith, or, indeed, of any religion, as merely a work of literature ; it is a much larger and more serious thing. The course of the Deist controversy in England forms an even more remarkable contrast to the history of the parallel movement in France, than do the men engaged in it. The two movements were indeed closely related ; the English was, in a sense, the source of the French Deism. The bosom at which both were suckled was the philosophy of Locke; but of the children the English was the elder and formative, the French was the younger and more imitative, though incalculably

the more potent. Voltaire did not deduce his Deism directly from Locke; he learned it from disciples less reverent and more audacious than the master. Nothing so astonished him during his English residence as the freedom with which religion was treated. He found, just as Butler did, that unbelief was fashionable: "Christianity was not so much as a subject of inquiry;" it had been "at length discovered to be fictitious." So Mr. Toland had proved that "Christianity was not mysterious." "The Sect of Free Thinkers" was the church of the wits, the synagogue of the socially select. Anthony Collins discoursed of their wisdom, and it needed the audacity of a Bentley to satirize their freedom as "thinking and judging as you find," "which every inhabitant of bedlam practises every day, as much as any of our illustrious sect." To him, indeed, their wise men were "idiot evangelists"; but to Voltaire they represented letters, culture, the men of sense. Bolingbroke, Pope's "guide, philosopher, and friend," became Voltaire's master in Deism; and he went home to France to preach what he had learned in England, with very different results from those that followed here. In England the victory was with the apologists; in France with the assailants of the faith. It was not simply that in England Deism was intellectually outmatched, while in France it had all the superiority of mind. The English deist, notwithstanding the general inferiority already noted, had still men who were, in the matter of intellect, the equals of the

5

English apologist. Hume was more subtle than
Butler. Gibbon was more learned and ponderous
than Lardner or Paley. Tom Paine was a greater
master of English and of argument than Beattie.
Yet, in spite of the number and social strength of
their opponents, the apologists triumphed ; when the
century ended the Christian religion was far more
strongly entrenched in the reason and heart of the
English people than it had been when the century
began. But in France there was another story.
When the century opened it was still the great age
of Louis XIV., where the Church was as illustrious in
intellect, in learning, and in eloquence, as the State
was in regal dignity, in military prowess, and in
skilful statesmanship. When the century closed the
Revolution had come, the terror had followed, Kingdom and Church had together perished. And to this
catastrophe no cause had contributed more potently
than the French movement which corresponded to
the English Deism.

Now why this remarkable difference ? To examine
all its roots and reasons would carry us much too far.
But the main reason is one which is not without its
bearing on our argument. In England the political
and social conditions were such that the religious was
not a civil question, but rather one intellectual and
ethical. The State had ceased to expect uniformity
of worship and belief, and was ceasing to enforce it
by civil disabilities and pains. The first step towards
toleration had been taken ; and Parliament had prac-

tically recognized that the civil and the ecclesiastical society, the State and the Church, were not identical and coextensive. And it so happened that the political situation, especially as concerned the king-ship, was such as to reduce to silence the only party in the State who could have resisted the principle of liberty. The old High Churchman, who believed in the divine right of the king and the duty of passive obedience, could not preach his doctrine in the face of the Hanoverian succession, or apply it to a sovereign who reigned by the will of the people and not of right divine. And so for the first time in English history since "the spacious days of great Elizabeth," religion had ceased to be a civil concern, and become the concern of the religious, a matter for the reason and the conscience, for the mind and the heart. And thus it was freely discussed, tested on its own merits, argued for, argued against, tried by logic, proved by evidence, dealt with as if it were of all subjects the one most germane to the intellect, the one thing absolutely common and accessible to all men. And the result stands written broad upon the face of the century: in a fair argument and on a free field religion easily and completely won.

But the situation in France was exactly the con-verse. In 1688 toleration began its reign with Dutch William in England; in 1685 Louis XIV. revoked the Edict of Nantes, and began the reign of in-tolerance. The Roman Church and the French State were henceforward so bound together as to be

in a sense one body breathing fateful breath. There
was no greater enemy of civil freedom than the
Church; no more vigilant foe of religious liberty than
the State. Each confirmed the other in the policy
that was most disastrous to its good. And so it
happened that the free-thinking spirit which had
returned from England incarnated in Voltaire, saw
that it could not teach religion without offending the
State; and so it had to strike at the State in order to
get at the religion which had become the very soul
of the tyrannical sway. And there was no lack of
provocation to assault. In popular feeling, dislike of
Voltaire, the mocker, has hidden from us how much
there was to justify his mockery, and what really just
and great ends it was often used to serve. We forget
that he was no mere spirit who denied, but one who
strongly affirmed where affirmation was at once most
necessary and most dangerous. He who loves freedom ought never to forget the services Voltaire
rendered to the cause he loves. On behalf of Jean
Calas, and in the name of justice and truth, he fought
the whole collective bigotry of France, and prevailed.
He confronted a church that in the age of Louis the
Well-Beloved dared to persecute, even though so
many of her priests and princes had ceased to
believe; and by his arguments, his scorn, his bold
mockery, he gained, almost single-handed, his
splendid victory. And here was the real reason
why in France reasonableness in religion or constructive religious thought never had a chance, or if

it had, never was able to use it. The tongue of the church was tied, she had to defend the indefensible, and so was silent; while the assault was delivered against the whole broad face of two flagrant offenders whose alliance made them appear as one: a State that, in its anxiety to repress a liberty which the church feared, forgot its own people; and a church that, in its desire to sanction and support a State which tried so hard to serve it, neglected its own duties and was faithless to the very end of its being. It was the civil independence of the question they discussed that made English positive thought so completely victorious; it was the league of the Roman Church and the autocratic State in France, so mischievous to the good of both, so provocative in both of evil, that contributed to their common and disastrous overthrow. The policy which the church either directed or approved was fatal to the faith its infallibility had been invoked to define and defend.

3. And it is now as then; it is Catholic countries that show the most radical revolt of the intellect from Religion, and a revolt not at one point, but at all. In Belgium the conflict is going on under our very eyes, political on the surface, religious beneath it; in Italy, where thought is most active, the claims and dogmas of the church are handled most freely; even in Spain political aspirations are wedded to ecclesiastical denials. There is no country in which unbelief is so strong and so vindictive as in France, so much a passion of hate, a fanaticism or zealotry

against, if not Religion, yet the church that claims to be its authoritative vehicle and exponent. The anti-clericals of the nineteenth century are more extreme than the encyclopædists of the eighteenth ; the resolute and rough-handed antagonism of the Senate and the workshop has superseded the fine criticism of the study, and the delicate yet well-spiced raillery of the *salon*. The very priesthood is not proof against the negative spirit ; the new political ideal steals the heart of a Lamennais from Rome, while German criticism turns the most hopeful pupil of Saint Sulpice into the freest and most famed critic of the creative Person and period of Christianity. No church has had such splendid opportunities as the Catholic ; everything that the most perfect organization and the complete control of rulers and their agencies could do for her and the faith she carried, has been done. And if she has yet allowed Free Thought, so often in its worst and extremest forms, to spring up all round her, it is evident that she of all churches most needs a relevant and living apologetic. She must reconcile the intellects that have revolted from her, or lose them utterly ; and the only way of reconciliation is the way of reason and argument. Grant belief in the papal claims, and authority and infallibility are powerful weapons. Create doubt or denial of them, and they are but empty words—the speech of exaggerated feebleness. Where they can only speak their claims, they but provoke to ridicule ; where these claims can appear as political or social forces, they beget the revolutionary and retributive fanaticism, the hate inspired by fear, which is so distinctive of unbelief in the Catholic countries. If, then, Catholicism is to win the revolted intellect, it must use reasonable speech; and the more reasonable it is, the more irresistible it will be. Protestantism frankly appeals to the reason, and so is bound to persuade it; Catholicism must humbly lay aside its high claims, and convince the reason before it can rule it. And so in either case a rational apologetic is necessary, though in the Catholic case, as there is so much more to prove, the proof must be correspondingly great and commanding.

4. It will not, I hope, be supposed that there is here any attempt at a *tu quoque.* It were an expedient fit only for a poor controversialist to excuse the weakness of the Protestant churches by charging the Roman Catholic with impotence; or to hide the failure of the Catholic to hold or control her peoples, by magnifying the feebleness of the Protestant. What is really intended is to emphasize this point :—the burden and responsibilities of the conflict with unbelief lie on all the churches, and no one can say to the other, "the work is thine, not mine"; or, with a more petulant insolence, " it is mine, and not thine." This duty, indeed, they have all on occasion been forward to recognize, and we rejoice to see men like Vives the Catholic, Pascal the Jansenist, Grotius the Arminian, Leibnitz the Lutheran, Butler the Anglican, Lardner the Presbyterian,

Schleiermacher the German Evangelical, and Martineau the Unitarian, united in unconscious harmony in doing for their several generations the same order of work. Yet it is necessary to make a distinction: an apology for Religion is not the same thing as an apology for a church ; nay, more—the best apologies for Religion have been in no respect apologies for specific churches. But, while the distinction is clear, a separation is not in every case possible. If the church is held to be the embodiment of the Religion, so necessary to it that the Religion were impossible without it, then the only complete and sufficient apology for the Religion is an apology for the church. And this is what we have a right to expect from Roman Catholicism ; what is an insufficient vindication of its claims as a church is, from its own point of view, an inadequate defence of the Christian Religion. For to the Catholic his church is his religion ; the two are not distinct and separable, but one and indivisible ; and therefore the apology which leaves the church unjustified leaves the Religion altogether condemned. That is a grave aspect of the matter, burdening Roman Catholicism and the Catholic with the heaviest responsibility church or man could bear ; and it is the aspect which gives significance to the question here proposed for discussion, viz., whether Catholic thought in England has given such an interpretation and defence of Religion as to make it more true and intelligible and real to critical and perplexed and doubting minds.

§ IV. *The Anglo-Catholic Movement and Religion in England*

1. Catholicism in England cannot be discussed apart from that Anglo-Catholic movement which did so much to revive it. As to the ecclesiastico-religious effects of that movement, there is no need for discussion. These are on all sides visible enough. Its ideal of worship has modified the practice of all the churches, even of those most hostile to its ideal of Religion. The religious spirit of England is, in all its sections and varieties, sweeter to-day than it was forty years ago, more open to the ministries of art and the graciousness of order, possessed of a larger sense of " the community of the saints," the kinship and continuity of the Christian society in all ages. Even Scotland has been touched with a strange softness, Presbyterian worship has grown less bald, organs and liturgies have found a home in the land and church of Knox, and some of the more susceptible sons of the Covenant have been visited by the ideal of a Church at once British and Catholic, where prelate and presbyter should dwell together in unity. On the other hand, it must be confessed that something of the old sterner Puritan conscience against priest-hoods and all their symbols and ways, has been evoked ; and in a sense not true of any time between now and the period of Laud, two ideals of Religion, each the radical contradiction of the other, stand face to face in England, and contend under the

varied masks supplied by our theological, ecclesiastical, and even political controversies. The one ideal is sensuous and sacerdotal, and seeks, by the way it construes and emphasizes the idea of the Church, to secularize the State, with all our daily activities and occupations ; the other ideal is spiritual and ethical, and seeks, by the way it construes and emphasizes the idea of Religion, to transform and transfigure the State, to sanctify all that belongs to the common life of man. The fundamental question is, whether an organized church which is, alike in history and administration, not in the civil but in the ecclesiastical sense, a political institution,—or a spiritual faith, which is in its nature a regenerative and regnant moral energy for the whole man, is to prevail. And the more obvious this question becomes, the more the issues are simplified, and men are forced to determine whether they are to be ruled by a church or governed by a Religion. The movement which has made or is making our people conscious of this vital issue, has rendered an extraordinary service to the men and churches of to-day.

2. But the most remarkable ecclesiastico-religious results achieved by Anglo-Catholicism are those to be found within the two churches chiefly concerned, the Anglican and the Roman. Though so many of the men who inaugurated and represented the movement left the English church, yet the spirit they had created, and many of the men they had inspired, remained within her. And the Anglo-

Catholic ideal has continued to live and work within her like a regenerative spirit, has filled all her
sons, even the most resistant, with new ambitions,
has both narrowed and broadened her affections and
aims, has changed old antipathies into new sym-
pathies, has made her devouter in worship and more
devoted alike in her practical action and ideal ends.
Rome is judged with more perfect charity, Dissenters
are judged with more rigorous severity. Unity is
loved, and historical continuity coveted, as the condition and channel of the most potent and needed
graces. The freedom and independence of the
church has become a watchword, Erastianism a
hated and unholy thing. The Sovereignty of the
Redeemer has become a living faith, and the symbols
that speak of His presence and work and activity
are invested with a solemn and sacramental and
even sacrificial significance ; while the acts that recognize His Deity and express man's devotion, are
performed with a new sense of awe and reverence.
The worship has grown at once statelier and more
expressive ; men have become more conscious of its
beauty and its power, have come to feel how completely it can articulate their needs, satisfy and
uplift their souls, bring them into the company of the
saintly dead and into communion with the Eternal.
The English church has a deeper sense of sin and
a greater love for sinners, and seeks to use her
symbolism and her service to bring Christ and His
salvation nearer to the hearts and consciences of

...the Catholic idea to... ...many elements, ...through the very ... ...symbolism, a materialized and so depressed limitation of the idea of the ... ...which ... ...remain "of Heaven," ...there it may reign ...on earth; but, what-ever it may be to such, no one can deny that it has been to the church of England ...spirit of life and energy. ...It is especially with the historical grounds on which it rests are considered ...splendid example of the power of faith, and of the creative and trans-figurative force of the religious imagination. From this point of view it has been, it is most pathetic tale; but its pathos need not blind us to the wonder-ful things it has accomplished. Though it may make ...which has accomplished ...wonder, for of old God ...to being to nought the things that were.

5. And as Catholicism itself the Anglo-Catholic movement has acted on us potently. It has changed its spirit and ethos to the English people, and the English people to it, has indeed, in a sense unknown since the Reformation, made Roman Catholicism English. Catholic emancipation supplied one of the conditions of the change, but the Oxford movement, and its issues, accomplished it. What Cardinal Newman describes as "the Protestant view of the Catholic Church" is an example of the remark-able limitation of his genius, his inability to under-stand where he does not sympathize. The "view,"

though, no doubt, vera ously reminiscent, is but a series of prejudices, all he more vulgar that they were those of cultureu n. What the true view is does not here concern s; only this: the English view was very much wh the course of history had made it. Catholicism h l been anti-English: in its interests foreign potent s had threatened England, and had tried to execute neir threats; Catholics had plotted against Elizabeth and against the first James; they had fought for at lutism under his son, had stood by the later Stuar and had intrigued for their return. Catholicism, in countries where the royal might threaten the pa l supremacy, had, by the mouth of men like Su z and Mariana, preached strong doctrines as to t: duties of kings and the rights of peoples. But in e later seventeenth century in England—where it hac verything to hope from the prince, and nothing from ie people—its loyalty was to the ruler, who promi l or seemed to promise to govern in its interests, no to the law or to the ruled. Indeed, nothing is so indi tive of the blindness which has happened to the Ron n church—and it is but a form of the fatal intellect l incompetence which falls upon all communities th live by an over-central-ized sovereignty—as it fatuous faith in reigning authorities, and its ina lity to understand and control that on which al authority must ultimately rest, viz., the mind and h rt and will of the people. To this there may be he proverbial exception, which proves the rule; bl as to the fact of the rule,

men. The Catholic ideal may be to many sensuous,
poor through the very wealth of its symbolism, a
materialized and so depraved translation of the idea
of the Kingdom, which must ever remain "of
Heaven," that it may reign over earth; but, whatever it may be to such, no one can deny that it has
been to the church of England a spirit of life and
energy. It is, especially when the historical grounds
on which it rests are considered, a splendid example
of the power of faith, and of the creative and trans-
figurative force of the religious imagination. From
this point of view it has, indeed, a most pathetic
side; but its pathos need not blind us to the wonderful things it has accomplished, though it may make
us wonder at the power which has accomplished
them. Yet we need not wonder, for of old God
chose the things that were not, to bring to nought
the things that were.

3. And on Catholicism itself the Anglo-Catholic
movement has acted no less potently. It has
changed its spirit and attitude to the English people,
and the English people's to it : has indeed, in a sense
unknown since the Reformation, made Roman
Catholicism English. Catholic emancipation supplied
one of the conditions of the change, but the Oxford
movement, and its issues, accomplished it. What
Cardinal Newman describes as "the Protestant view
of the Catholic Church" is an example of the remarkable limitation of his genius, his inability to understand where he does not sympathize. The "view,"

though, no doubt, veraciously reminiscent, is but a series of prejudices, all the more vulgar that they were those of cultured men. What the true view is does not here concern us; only this: the English view was very much what the course of history had made it. Catholicism had been anti-English: in its interests foreign potentates had threatened England, and had tried to execute their threats; Catholics had plotted against Elizabeth, and against the first James; they had fought for absolutism under his son, had stood by the later Stuarts, and had intrigued for their return. Catholicism, in countries where the royal might threaten the papal supremacy, had, by the mouth of men like Suarez and Mariana, preached strong doctrines as to the duties of kings and the rights of peoples. But in the later seventeenth century in England—where it had everything to hope from the prince, and nothing from the people—its loyalty was to the ruler, who promised or seemed to promise to govern in its interests, not to the law or to the ruled. Indeed, nothing is so indicative of the blindness which has happened to the Roman church—and it is but a form of the fatal intellectual incompetence which falls upon all communities that live by an over-centralized sovereignty—as its fatuous faith in reigning authorities, and its inability to understand and control that on which all authority must ultimately rest, viz., the mind and heart and will of the people. To this there may be the proverbial exception, which proves the rule; but as to the fact of the rule, the student of modern history will be the last person to doubt. And largely because of this rule the English Catholics lived as aliens in the land, under heavy civil disabilities, with the home of their religious interest and the source of their religious inspiration elsewhere. Time brought amelioration; Spain fell, and could launch no second Armada, raise no army England need fear; the Stuarts were expelled, and France was soon too completely broken to have either the will or the power to interfere on their behalf. Freed from fear of invasion or rebellion, the attitude of England changed. She became tolerant, came to understand what civil and religious liberty meant, celebrated—moved in great measure by the persuasion of the men most radically opposed to Catholicism—one memorable moment in her process of learning by "Catholic Emancipation." Liberty allowed a completer incorporation with the English people, a new baptism in the English spirit, a healthier, because a freer, profession of faith. And this had been prepared for from within. The saintly Challoner and the brave Milner had quickened Catholic religious zeal; Lingard, with notable erudition and independence, had made English history its apology; and Cardinal Wiseman improved the new day that had dawned by an apologetic of rare skill and eloquence. But the foreign taint still clung to Catholicism; it wanted English character and breeding, national traditions and aspirations. Even Wiseman was but an Italian priest, a professor from

Rome, Irish by descent, Spanish by birth. What it wanted the Oxford movement gave, a distinctively English quality and aspect. The men carried over to Rome had received the most typical English education, their leader was the greatest living master of the English tongue. They had been nursed in Anglican traditions, were, some of them, learned Anglican divines, who could not forget their learning or change their blood and breeding with their church, or cancel and cast out the ancient inheritance they had so long possessed and loved. They were Catholics of an altogether new type; their memories and instincts were not of a persecuted sect, hated and alien in England, but of a church proudly and consciously English ; the superstructure of their faith and life might be Roman, but the basis was Anglican, and the superstructure had to be accommodated to the basis, not the basis to the superstructure. Cardinal Newman does not build on Thomas Aquinas or Bellarmine or Bossuet ; they only supply the buttresses and pillars, the arches and gargoyles of his faith : his fundamental principles are those of Butler ; he reasons when he is gravest, fullest of conviction and most anxious to convince, in the methods and on the premisses of the *Analogy.* For polemical purposes he is all the better a Catholic for having been an Anglican ; and, indeed, in a very real sense, he did not cease to be an Anglican when he became a Roman Catholic. And it is this persistence of the primitive type that has been the strength of the derivative. Though the men went to Rome, they yet remained English; the principles that carried them had been educed and developed within the Anglican church and in its interests; and so men and principles alike tended to naturalize Catholicism on the one hand, and to beget a patient and respectful hearing for it on the other. People wished to believe that men they admired and loved had acted with reason and had accepted what was reasonable; the old attitude to Romanism ceased, and a public, well disposed for conviction, invited the best efforts of men so well able to convince.

§ V. *Whether the Catholic Apology was equal to the Need*

1. Now, whether Catholicism has profited by this extraordinary change, and the gains that caused it, as much as she hoped to do, or as she might and even ought to have done, or whether her once high hopes have been dashed with bitterest disappointment, is not a matter that concerns us. But here is a matter that does—the movement that made Religion more real and living to a large number of cultivated men did a true interpretative and so apologetic work. It is a blunder of the worst kind to imagine that any one form of Christianity can be served by any other being made ridiculous. It belongs to the madness of the sectary, whether Catholic or anti-Catholic, to believe that his own system grows more sane as others are made to seem less rational. But the

Protestant ought to be as pleased to discover the reason in Catholicism, as the Catholic to find the truth in Protestantism; what makes either ridiculous makes the other less credible. For if there is difference there is also agreement; and while the difference is in man's relation to the truth, the agreement is in the most cardinal of the truths that stand related to man. If Christ lives within Catholicism, He ought to seem the more wonderful, and it the less odious to the Protestant; if within Protestantism, He ought to appear the more gracious, and it the less void of grace and truth to the Catholic. Unmeasured speech is either insincere or unveracious; and the worst unveracity is the one that denies good to be where both good and God are. Now, the movement that made many men better Christians by making them Catholics, did a good deed for Religion. By showing that there was reason in Catholicism it made history more reasonable; it made, too, the honesty, saintliness, intellectual integrity and thoroughness of many schoolmen and thinkers more intelligible, and evoked the charity that dared to love and admire where religious and intellectual differences were deepest. There were, indeed, more irenical influences in the movement than the men who conducted it either imagined or desired.

2. But when we have said all that can be justly or even generously said in praise of the ecclesiastico-religious effects of this movement, have we said enough? England had some claim on the

6

men who led it, and so had the Christian Religion. England had done something for the men,
had borne, nursed, reared, educated them ; had endowed them with her best learning, the wealth
of her choicest teachers, the noble inheritance of
her traditions and aspirations. The Christian Religion had quickened and cultivated them, had inspired them with high faith and lofty ideals, had
given them a splendid opportunity for service and
equal ability to serve. The land and the faith that
had so entreated them, had a right to expect from
them a correspondent measure of help. They stood
at the breaking of a day that dawned with abundant promise of new life ; yet with the certainty of
all the difficulties new life ever encounters, and must
overcome or die. The century of hard rationalism
was ended ; its Deism, Free Thought, Encyclopæd-
ism, Materialized Religion, and Secularized Church
had perished in revolution ; and in revolution, and
through it, the spirit of the new age had been born.
In philosophy a constructive, though critical, Transcendentalism replaced the subtle and barren Empiricism that by the mouth of the sceptic Hume had
confessed that it knew not what man or nature
was, whence they had come or whither they tended.
In literature the genius of Goethe had created an
ideal of culture that seemed higher and completer
than the ideal of religion. Byron had assailed the
old moral and social conventionalisms, magnifying
independence of them into, if not the chief virtue,

yet the best note of the nobler manhood. Shelley had given clear and musical voice to the passion for freedom and hatred of the hoary despotisms that had hindered the progress and marred the happiness of man. Wordsworth had made nature radiant with the light of indwelling spirit; Scott had evolved from the past visions of chivalry and nobleness to rebuke, to cheer, and to inspire the present; Coleridge had made the speculative reason and the creative imagination become as sisters ministrant to faith; everywhere a brighter, more genial and reasonable spirit possessed man. In politics the old dynastic and despotic ambitions had fallen before the uprisen peoples; they were possessed by a new sense of brotherhood, a passion for ordered freedom, for justice, for the reign of the law that would spoil oppression, secure to each his rights, and require from all their duties. In such an hour of regeneration and the activity of the regenerated, Religion could not be allowed to escape change; the day of humdrum respectability was over. It was not enough that the church should stand by the throne, indifferent to the character of him who filled it; it must feel the new spirit, and either open its heart to it or by shutting the door against it seal its own doom. And when the new spirit knocked at the door of the English church, her then most potent and active sons knew not what better thing to do than to evoke an ancient ecclesiastical ideal to answer and withstand it. And it was out of this

appeal to a tried and vanquished past against a
living present, that the Anglo-Catholic movement
was born. It was less the child of a great love than
of a great hate, hatred of what its spokesman and
founder called " Liberalism." What he so called he
never understood ; his hatred was too absolute to
allow him to get near enough to see it as it was.
He was a poet, and had the poet's genius and
passion ; where he did not love he could not understand ; what he hated he held before his imagination, and took a sort of Dantesque pleasure in
making it hideous enough to justify his hate. This
abhorred " Liberalism " might have had a threaten-
ing front to mole-eyed prerogative and privilege ;
but the eye of the spiritual ought to have read its
heart, seen the probabilities of danger, but the infinite possibilities of good—its hatred of wrong, its
love of justice, its desire for sweeter manners, purer
laws, its purpose to create a wealthier, happier and
freer state. And the spirit that so discerned would
have helped by bringing Religion into " Liberalism "
to make " Liberalism " religious. But John Henry
Newman saw nothing of the enthusiasm of righteousness and humanity that was in its heart ; saw only
its superficial antagonisms, to political injustice, to
ecclesiastical privilege, to the venerable but mischievous, because richly endowed, inutilities of Church
and State ; and so he faced it as if it were the very
demon of revolution, the fraudulent disguise of Atheism and impiety. To counteract it he did not fall

back on the Christianity of Christ—that was too closely allied to the thing he hated; but he tried to recall the lost ideal of an authoritative church, the teacher, interpreter, and embodiment of Religion. His bulwark against "Liberalism" was authority; the organized illiberalism of a body ecclesiastical. The ghost of a mediæval church was evoked to exorcise the resurgent spirit of Christ in man.

That was a most calamitous choice, the loss of a golden opportunity for the highest service. Newman, though not the most gifted religious teacher of the century, had in him above any man of his day the quickening spirit, the power to search the conscience, to rouse the heart, to fire the imagination, to move the will. He was without the speculative genius of Coleridge; the swift insight that could read the heart of a mystery; the mental heroism that could explore every part of an opposed system; the chivalry that could entreat it nobly; the synthetic mind that could resist the fascination of false antitheses and antagonisms; the constructive intellect that could bring into order and unity elements that seemed to hasty and shallow thinkers chaotic and hostile. But he had, in a far more eminent degree, the qualities that teach and persuade men; a concentration of purpose; an intensity, even as it were a singleness, of conviction; a moral passion, a prophetic fervour, which yet clothed itself in the most graceful speech; a strength and skill of spiritual inquisition or analysis, enabling him to reach the inmost recesses of the heart and probe the sensitive secrets of the conscience; a humour now grim and fierce, now playful and tender; an imagination that often dominated, yet always served his intellect, and was most restrained when most indulged, its pictures but making his meaning more clear and distinct. He had not the large charity of Maurice, the power to read the system through the man and make the man illustrate the system, finding the good in both. Indeed, especially in his early days, he could not differ without disliking: dissent from a man's opinions rose almost into personal contempt or even hate of the man. Nor had he the massive and human-hearted manhood of Arnold, who ever loved persons and humanity more than systems and things; while of Newman it may be said, he valued persons only as they were the representatives of systems and typical of things. Nor had he Whately's sober integrity of mind, the English sagacity that liked to look things straight in the face and see them as they were. But he had as none of these had, as no man in this century has had, command over the English people through his command over the English tongue; the enthusiasm of a reformer who believed in the absolute sufficiency of the reform he was conducting; who lived, thought, spoke like a man who had a mission; and whose mission it was to reclaim the people of England for their church and their God. And the gift he had he could not exercise without moving men; they rallied to him or recoiled from him; his speech made disciples, agitated his church, filled it with strong hopes and strange fears, raised high expectations at Rome, and made England resound with the noise and confusion of long silent controversies. When we look into those disturbed times, the thing that most strikes and abides with us is, the presence and personality of the man that moved them.

3. We may, then, represent the matter thus :— the formative period of Newman's life, 1826–1833, and the decade that followed, may be described as a period during which men were waiting for a relevant constructive interpretation of the Religion of Christ. The revolutionary forces were spent, constructive forces were at work in every region of thought and life; and they needed but the electric touch of a great religious ideal to be unified and made ministrant to Religion. The old monarchical and oligarchical theories having perished, the Philosophical Radicals were seeking, with but poor success, a new basis for politics, that they might determine what was the chief good'; and new methods in legislation, that they might promote and secure the greatest happiness of the greatest number. John Stuart Mill had just escaped from the dogmatic Empiricism of his father; had been spiritually awakened by the poetry of Wordsworth and the philosophy of Coleridge; and was looking about for a faith by which to order his life. Charles Darwin was just beginning to watch the methods of nature and to

learn how to interpret her; and while Newman was
making verses and gathering impulses in the Medi-
terranean, he was away in the *Beagle* exploring many
seas and lands. In the "loneliest nook in Britain,"
under the shadow of hills and within sight of moorlands consecrated by the heroism and martyrdoms
of his Covenanting forefathers, Thomas Carlyle was
doing his strenuous best to wed the thoughts that had
come to him from German literature and philosophy,
with the substance and spirit of his ancestral faith ;
the effort taking visible shape in the egoistic idealism of his *Sartor Resartus*, and leading him to look
into man and his recent history with the eyes that
were to see in the French Revolution the tragedy
of retribution and righteousness. Transcendental
Idealism was in full career in Germany ; Hegel and
Schleiermacher were lecturing in Berlin, the one applying his philosophy to the explication of religion
and history, the other his criticism to the documents,
facts, and doctrines of the Christian faith ; while in
Tübingen, Strauss was combining and developing
the two, with results that were to break upon the
alarmed world in a certain *Leben Jesu.* In France,
Saint Simon had developed his *Nouveau Christianisme*, pleading that Religion might be more an
energy directing all "social forces towards the moral
and physical amelioration of the class which is at
once the most numerous and the most poor " : and
Comte had begun the *Cours de Philosophie Positive*,
explaining how the theological and metaphysical

states had been passed, and the final and positive state had come; and what were the new ideas of Society, of God, and of Religion on which it was to rest. Everywhere the struggle was towards positive ideas, constructive ideals, such an interpretation of man's nature, history, and universe, as would tend to a more perfect organization of society and a better ordering of life. It was indeed a splendid moment for an Apologist built after the manner of Augustine, with his insight into the actualities of the present and the possibilities of the future, with his belief in God and truth, the infinite adaptability and comprehensiveness, imperial authority and pervasive spirit of Religion. He would have seized the new ideas, translated them into their Christian equivalents, realizing, elevating, vivifying, organizing them by the act of translation. He would have found that every attempt to find law and order in nature, to discover method and progress in creation, without leap or gap, violence or interference, whether with Hegel, by the evolution of the transcendental idea, or, what was indeed only the empirical side of the same, with Darwin, by the gradation and blending of genera and species,—was no attempt to expel God from nature, but only to make nature more perfectly express Him, and be more wholly His. He would have welcomed every endeavour to read anew the past of man, to find law in it, to discover the affinities of thought and custom and belief—as evidence that men were at last awakening to the truth

that the race was a vast whole, a mighty organism,
whose parts lived in and through each other, and were
bound to live each for the other and all for the whole ;
and an organism which lived and grew not simply
by intercourse and conflict with its environment, but
under the reign and for the ends of a universal
Reason, an omnipresent Providence. He would have
seen in the ambition for freedom ; for more and more
equitably distributed wealth ; for a more perfect state,
a society where the hated inequalities of the past had
ceased, and a true human brotherhood was realized—
an ambition inspired by Christ, the direct fruit of His
humane and beneficent spirit. And he would have
hailed the love, which was even becoming a worship
of humanity, as proof that the first principles of
"the kingdom of God" were at last beginning to be
understood. And this relation to the new thought
would have determined his apology. It would not
have invoked the authority of a church that, whatever its claims, had proved its impotence by the
inexorable process of history in the indubitable
language of fact ; but it would have said :—" This
awakening is of God, and must be accepted as His,
not dealt with as if it were the devil's. These new
ideas of order in nature and history, of social justice
and human rights, those ambitions for a larger good
which 'Liberalism' so ill expresses, and Socialism
so badly embodies and fails to realize—are all of
Christ ; they mean that men are getting ready to
understand the idea of His Kingdom. It compre-

hends, for it created these new ideas; into its language they must be translated, that they may find
their most perfect forms, live in the organism and
possess the energy that will enable them to do their
work. The progress of man and the Church of God
are two kindred things; all true knowledge is knowledge of truth, and truth is holy; to know it is to
be made better, more like what God meant man to
be. Let knowledge grow—whatever truth science discovers religion blesses and appropriates; let research,
whether as physical investigation or historical criticism,
pursue her quest; for love of truth is love of God, and
the more we find of it, the more we know of Him."

4. What has just been said is meant to indicate
what would have been the attitude of a really constructive Christian thinker in face of the new and
nascent thought. He would have recognized as
Christian, and claimed for Christianity, the new
spirit, with all its nobler truths, ideals, aims. What
belongs of right to the Christian Religion ought to
be incorporated with it; what is so incorporated
can never become a facile and deadly weapon in the
hands of the enemy. But Newman's attitude was
precisely the opposite. Change was in the air; he
felt it, feared it, hated it. He idealized the past, he
disliked the present, and he trembled for the future.
His only hope was in a return to the past, and to
a past which had never existed save in the imagination
of the romancer. What he hated and resisted he
did not take the trouble to understand. He was in

this respect a conspicuous contrast to his friends, Hugh James Rose and Edward Bouverie Pusey, especially the latter, who, in his memorable, though, unhappily, afterwards recalled reply to the famous sermons of the former against German Rationalism, showed thorough knowledge of the older Continental criticism,—though, as it turned out, the knowledge was not his own,—as well as the chivalry that could dare to speak the truth concerning it. But one seeks in vain in Newman's early writings—poems, essays, articles, pamphlets, tracts—for any sign or phrase indicative of real comprehension of the forces he opposed. He does not comprehend their real nature or drift; what reasons they have for their being, what good they have in them, what truth; what wrongs to redress, what rights to achieve : he only feels that they are inimical to his ideals. There is no evidence that he ever tried to place himself in the position of the philosophical radical, or the rational critic, or the constructive socialist, or the absolute idealist ; and look at his and their questions through their eyes and from their standpoint. He hated them and their works too utterly to attempt to do so—perhaps he was haunted by a great doubt as to what might happen if he did ; but the result was, he resisted he knew not what, and knew not how to resist it. As a simple matter of fact, he resisted it in the least effectual way. He emphasized the church idea, the historical continuity, sanctity, authority, rights, prerogatives and powers of the organized society or body which called itself here the Anglican, there the Catholic church. The idea grew on him ; the more he claimed for the church, the more he had to claim ; the more he set it in opposition to the movement and tendencies of living thought, the more absolute and divine he had to make its authority. The logic of the situation was, inexorable,—if the church alone could save man from the spirit embodied in " Liberalism," then it must be a divine and infallible church, the vicar and voice of God on earth. But the logic of the situation was one, and the logic of history another and tragically different. In the past Catholic authority had bent like the rush in the river before the stream and tendency of thought ; if it had had divine rights it had been without divine wisdom ; men and countries it had owned, it had been unable to hold ; and for centuries the noblest life, the best minds, the highest and purest literatures of Europe had stood outside its pale. And what had been, was to be. Newman went to Rome, and carried with him, or drew after him, men who accepted his principles ; but the " Liberalism " he hated went its way, all the mightier and more victorious for the kind of barrier he had tried to build against it. He succeeded wonderfully in making Roman Catholics of Anglicans ; but he failed in the apologetic that saves the infidel, and baptizes the spirit of a rational and revolutionary age into the faith of Christ.

February, 1885.

CATHOLICISM AND RELIGIOUS THOUGHT

THE Catholic Revival ought not to be conceived as a mere English or insular movement: so far as English, it was rather like a wave which reached our shores from a larger continental flood. It took indeed, here, a form and character of its own; but it would be a grave mistake to regard it as isolated, or as simply the creation of a few able and resolute men. That was what it seemed to many contemporary critics, but it was nothing so accidental and arbitrary. The men who led it were, in a sense, spokesmen of a common intellectual and religious tendency. The revival they effected was part of the general European reaction against the Illumination and the Revolution. The reaction was not simple but complex, at once religious, intellectual and political; a recoil of the conservative spirit from the new ideals that had been so suddenly translated into portentous realities. And it was marked everywhere by the same hatred of the eighteenth century and all its works, embodied everywhere the same hopes and fears, expressed the same motives and ends. On the one side stood the revolutionary theses, the rights of reason and of man, the watchwords "liberty, equality, fraternity"; and these were construed not in their high ideal sense, but through the accidents and atrocities, the terror and ruin that had attended the attempt at realization. On the other side the reaction emphasized its own antitheses—the rights of the community before those of the individual; the rights of God and of the sovereigns, spiritual and civil, He had appointed, above those of the reason and the peoples; authority as the only sufficient basis of order; and order as the condition necessary to the highest common good. But not satisfied with opposing antitheses to theses, it became concrete and practical; confronted the recent revolutionary frenzy, its passion for iconoclasm and violent change, with an idealized mediæval history; attempted to resuscitate and realize its ideals; and in order to this, invested the church—which was its most splendid and persistent creation—with the authority that was held to be alone able to revive religion and create order, curb and turn back the loosened and lawless forces which had achieved the revolt. This radical contradiction, ideal and historical, seemed at once the surest and the most direct way to victory; but to build a dam across a river is not to arrest the gathering or change the course of its waters, as the men who securely pitch their tents in the shelter of the dam will be the first to experience.

§ I. *The Catholic Revival as the Counter-Revolution.*

The Catholic revival was the principal phase or feature of this reaction, and the literature that was its most operative factor may be described as the literature of the new Catholic Apologetic.[1] Our reference to its distinctive principles and work must be brief.

1. The reaction was a complex movement, at once literary, political, religious. In literature it appeared as Romanticism, in politics as legitimate and theocratic theory, in religion as Ultramontanism. These three were but different phases or expressions of the one spirit; and they may be said to represent the organization of the more conservative instincts against the new agencies of progress and change. The oneness of the spirit is evident from the ease with which its phases melted or passed into each other. Romanticism was a revolt against the reign

---

[1] What is here described as the literature of the new Catholic Apologetic, may be held as represented by the following :— Joseph de Maistre : *L'Eglise Gallicane* (Ed. 1882), *Les Soirées de Saint Petersbourg* (Ed. 1874), *Du Pape* (Ed. 1819). De Bonald : *Théorie du Pouvoir Politique et Religieux dans la Société Civile, La Législation Primitive* (Ed. 1819). Chateaubriand : *Génie du Christianisme* (Ed. 1802). Lamennais : *Essai sur l'Indifférence en Matière de Religion* (Ed. 1859). This literature may be said to be devoted to the exposition of the function of Catholicism in an age of revolution, and so represents what we have termed the new Apologetic. Good examples of the older are :—Houteville : *La Religion Chret. prouvée par les faits* (1740). 3 vols. Bergier : *Traité Historique et Dogmatique de la Vraie Religion* (1780). 12 vols.

of the classical and rational spirit in literature, with its intense individualism, its severe sense of justice and of personal rights. The Romantic movement rose outside Catholicism, was indeed German in its origin and had its source in the strenuous Protestant soul of Herder ; but it received full development at the hands of men like the Schlegels, Tieck, and Novalis, who loved the realm of the imagination, and hated the rationalism that had expelled miracle from nature, and mystery from man, making the universe the home of prosaic commonplace. They disliked the cold classicism of Goethe and even the warmer humanism of Schiller ; and said : " Poetry and religion are one. Man needs an imagination to interpret the universe, and he is happy only as he has a universe peopled by it and for it. These three —poetry, religion and imagination—are one, and are never found singly. When man has most religion he has also most poetry and is fullest of imagination ; and the times when he had these three divine graces in the highest degree were the mediæval." And so they glorified these times, edited their ballads and romances, praised their ideal of life and duty, their bravery, courtesy, devotion ; their indifference to the market and the exchange, their loyalty to beauty and honour and religion, their glorious Gothic archi- tecture, with the faith it at once embodied, illustrated and made illustrious. Admiration for the past, though it was a past that was a pure creature of the imagination, easily became belief in the church

7

that claimed it as its own ; and so Romanticism in
men like Stolberg, Friedrich Schlegel, and Werner,
passed by a natural gradation into Catholicism.

The reaction in politics was conducted in a still
more courageous and thorough spirit, for it was
directly polemical, a *guerre à outrance.* It was as
specifically French, or, let us say, Latin, in origin
and form, in atmosphere and purpose, as Romanticism
had been German. Authority must be made divine
if the rights of man were to be denied and his reason
subdued and governed ; but the dynastic idea had
been too rudely broken to be capable of again standing up, and in its own name claiming divine authority.
Its hour of weakness was the church's opportunity ;
it alone had braved the storm, it had been shaken
but it had stood, manifestly, not in its own strength,
but in God's. In the lurid light of the anarchy Rome
was seen to have a mission ; as the seat and home of
supreme authority, in her ancient rôle of the Eternal
City, universal, immutable, infallible, she could stand
forward as the saviour of society, now gone or going
to destruction for want of its most Christian kings.
She was the church God had founded, had supernaturally endowed and guided, had made the sole
bearer and teacher of His truth, and had graced and
crowned with an Infallible Head. Here was an
authority so awful, so august, and so inviolable as
to be alone able to end the conflict of rival rights,
and restore order by enforcing the one universal duty
—obedience. If divine authority was to rule in the

State, it must be got through the church. Round her, therefore, the broken fragments of the ancient order crystallized; to her the resolute spirits that headed the counter-revolution rallied with sure pre-science of her power, ideal and actual; and called upon the whole army of her supernatural claims and beliefs and sanctions for help in the new crusade. Joseph de Maistre formulated his hierocratic doctrine, making the Papal at once guarantee and condition the royal power. De Bonald wove the political into the religious revelation, ascribing sole sovereignty to God, but building upon it the Pope's, and upon his the king's. Chateaubriand described Christian Rome as being for the modern what Pagan Rome had been for the ancient world—the universal bond of nations, instructing in duty, defending from oppression. Lamennais argued that without authority there could be no religion, that it was the foundation of all society and morality, and that it alone enfranchized man by making him obedient, so harmonizing all intelligences and wills. And thus the Roman church, as the supreme authority, was conceived as the principle of order, the centre of political as well as religious stability; the only divine rights were those she sanctioned; in her strength kings reigned, and through obedience to her man was happy and God honoured.

2. The Counter-Revolution thus gave Catholicism a splendid opportunity for a new Apologetic; summoned it to occupy a more important and command-

ing position than it had held since the Renaissance.
The Apologetic may be described as the principle of
authority done into a philosophy which explained
the past and promised to save the present. It may
be said to have consisted of two parts, a theoretical
and an historical—the first being a vindication of
authority as the only sure basis of religion, and, con-
sequently, the only solid ground and guarantee of
order ; the second being a justification of the Roman
church as it had lived and acted in history.

i. The theoretical apologetic was on the positive
side a philosophy of religion, society, and history ; on
the negative, an absolute contradiction of the modern
philosophies, the governing principles or ideas of the
modern mind. The Apologists saw that the Revolution had not been an accident, but a logical issue
from the premisses of the sixteenth century ; *i.e.*, it
was an attempt to realize a political ideal correlative
and correspondent to the ideal of religious freedom.
The anarchy, the bloodshed, the social misery and
ruin, were held to be the direct result of the movement
which Luther had instituted ; to this, along many lines,
it had been inevitably tending ; in this, its true
character stood revealed. What appeared before the
Revolution as innocent abstractions, or speculations
that flattered human pride in the degree that they
exercised human reason, appeared after it as disintegrative forces capable of doing the most disastrous
work. It was not a question of Catholicism against
Protestantism, but of Catholicism against the modern

movement as a whole. Humanity must be turned back in its course three centuries that society might be saved. The literary revolt of the fifteenth century, the religious revolt of the sixteenth, the philosophical systems of the seventeenth, the political revolution of the eighteenth, were all parts of a whole, successive steps in the dread argument that had been fulfilling itself in history. To deal with this in the most radical way, modern philosophy, as supplying the principles and premisses, was fiercely attacked. It was not necessary that it should be understood or be treated with justice and truth; it was only necessary that it should be overturned and deprived of all its spoils. De Maistre, with what in him may have been a holy fury, but what in more worldly men would have been delirious unveracity, assailed both the philosophers and their philosophies, discrediting the systems through their authors. Bacon was a presumptuous and profane scientific charlatan, whose bad philosophy was the fit expression of his bad morality. "Contempt of Locke was the beginning of knowledge."[1] Hume "was perhaps the most dangerous and the guiltiest of all those baleful writers who will for ever accuse the last century before posterity."[2] Voltaire "was a man Paris crowned, but Sodom would have banished."[3] Even Herder was described as "the genteel (*honnête*) comedian who preached the gospel in the pulpit

---

[1] *Soirées*, vol. i., p. 442.   [2] *Ibid.*, p. 403.   [3] *Ibid.*, p. 243.

and pantheism in his writings."[1]   Lamennais argued
that the philosophies and the heresies had one principle, "la souveraineté de la raison humaine," the
end whereof was universal disbelief.[2]   Admit it, and
from the end there was no escape; the inevitable
way was from heresy to deism, from deism to
atheism, from atheism to universal scepticism.
Hence, by an exhaustive process, the necessary
conclusion was reached: we must have authority if
we are to have faith; the true religion is that which
rests on the greatest visible authority, which from
sheer lack of actual or possible claimants can be no
other than Rome.   The variations of philosophers as
of Protestants proved their want of truth; the consistencies and harmonies of Catholics proved their
possession of it.   Authority being the creative and
fundamental principle in religion, to despise or deny
it was sin—order was Heaven's first law; contempt
of authority was man's first disobedience.   The
systems that denied it were not simply false, they
were evil; at once causes and fruits of sin.   Of sin
and its inexorable penalties, the new Apologetic had
much to say; sin explained the revolt, the Revolution
illustrated the penalty.   To end the revolt the church
must triumph; and its victory would be the creation,
not of religion only, but of order, of a stable, contented, happy society.   But, as Lamennais was destined later fatefully to discover, if authority was to

---

[1] *Soirées*, vol. i., p. 258.   [2] *Essai sur l'Indifférence*, vol. iv., pp. 242-3.

rule at all, it must rule everywhere, in both Church and State; if freedom reigned in either, it would reign in both. So de Maistre saw and victoriously argued : both authorities are of God, but the spiritual is the higher; the king's does not qualify the Pope's, but the Pope's limits the king's. Power may be limited from above, but not from below; the subjects may not judge the sovereign, or impose conditions on him, but he may be judged by the Pope, and the judge of the Pope is God. Absolute authority thus, as political, personified in the king, confronted revolution; and as spiritual, personified in the Pope, confronted the Protestant reason; and by its strength religion was to be saved, society re-constituted, order created, and humanity made obedient to God.

ii. But it was not enough to be critical and theoretical; it was no less necessary to show the fine· correspondence of the theory with history, the speculation with fact. And so the discussion became historical; the church was exhibited as the maker of civilization, the mother of the arts and sciences, the creator of the humanities, the enemy of vice, the nurse of virtue, the home of all the graces. When the Roman empire fell the church mitigated the miseries, lessened the evils, conserved the good that but for her would have perished in the ruins. When the young peoples came pouring into the older states, she received them into her bosom, tamed them, organized their energies, built them into a new order and new civilization. She protected its tender years ; hers was the arm which turned back the Moor, the Saracen, and the Turk. In her the conquered peoples had their true and strongest friend ; the conquerors, a common sovereign who ruled their fierce wills into obedience and humanity. The church united the divided nations, created out of a multitude of turbulent tribes a brotherhood of peoples, made the hostile kingdoms become a single Christendom. Modern Europe without the church were inconceivable; whatever most distinguishes her, whatever she most admires, she owes to the church. The church has put her stamp on the literature of every modern people ; the drama rose out of her miracle plays ; it was her faith that bade the first and greatest of modern epics live, and that will not let it die. Art was her peculiar creation ; she inspired the genius of the builder, and he built the large faith he lived by into cathedral and monastery ; her vivid and fruitful imagination formed the painter, and the wondrous beauty of his work but witnesses to the sublimity of her spirit and the truth of her beliefs. Her mysteries, the sacraments, and miracles that offend the prosaic rationalism of a godless age, disclose their true significance, their power at once to awe, to humble, and to uplift, when seen reflected in the mirror of mediæval art. Science, too, the church had made ; her sons loved, and cultivated, and enlarged it when the world was dark, and kings and nobles lived but for war and plunder. All beneficent and ameliorative agencies were of her making: hospitals, charities, schools, colleges, the laws that shielded the serf from the savagery of his master. For all this, and kindred work, her very constitution qualified her. The clergy had no land, no home, no worldly affections, no secular care, were separated to her service, consecrated wholly to her ends, which were those of man's highest good. Her very organization showed her to be the bearer and organ of divine truth, throughout adapted to secure its recognition and realization among men. For above all stood the supreme Pontiff, the spiritual Sovereign, source of unity, law, order, directing the energies, formulating the judgments, determining the faith of the church; so much the Vicar of God as to be His audible voice; gifted with speech that he might control kings and command peoples, maintain religion, and compel obedience. What the church had been the church would continue to be; she had saved Europe when Rome perished, and would save it again even though it were out of the very jaws of the destroyer.

3. In this outline the hierocratic Apologetic is briefly but not unfairly or inaccurately represented. The historical part was at once confirmatory and illustrative of the theoretical. And so far as it was true to history it did a needed service. It did not indeed speak the whole truth, nay, it left much of the truth unspoken. Its past was largely a creation of the imagination; or a reality so highly idealized

as to have become the likeness of a vision. One
thing indeed must not be forgotten, viz., that the
objective and historical mode of viewing and representing the church and its work in the Middle
Ages rose outside Catholicism ; was due to liberal
and scientific thought, not to ecclesiastical and
polemical. To it, looking only from the historical
point of view, it seemed hardly possible to exaggerate
the obligations of Europe to Catholicism. The
Catholic church in the Middle Ages had nobly
served humanity ; moderated for the old world the
miseries of dissolution, moderated for the new the
perhaps still greater miseries of organization and
evolution. But suppose we grant, not the vigorously
historical and scientific view of the mediæval church,
but the highly imaginative and richly coloured
picture of those Catholic romances, what then ? Why,
this justice to mediæval must not make us unjust
to modern history. The question is, not what the
Catholic church had done in the early or middle
centuries, but what it has done in the modern world.
An organization that had served and saved a society
penetrated with pagan ideas, may be little qualified
to serve a society possessed and moved by Christian
ideals. Laws good for childhood may be bad for
manhood ; what makes a man of a child is excellent,
but what makes a child of a man is evil. The
Apologists were as weak in the modern as they
were strong in the mediæval question. In the one
case, they were eloquent and philosophic about the

church and its work; in the other, they were re-
proachful and severe concerning the pride and
wickedness of man, though he was no prouder or
more wicked than the men who had been in either
pagan or mediæval times. They did not see that
there was an absolute change in the conditions; in
the earlier period it was the secular empire that
had broken down, but in the later the breakdown was
in the spiritual. In the days of the decadence of
imperial Rome and in those of the barbarian invasions
and the formation of the European States, the church
had indeed been an ameliorative agency and an architectonic power; but in the days of the Reformation
and the Revolution it was the church that had
fallen into feebleness and become a disintegrative
force. The Europe she claimed to be alone able
to reorganize and restore, was the very Europe
that her own hands had disorganized. Chaos had
come into the world because she had not been
able to govern it. She was in the place of the
Roman Empire, while the modern spirit was claiming to occupy the place that had once been hers
The Pope was the new Julian; de Maistre the
new Libanius. As a simple matter of fact, the
very revolt of the intellect was the gravest possible
reflection on the capacity of the church. The intellect had been in subjection for centuries; to allow
it to escape implied infirmity in the ruler, deficiency
in wisdom, inefficiency of energy and will. The
claim of infallibility is a tremendous claim, not be-

cause of what it requires from man, but because
of what it demands in and from the church. Infallibility in truth is significant when conjoined with
infallibility in wisdom ; but the one without the other
is significant only of the incapacity which springs from
uncorrelated faculties. And when infallibility in matters of opinion is conjoined with the most pitiful
fallibility in conduct, the situation becomes worse
than absurd. To be under an authority so ill-
balanced and so badly guided where guidance is most
necessary, is like being under a creator, almighty
but not all-wise ; to possess it is, as it were, to have
the mechanical gift, the skill to make instruments ;
but not the political, the power to handle and govern
men. For if the revolt of the sixteenth century
were a sin, the men who achieved it were not the
only sinners—still guiltier was the church that made
it possible, and allowed it to become actual. During
centuries she had been supreme ; hers had been
the hands that made the men, hers the mind that
made Europe ; and if the issue of all her doings
and endeavours were the revolt, could she be guilt-
less, or as wise as she must be to make her infallibility of any avail, or make it anything more than
an ability to do great things if she only knew how ?

But more : why had the Revolution happened ?
and why amid so much hideous terror and blood ?
Modern philosophy was not altogether or alone to
blame ; neither was suppressed and expatriated
Protestantism. The men were sons of France,

France was the eldest son of the church, and the
son ruled as the church had taught him, with results
dreadful to both. The responsibility for the horrors
of the Revolution does not lie with its principles,
but with its causes; and who will now say that to
these causes the church did not powerfully contribute? But if she were a contributary cause, what
becomes of her claim to the sole ability to organize
and order the modern, because she had ordered
and organized the mediæval world? To be a cause
of the evil can hardly be regarded as guarantee-
ing the possession of the power to cure it. The
philosophy of history is guided in its judgments by
rigorous and impartial principles. It cannot, merely
in the interest of dogma or sect, accord or deny
honour to a church; but the honour it accords at
one period may be changed into deepest blame at
another. The very reasons that lead it to praise
the work and services of early and mediæval
Catholicism, compel it to hold the later Catholicism
mainly responsible for evils the Revolution was
needed to cure.

If the historical doctrine was no good philosophy
of history, still less was the theoretical a good
philosophy of religion. To base religion on authority is the most fatal of all scepticisms. The arguments that prove it, prove man possessed of an
inherent and ineradicable atheism of nature. But
what is to be said on this point can better be said
later on. Enough to remark here, the new Apolo-

getic was an apologetic for Catholicism, not for
Christianity. Its interest was the church, not the
religion, at least the religion only so far as identical
or co-extensive with the church. This gave to it
its two most distinctive characteristics — it was
political or sociological and historical. It was a
theory of society and the State illustrated by specific
periods and events in history. It was a speculation
as to the best methods for the creation and maintenance of order. De Maistre, as has been well
said, was a publicist, and looked at the whole matter
from the publicist's point of view. He was a sort
of ecclesiasticized Hobbes, with the strength, courage,
keenness, directness, and, we may add, coarseness
of the original; only with the Pope substituted for
the king. But even so, the hierocratic system had
its place, and did a not unneeded or ignoble work.
It did for the Papacy what Hobbes had done for the
Monarchy, formulated a theory of government where
order was created by absolute authority being given
to the one, and absolute subjection to the many.
Both marked the reaction that succeeded revolution, though in the one case the revolution was
religious, an attempted reign of the saints; in the
other secular, an attempted reign of reason. It was
no less characteristic that the theory opposed to
the religious revolution based authority on might,
but the theory opposed to the secular based might on
authority. Hobbes' king created the church, but de
Maistre's church created the king. Yet each is

explained by its occasion. The Restoration would have been incomplete without the Leviathan ; the Catholic revival and the Counter-revolution would have lacked theoretical justification without Ultramontanism.

§ II. *The English Counterpart of the Continental Revival*

1. We must now pass from the Continental to the English Catholic movement. The conditions in the two cases were altogether different. In France the Revolution had been swift, imperious, destructive ; but in England the genius of the people, their prosaic sagacity and insular pride, sobered and disciplined by the long struggle towards completer freedom, first held it at bay, then graduated its approach, and, at last, peacefully and legally accomplished it. Hence the Catholic revival could not appear here as the counter-revolution, as the source and ground of order to a disordered State ; for order reigned, and our very revolutions had increased rather than disturbed it. Indeed, our combined freedom and order had so perplexed and bewildered the hierocratic theorists, that de Bonald calmly dismissed from consideration the English people, because they were, " mainly on account of their defects, by far the most backward of civilized peoples," and de Maistre described our constitution as " an insular peculiarity utterly unworthy of imitation." But even here the forces of change were active, and their movement was the more resistless that it

was so regulated and, as it were, so constitutional. These forces were not simply in the air but immanent in the English nature, embedded in the customs and habits, laws and institutions, mind and method of the people. They were forces universal and supreme; govĕrning the men who governed. While they appeared political, they were really religious; they threatened the Church even more than the State; they questioned the accepted principles, doctrines, facts, and authorities in religion, much more severely than the ancient and established customs and methods in politics. In their collective and corporate character these forces constituted what was termed "Liberalism," which was the milder but more fatal English equivalent for the fiercer but less insidious Gallican "Revolution." If, then, they were held to be forces mischievous in character, evil in tendency, and ruinous in result, to resist them was a most manifest and absolute duty. But how? The Sovereign could not, for the Sovereign was simply the greatest subject in the realm, the creation of its laws; nor could the Parliament, for it was but the nation in Council; nor could the church, for the church was the people's, rather than the people the church's. There was nothing then to hinder the people, were they so minded, from going so far wrong as even to abolish the law and worship of God. It was necessary, therefore, to discover an authority able to bridle and govern the forces of change. God was the supreme authority;

the church in which He lived and through which He worked was His visible presence; in it, therefore, the Divine authority must dwell. Of this the English people had hitherto been negligent or unconscious; only here and there a Catholic divine had understood and believed; but once make it thoroughly evident, and men, no longer ignorantly free to believe and worship as they pleased, will feel bound to hold the faith and obey the law of God.

This was, in brief, the genesis of the Anglican movement. While formally and incidentally affected by many collateral influences—the romances of Scott, which supplied it with an idealized past, and inspired the passion still further to idealize it; the speculation of Coleridge, which touched it with mysticism, and imparted, in some degree, the gift of spiritual insight; the poetry of Wordsworth, which revealed the symbolical and sacramental significance of common things—yet it was essentially an endeavour, in a period when political change threatened to affect religious institutions, to find a stable religious ground on which to build the faith, an absolute authority by which to govern the life, first of the individual, next of the nation. It assumed that the truth of God did not live in the common reason, or His authority reign in the collective conscience; and that, without a special organ or vehicle for their transmission and embodiment, they could not continue to live and reign at all. It thought that if the State touched even the abuses of the church,

8

it would act profanely ; and it desired therefore to
make the church inviolable by the State. What
was needed to set a limit to the forces of encroach-
ment and aggression was an authority—valid, visible,
supreme. To be supreme, it must be religious ; to
be visible, it must be a realized polity or constituted
society; to be valid, it must have independent legislative and efficient executive powers. With these
attributes the Anglican church was invested, but
they were too immense for her ; she bent and failed
beneath the burden. Her weakness but set off the
strength of Catholicism. What the one church
could not bear, was the very vital principle of the
other ; she had for centuries been testifying her
possession of it to the perverse and incredulous
English people. The ancient cause of offence became the new feature of commendation; and those
who felt that they could not believe and be Christian
without authority, found in her bosom the authority
they needed.

2. The English Catholic movement, then, was
distinguished from the Continental by its being more
personal and religious in character, aiming at reform
and resistance rather than counter-revolution. The
publicist view did not exist here ; the conditions did
not call for it. But what national events occasioned
in France, personal experiences accomplished in
England, though they were experiences of disquiet
in the face of forces which Europe had learned to
dread. Still the arena of action and change was

mainly subjective, in minds that had feared the un-
settling influence of the critical and progressive tendencies then active, and were alarmed for religion
in the degree that they loved it. The revolution
that was dreaded was internal, in the region of
thought and belief. Superficial readers of the
Apologia have wondered at the determinative
influence attributed to such incidents as the Jerusalem Bishopric; but, in truth, nothing could be
more just than the place assigned to it, or more
impressive and significant. It was not only a fact
fatal to a theory; but Newman's mind had become
hyper-sensitive, it had lost the sense of proportion;
little things troubled even more than large; and his
doctrine of the church had become so nearly equivalent to the truth of religion, that what touched the
one seemed to threaten the other with ruin and
disaster. It had become a matter of personal necessity that he should find an immutable and infallible
church, in order that he might have a stable and
true religion. This need was altogether distinctive
of him and the men he moved, and belongs rather
to their natural history than to the nation's. It did
not rise out of the native conservatism of the English
people, seeking to find the religious principle or constitutional doctrine that could best resist the tides
of revolutionary thought and action; but it rose in
the spirits and out of the experiences of men who
believed that religion could not be saved, either for
themselves or the people, unless in the strength of

a greater and more efficient authority than any their church knew or could allow.   Hence the English Catholic movement proceeded from and expressed the religious necessities of persons, not the needs of the State or the aspirations of the people.   And what it was, it is—a thoroughly individual movement, with less national promise now than it had at first ; and, what we may term its fundamental principle— an organized authority as the basis of Religion, and this authority as embodied in the infallible church of Rome—was formulated to satisfy these individual needs.   What we have now to consider is the validity and constructive value of this principle, as repre- sented and interpreted by modern English, as dis- tinguished from Continental, Catholicism.

§ III.   *Philosophical Scepticism as the Apology for Ecclesiastical Authority*

1. Cardinal Newman [1] is here, beyond question, the

---

[1] If the subject had been Apologetics by English Catholics, instead of, as it really is, English Catholicism as an Apologetic, there are many men I should have liked gratefully to review, such as Cardinal Wiseman, Dr. Ward, Father Dalgairns, a thinker of exquisite subtlety and refinement, Mr. St. George Mivart, Father Harper, and others hardly less worthy of regard.   The extensive work of the last, *The Metaphysics of the School* (Macmillan & Co., 3 vols., 1879–84), deserves a more careful criticism than it has yet received.   Its worth for the historical student is considerable : but its polemical, critical, and constructive parts, though most painstaking and laborious, are of another order and quality than the expository.   Thomas Aquinas is indeed more real and intelligible in his own Latin than in any English exposition.   He is in the one case a living

representative man, and so it is through him that we must construe and criticise the principle. Its acceptance was a necessity to his own faith; he has done more than any living man to make it a necessity to the faith of others. He is here regarded under only one aspect, as the disciple and defender of Roman Catholic authority, that he may be the better and more victorious a Christian Apologist. We have the right so to regard him. Disciples have represented him as the foremost apologist of the day; his *Apologia* was the recognition of his own significance, the history was the justification of " his religious opinions." There is no man living whose works are so thoroughly autobiographical; they are but various illustrations of his own principle—in

---

teacher, handling relevant problems, holding his own place in history, determining much both of the form and matter of later thought ; but in the other case he is only an adapted teacher, not very capable of the sort of adaptation he has received, rather lustily resisting it, justly refusing to be forced to shed light on problems that had not emerged in his own day. Descartes, Hume, and Kant are not to be so answered and superseded ; their questions underlie the " Metaphysics of the School," determining alike their possibility and worth, and Father Harper's criticisms are incidental and verbal rather than material and real. He must go to work in a more radical fashion, both in the criticism of modern philosophy and the adaptation of the schoolman, before he can effect either the displacement of the one or the substitution of the other. Yet we gladly acknowledge that the increased attention, so largely due to the present Pope, which has now for many years been paid in Catholic schools to Thomas Aquinas is a most hopeful sign for Catholicism.

religious inquiry egotism may be true modesty.[1]
There is as much autobiography in, to mention no
others, the *Sermons*, the *Discourses to Mixed Congregations*, the *Development of Christian Doctrine*,
Present Position of Catholics in England, the *Letters
to Dr. Pusey* and *to the Duke of Norfolk*, and the
Grammar of Assent, as in the *Apologia*. Indeed, the
Apologia loses half its significance when read alone ;
it needs to be studied in the light of the works, tracts,
essays, lectures, histories and treatises, chronologi-
cally arranged. Conscious revelation of self, even
when most careful and scrupulous, hides even more
than it reveals ; it is the unconscious and undesigned
that testify more truly of a man. Newman was
always supremely conscious of two beings—God and
himself—and his works are a history of his successive
attempts to determine and adjust the relations between these two. This is significant ; in the heart
of this chief of English Catholics there is an intense individualism—indeed, it was the strength of
his individualism that made a Catholic of him. The
Apologia is the history of an individual mind ; the
Grammar of Assent is its dialectic—*i.e.*, the translation of the causes and course of the changes which
the history records, into logical forms and reasoned
processes. But this exactly defines the worth and
describes the range of Newman's apologetic work
—it is distinctively individual—first explicative of

---

[1] *Grammar of Assent*, p. 384 (fifth ed.). Cf. Mr. Lilly's
Ancient Religion and Modern Thought p. 48.

himself, and then cogent for men who start with his ecclesiastical assumptions and are troubled with his spiritual experiences and perplexities; not for those outside the churches, seeking for a reasoned and a reasonable belief.

In order to a radical and just discussion, it will be necessary to discover, if possible, Newman's ultimate ideas or the regulative principles of his thought; for they determine not only his ratiocination, but his mode of viewing things, and the kind and quality of the arguments that weigh with him. He is by nature a poet, by necessity rather than choice a metaphysician and historian. Truth finds him through the imagination, is real only as it comes to him in image and breathing form, a being instinct with life. And so he hates the abstract and loves the concrete; a truth grows real to him only when it is so embodied as to speak to the imagination and fill it. He is ill at ease when the discussion carries him into the region of abstract principles; he is happy only when he can handle what his intellect conceives to be the actual. For the same reason he is averse to historical criticism. No man had ever less of the analytical and judicial spirit, that must search and sift and separate till the original and unadorned fact be found. He can well understand the love that idealizes the past; he cannot so well understand the love that is so bent on the truth as to be able to analyze and sacrifice the dearest traditions and beliefs to reach it. He loves the past which fills and satisfies the imagination, not the one dissected and disclosed by the critical reason. Now, these characteristics make it a difficult, almost a cruel, thing to attempt to reach the ultimate principles that govern his thought. His is a mind to be handled as he loves to handle things, imaginatively and in the concrete, not coldly analyzed ; but unless his governing ideas are reached, neither his mind nor his method can be understood.

2. The true starting-point for the critical analysis and appraisement of Newman's apologetic work is the famous passage—

" I came to the conclusion that there was no medium, in true philosophy, between Atheism and Catholicity, and that a perfectly consistent mind, under those circumstances in which it finds itself here below, must embrace either the one or the other. And I hold this still : I am a Catholic by virtue of my believing in a God ; and if I am asked why I believe in a God, I answer that it is because I believe in myself, for I feel it impossible to believe in my own existence (and of that fact I am quite sure) without believing also in the existence of Him, who lives as a Personal, All-seeing, All-judging Being in my conscience." [1]

The points here noteworthy are—(1) Atheism and Catholicism are to his own mind the only logical alternatives ; (2) he is a Catholic because a Theist ; and (3) a Theist, because he believes in his own existence, and hears God speak in his conscience. Now, in a case like this, it is a matter of moment to see how the principle and the ultimate deduction are

---

[1] *Apologia,* p. 198 (ed. 1883).

related—the process by which he passes from conscience to God, and from God to Catholicism. It
may be true that " he has not confined the defence
of his own creed to the proposition that it is the
only possible alternative to Atheism ";[1] but it is
certainly true that he believes it to be the only real
alternative, and his belief looks ever and again
through the joints and fissures of his cumulative
argument, especially as pursued and presented in
his great dialectic work. The position, a Catholic
because a Theist, really means, when translated out
of its purely individualistic form, a Catholic in order
that he may continue a Theist; for, as Dr. Newman
conceives the matter, Catholicism, though it did not
create Theism, is yet necessary to its continuance
as a belief. " Outside the Catholic Church, things
are tending to Atheism in one shape or another."[2]
The Catholic church is the one " face to face antagonist," able " to withstand and baffle the fierce
energy of passion and the all-corroding, all-dissolving
scepticism of the intellect in religious inquiries."[3]
As Dr. Newman conceives the matter, Catholicism
is for the race as for the individual, the only alternative to Atheism, the necessities that govern the
individual governing also the collective experience.
Without Catholicism, faith in God could not continue
to live. There is, therefore, in spite of the con-

[1] Mr. Lilly's letter, *Grammar of Assent,* p. 500.
[2] *Apologia,* p. 244.   [3] *Ibid.,* p. 243.

science, so much latent Atheism in the nature, and, especially, the reason of man, that without an organization, miraculously created and governed, God would be driven out of human belief and reverence. A theory of this sort may in a high degree honour the church, but in the same degree it dishonours God. If " the Church's infallibility " be " a provision adapted by the mercy of the Creator to preserve Religion in the world," [1] then the provision has been not only, as the history of European thought testifies, singularly ill-adapted to its end ; but it implies a strange defect in the original constitution of the world, and a still stranger limitation, alike in the intensive and extensive sense, of the divine relation to it.

The relation between Theism and Catholicism being so conceived, the one must be made to involve the other ; the Theism becomes the implicit Catholicism, the Catholicism the explicit Theism. The question here is, not why the Theism needs the Catholicism, but how Catholicism is involved in and evolved from the Theism ?   The questions are related : for if the how can be found, the why will at once become apparent.   Yet it is necessary to hold them distinct, for only so can we get at those ultimate principles or ideas we are here in search of.   It seems, at first, curious that the Theism, which does not need Catholicism for its creation, should need it for its continuance.   One would have thought that what existed before it, and independently of it, could

---

[1] *Apologia*, p. 245.

exist without it ; but this is the very thing the position will not allow.   Theism must grow into Catholicism or die, become Pantheism, or Atheism, or
something equally bad and unlike the original.   If
we ask, why ? the answer is more or less rhetorical,
a survey of modern schools and tendencies of
thought ; and a comparison of their conflict and
varieties of opinion, with the certainty, harmony, and
tenacity of Catholic belief.   But if we ask, how the
one involves and leads up to the other ? we shall
find that it was really and only due to the concatena-
tion of ideas in Newman's own mind.   What made
him, because a Theist, become a Catholic ?   There was
nothing generic, or common, or logical in the process,
to give it validity apart from the assumptions and
peculiar history of the man himself.

But, to pursue the analysis, it is evident that the
answer to the question, What made him because a
Theist become a Catholic ? depends on the answer
to a still prior question, Why is he a Theist ?   What
is the basis and reason of his Theism ?   He tells us
that he came to rest in the thought of two, and two
only, absolute and luminously self-evident beings, himself and God.[1]   But why was the being of God as
certain and luminous to him as his own ?   Through
conscience, which he holds to be the theistic and
religious faculty or organ in man.[2]   " Were it not
for the voice, speaking so clearly in my conscience

---

[1] *Apologia*, p. 4.
[2] *Grammar of Assent* pp. 105–110, 389 (fifth ed.).

and my heart, I should be an Atheist, or a Pantheist, or a Polytheist when I look into the world."[1] "As we have our initial knowledge of the universe through sense, so do we in the first instance begin to learn about its Lord and God from conscience."[2] In each case the knowledge is instinctive; "the office which the senses directly fulfil as regards creation," is indirectly fulfilled by the sense of moral obligation as regards the Creator.[3] It is therefore conscience not as "moral sense," but as "sense of duty," as "magisterial dictate," which "impresses the imagination with the picture of a supreme Governor, a judge, holy, just, powerful, all-seeing, retributive."[4] As a consequence "conscience teaches us, not only that God is, but what He is"; "we learn from its informations to conceive of the Almighty, primarily, not as a God of wisdom, of knowledge, of power, of benevolence, but as a God of justice and judgment." "The special attribute under which it brings Him before us, to which it subordinates all other attributes, is that of justice—retributive justice."[5] The "creative principle" and the contents of religion necessarily correspond; the correlative of the "magisterial dictate" within, is the dictating magistrate without.

Conscience, then, is the theistic and religious

---

[1] *Apologia*, p. 241.   [2] *Grammar of Assent*, p. 63.
[3] *Ibid.*, p. 104.   [4] *Ibid.*, pp. 105–110.
[5] *Ibid.*, pp. 390–391.

faculty; but what of the intellect, the reason? While "the unaided reason, when correctly exercised, leads to a belief in God, in the immortality of the soul, and in a future retribution," "the faculty of reason," considered "actually and historically," tends "towards a simple unbelief in matters of religion." The intellect is "aggressive, capricious, untrustworthy"; its "immense energy" must be smitten hard and thrown back by an infallible authority, if Religion is to be saved. Its action in religious matters is corrosive, dissolving, sceptical.[1] Hence while the conscience creates religion, the reason tends to create unbelief; the one is on the one side of God, the other against Him. Of course he speaks of "reason as it acts in fact and concretely in fallen man"; but the conscience he speaks of is also the active and actual "in fallen man." If sin puts either, it must put both, out of court; what does not disqualify the one as a witness, ought not to be used to stop the mouth of the other.

3. But why is so different a measure meted out to the two faculties? The reason must be sought in Dr. Newman's underlying philosophy. That philosophy may be described as one empirical and sceptical, qualified by a peculiar religious experience. He has a deep distrust of the intellect; he dare not trust his own, for he does not know where it might

---

[1] *Apologia*, pp. 243–246. Cf. *Discourses to Mixed Congregations*, p. 283.

lead him, and he will not trust any other man's. The mind "must be broken in to the belief of a power above it"; to recognize the Creator is to have its "stiff neck" bent.[1] The real problem of the *Grammar of Assent* is, How, without the consent and warrant of the reason, to justify the being of religion, and faith in that infallible church which alone realizes it.[2] The whole book is pervaded by the intensest philosophical scepticism; this supplies its *motif*, determines its problem, necessitates its distinctions, rules over the succession and gradation of its arguments. His doctrine of assents, his distinction into notional and real—which itself involves a philosophy of the most empirical individualism—his criticism of Locke, his theories of inference, certitude, and the illative sense, all mean the same thing.[3]

---

[1] *Discourses to Mixed Congregations*, pp. 275, 276.

[2] Mr. Froude, in a for him rather innocent way, describes the *Grammar* as "an attempt to prove that there is no reasonable standing-ground between Atheism and submission to the Holy See."—*Short Studies*, second series, p. 83. If he had said—"a book intended to show how a sceptic in philosophy could, in the matter of Religion, find no standing-ground," etc., etc., he would have been nearer the truth.

[3] The philosophical scepticism is, of course, implicit, not explicit. From the latter he has tried carefully to guard himself; cf. *Gram.*, 64. In this connection the paragraphs, pp. 60, 61, which the late Dr. Ward thought a veiled attack on himself, ought to be studied : cf. *Philosophical Theism*, vol. i., pp. 30, 31. The two men were alike in their religious profession, but not in their philosophical principles. The sort of analysis in which Dr. Ward delighted, was not agreeable to Dr. Newman ; it savoured too much of the abstract and *a priori* to please so

His aim is to withdraw religion and the proofs concerning it from the region of reason and reasoning
into the realm of conscience and imagination, where
the reasons that reign may satisfy personal experience without having objective validity, or being able
to bear the criticism that tests it. And so he feels
" it is a great question whether Atheism is not as
philosophically consistent with the phenomena of the
physical world, taken by themselves, as the doctrine
of a creative and sovereign Power." This is the
expression of real and deep philosophic doubt, which
is not in any way mitigated by the plea that he
does not "deny the validity of the argument from
design in its place."[1] Neither did John Stuart
Mill.

We are now in a position to see why to Dr. Newman Theism involves Catholicism. It does so for two
reasons, springing respectively out of his doctrines
of the conscience and of reason. He interprets conscience as the consciousness of a "magisterial dictate," the echo within the breast of an authoritative
voice speaking without it; and to him the legitimate
deduction is the organization of the authority in an
infallible church, and the articulation of the voice
through its infallible head. But the other is the

---

great a lover of the concrete and experimental. And Dr.
Ward's trust in his faculties and their avouchments, came
nearer a belief in the sufficiency of reason than Dr. Newman
liked to go.

[1] *University Sermons*, p. 194. Cf. Mr. Lilly, p. 99.

more imperative reason : the intellect is not to be trusted ; left to themselves the conscience may succeed at first, but the intellect prevails at last. There is no possible escape. "Unlearn Catholicism," and the "infallible succession" is, "Protestant, Unitarian, Deist, Pantheist, Sceptic."[1] The "formal proofs" for the being of God may amount to "an irrefragable demonstration against the Freethinker and the Sceptic"; but they are able so "to invalidate that proof" as to "afford a plausible, though not a real, excuse for doubting about it." And without Catholicism the doubt is invincible. "When a man does not believe in the church, there is nothing in reason to keep him from doubting the being of a God." "There is nothing between it (the church) and Scepticism, when men exert their reason freely."[2]

4. Atheism and Catholicism are then to Dr. Newman the only possible logical alternatives, because, if we are not driven by the inner and ethical authority, *i.e.* conscience, to rest in an infallible outer authority, *i.e.* the Roman church, we must follow whither the intellect leads, and make the *facilis descensus Averni.*

---

[1] *Discourses to Mixed Congregations*, p. 283. Cardinal Newman here but repeats Lamennais. It is interesting to compare the agreements of the *Essai sur l'Indifference* with the *Grammar* and the *Apologia.* They differ in some important respects, but in one fundamental point they agree—their philosophical basis for the dogma of authority is the most absolute of all scepticism—doubt of the sanity and divine contents of human reason. They believe in its native and ineradicable Atheism.   [2] *Ibid.*, pp. 262, 263, 283.

But what sort of basis have we here for Theism? and what sort of Catholicism have we built on it? The nature of man is divided, and its two parts set in contradiction and antagonism to each other. The conscience is "the aboriginal vicar of Christ, a prophet in its informations, a monarch in its peremptoriness, a priest in its blessings and anathemas;"[1] but the reason is critical, sceptical, infidel, even atheistic. This division of nature is the death of natural proof; it is a confession that proof is impossible. He may recognize "the formal proofs on which the being of a God rests"; but his recognition must be criticized in the light of his fundamental principle. It is to him entirely illegitimate. Conscience he holds to be authoritative, but not reason. He deduces Religion from conscience, but leaves reason to be crushed and subdued by authority. Now to build Religion on a doctrine that implies the radical antagonism of these two, is to make their reconciliation impossible to Religion; the one must be sacrificed to the other if man is ever to have peace. The Catholicism that achieves this may be extensive, but is not intensive; it may be political and local, but is not ideal and human; it may be externalized authority, but is not externalized reason. It may include all men, but it does not include the whole man. But more: the reason within man im-

---

[1] *Letter to the Duke of Norfolk.—Anglican Difficulties,* vol. ii. p. 248.

plies the reason without him; he develops into a
rational being because he lives in a rational world.
To leave the theistic contents of the reason unexpli-
cated, is to leave the theistic reason of the world
unexplored and unrecognized; only as they are conceived in their correspondent and reciprocal relations
can we have a Theism satisfactory to the whole
nature of man and explicative of the system to
which he belongs. It is only through reason we find
an argument of universal validity; but Cardinal
Newman's doctrine is the purest individualism. The
deliverance of his conscience avails for himself—can
avail for no other; it has interest as a fact of personal
testimony, but has no value as a ground of general
belief. It is significant, too, as to the temper of his
own mind; in his intellect as he knows it, in his
reason as he interprets it, he finds no Religion, no
evidence for the being of God : he dare not trust or
follow it, for its bent is sceptical; and so he has to
invoke the voice of authority to silence and to command. The need he discovered in history for an infallible church, he had first found in his own breast.

§ IV. *Whether either the Scepticism or the Authority
be Valid*

Detailed criticism of Newman's position, with
its various assumptions and complex confusion of
thought, is, of course, here impossible; but it is hardly
possible to conceive a worse basis for a constructive
Theism, especially in a critical and sceptical age. It

turns Catholicism into a new and feebler Protestantism, one directed against the modern movement of mind. The Freethinker sacrifices religion to reason in one way, by declaring that his individual mind is the measure of religious truth ; the Catholic does it in another way, by declaring that unless religion come under the ægis of his church, it will assuredly perish before the corrosive action of the intellect. Each position is an awful degradation of religion, but the latter is the greater ; for the intellect will not, indeed cannot, cease to be active and critical, and what is declared incapable of resisting its criticism is handed over to death. There is surely a nobler Catholicism than this, one not of Rome, but of man, based, not on the excommunication of the reason, but on the reconciliation of the whole nature, intellect, conscience, heart, will, to God and His truth.

1. In Cardinal Newman's position, those elements that belong to his Apology for Theism must be distinguished from those that belong to his Apology for Catholicism. They are not only distinct, but incompatible. Theism is so rooted in his being, that he must believe in God because he believes in his own existence ; but, on the other hand, his reason is so inimical to Theism that if he had not become a Catholic, he must have become an Atheist. Now, this is an important psychological fact, a valuable testimony concerning personal experience ; but when it is erected into a dialectic position and elaborated into an Apology for Catholicism, as the only possible

permanent form of the Christian Religion, the matter
is altogether changed. It is then necessary to say,
the position is at once philosophically false and
historically inaccurate. To exercise the intellect
is to serve God; Religion has been most vital
and most vigorous when the intellect was most
critically concerned with it. This is a simple historical fact. In the *Apologia* [1] it is said: "No truth,
however sacred, can stand against it (the faculty of
reason), in the long run": and the illustration is, the
pagan world when our Lord came. But the intellect
in the ancient world ennobled and spiritualized Religion; the period of its greatest activity in Greece
was also the period when the religious faith became
purest and strongest. The poets made its gods more
august, moral, judicial. Plato made its ideas sub-
limer, purged its mythology, transfigured the theistic
conception, made the world articulate the perfect
reason, and time sleep in the bosom of eternity. The
Stoics, by finding a moral order in the universe and a
moral nature in man, breathed a new ethical spirit
into both their religion and their race. In the ancient
world the activity of the intellect in the field of
religious knowledge was the life of Religion; and
when it ceased to be active, Religion ceased to live.
In the days of our Lord, the places where the intellect was most active were also the places where
Religion was most real.

---

[1] Page 243.

And what was true of the ancient, is true of the modern world. The activity of the intellect in Religion has been altogether beneficent; its criticism has been but the prelude to construction; what has died under its analysis has but made room for higher forms of thought and larger modes of life. Did space allow, illustration were easy and abundant, especially from the highest of all regions—the action of speculation on the idea of God. To take the strongest illustration, it is no paradox to say, the system of Spinoza was, from the standpoint of the Christian Religion, a greater benefit to Europe than any—I had almost said than all the conversions to Catholicism in the seventeenth century, whether of kings like James II., or men of letters like John Dryden. For it raised the problem of Theism to a higher platform, directly tended to enlarge and ennoble the conception of God, to enrich the idea of Religion, to promote the study and criticism and appreciation of its work in history; placing it in a higher relation to the nature and action of God on the one hand, and the spirit and life of man on the other. When Newman says that, without Catholicism, we must proceed "in a dreadful but infallible succession," from Protestantism through Deism or Pantheism to Scepticism, or that "outside the Catholic Church things are tending to Atheism in one shape or other," he writes mere rhetoric. The statement might be reversed; the "infallible succession" might be charged upon Catholicism with quite as much truth and charity, or rather with more

historical warrant and justification. Pantheism was
known in the Golden Age of Catholicism, the Middle
Ages ; to it must be reckoned the systems of Scotus
Erigena, Meister Eckhardt, the Dominican, as well as
whole Schools of Mystics ; the man who revived it,
Spinoza's forerunner, if not master, was another
Dominican, Giordano Bruno. The most pronounced
modern materialism was developed in Catholic
France; certain of its earliest masters were Catholic
dignitaries. One of the earliest martyrs to Atheism
was the pupil of Catholic Divines, the whilom priest
Vanini. The Deism of eighteenth-century England
was innocence compared with the revived paganism
of fifteenth-century Italy. The man whom Buckle
selected for special praise as having been the first to
apply the rationalist method to morals and to history,
had been a Catholic priest and preacher. Catholicism
converted Bayle, but only to make a more utter
sceptic of him ; converted Gibbon, but only to see
him recoil into completer infidelity.[1] All this may be
poor enough, but it is after Newman's manner. Over
against his charge, "outsidé Catholicism things are
tending to Atheism," I place this as the simple record
of fact, verifiable by all who choose to pursue the
necessary inquiries—inside Catholicism things have

---

[1] I hesitated long about Gibbon ; but after carefully weighing
the statement in the "autobiography," and one or two significant passages in the *Decline and Fall*, I determined to let his
name stand. Yet the argument does not depend on one or two
names : it represents tendencies operative through centuries.

tended, and still, wherever mind is active, do tend, to the completest negation. If his argument be held equal to the proof of the need of infallibility, mine must be held to prove its perfect insufficiency. Men may need it, but it is not adequate to their needs; and an inadequate infallibility is certainly near of kin to common fallibility. The arguments are parallel, but the cases are not. Catholicism professes to be able by its authority to do what history has proved it unable to accomplish, and so is justly chargeable with the most serious incompetency; but Protestantism, making no claim to authority, professing indeed to be quite without it, may justly refuse to bear the responsibility of failure. Incompetency in a system like the Roman is the most invincible disproof of claim; the competence that comes of supernatural gifts and authority is no part of Protestantism.

2. But Cardinal Newman's position raises another question, whether an infallible authority, such as he attributes to the Church and Pope of Rome, and exercised for the purposes he describes, would be a help or a hindrance to Religion? Would it make Religion more or less possible, more or less stable and real? Differences on such matters are, as a rule, apprehended in their superficial aspects rather than in their determinative principles and causes. One of these is the idea of Religion; it is one thing to me, another to Cardinal Newman. The Catholic criticizes Protestantism as if it were or professed to be a sort of substitute for Catholicism; but it is not this, and

never can become it. They are not simply opposites, but incommensurables. The one represents an organized and finely articulated hierarchical system, legislative, administrative, administered, able to comprehend men and nations, and cover the whole life from the cradle to the grave; but the other denotes only an attitude of mind or the principle that regulates it. Catholicism claims to be a Religion; Protestantism cannot be truly or justly described as making any such claim, or as seeking to be allowed to make it. It is simply the assertion of a right to perform a duty, the right of every man to fulfil the holiest and most imperial of his duties, that of knowing and believing the God who made his reason, of worshipping and serving the God who speaks in his conscience. It is significant as the contradiction and antithesis to a system of collectivism, which hindered the clear sense of personal relation and responsibility to God; but the creation of this sense was the work of God alone, and its realization in Religion was due to His continued and gracious activity among men. Protestantism is thus only an attempt to make religion possible, to create the conditions that will permit and require the Religion of Christ to become actual. It implies the being of this Religion, but neither creates it, nor represents it, nor embodies it; only insists on removing whatever hinders God and man, or man and the Religion, coming face to face, that it may be realized in and through his spirit. It may be construed to signify the supremacy of reason, and so it does; but this only means the supremacy of the truth, or, in religious speech, the sovereignty of God. The reason, indeed, is not particular, individual, arbitrary, but universal, law-abiding, reasonable—the thought which cannot think without following the laws of its own being, and cannot follow them without finding the truth. The whole truth may not be found, but what is found is reality, divine and sovereign to the man who finds it.

In a certain sense, submission to Catholicism is the victory of unbelief; the man who accepts authority because he dare not trust his intellect, lest it lead him into Atheism, is vanquished by the Atheism he fears. He unconsciously subscribes to the impious principle, that the God he believes, has given him so godless a reason that were he to follow it, it would lead him to a faith without God. Now, there is more religion in facing the consequences than in turning away from them; for the man who faces the consequences remains truer to the truth, obeys the most immediate and inexorable law of God, that given in his own being. I can understand the man who says : " I do not wish to be either a Pantheist or Agnostic ; but I must be what the best thought and light within me— beams as they are of the universal and eternal— determine ; and if they conduct me to either Panthe- ism or Agnosticism, then to either I will go, obedient to the laws under which I live and think." But I cannot so well understand or admire the man who says : " If I follow my reason, it will make an Atheist or a Sceptic of me; therefore, I will flee for refuge to the arms of infallible authority." There is a harmony, and so a religion, in the one nature that is absent from the other; the one has faced the issues, and knows them; the other has evaded their touch, and is haunted by possibilities he cannot but fear. There is victory, even in defeat, to the man who has dared the conflict; there is defeat, even in the rest he wins, to the man who, that he may keep a whole skin, turns and runs from the battle.

3. But there is another and still deeper difference, the conception of the Reason. Here the ideas are again opposite and incommensurable. Dr. Newman's language seems to me often almost impious, a positive arraignment of the God who gave man his intellect. I may say, and the saying need not be misunderstood, reason is to me as holy as his church is to him. It is too godlike to be inimical to God; scepticism is not the essence but the accident of its activity. It is critical when confronted by authority or authoritative formulæ, and it ought to be critical then; but its history does not record the growth of scepticism, rather narrates the expansion and elevation of belief. Reason, while realized in individuals, is universal; while conditioned in its working, it is transcendental in its nature and worth; while it acts in and through millions of natural agents, it has a supernatural source and end. It represents law, while authority represents the violation of law; the one expresses an order instituted of God, but the other

man's most violent attempt at its suspension or super-session. Hence reason is here conceived as essentially architectonic ; its action, where most analytical, is always with a view to a more perfect synthesis. It cannot realize its idea, or be itself, without being constructive. Every attempt to do justice to it has emphasized this as belonging to its very essence, that without which it could not be reason. Take, for example, Kant. He and Newman have been compared or rather contrasted as, respectively, the one the source of modern scepticism and agnosticism, and the other the ideal teacher of religion. But the positions ought to be reversed ; Kant is the great teacher of faith, Newman, in the region of the reason or the intellect, is the master of scepticism. Kant's reason was architectonic, made nature, supplied the forms and the conditions of thought by which alone she was interpretable and interpreted. Reason was a latent or implicit universe, real in its very ideality, so determining phenomena as to constitute a cosmos. But where Kant treads firmly, Newman walks feebly, speaks of instinct and presumption, and feels as if he dare not trust reason with nature, lest he have to trust her with more. Kant, indeed, does not allow that the mere or pure reason, which is equal to the interpretation of nature, is equal to the cognition of God ; and he builds, like Newman, his argument for the Divine existence on conscience. But to him conscience is still reason, all the more that it uses the " categorical imperative," and his argument, unlike Newman's, is reasoned ; it is not the mere echo of a " magisterial dictate," but is based on a universal principle, and articulates a complete theory of moral sovereignty and government. Kant's moral religion was at once natural and transcendental ; Newman's is positive and legislative. The former was inseparable from the ideal of humanity ; but the latter is institutional, comes *ab extra*. Kant's position is the vindication of faith through nature ; Newman's is the surrender of nature to unbelief. For with Kant the practical is not the contradiction of the pure reason ; the one is but the supplement of the other. They are conceived by their author not as mutually independent, still less as opposed, but as so constituting a unity and a synthesis that what the one does for nature the other does for eternity and God. But Newman finds such a dualism in nature that he has to introduce a *Deus ex machina* to rectify it. Conscience demands God, but reason will not allow the faith in Him to live ; and so an infallible church is called in to determine the issue, confirm and support the conscience, and "preserve religion in the world" by so restraining " the freedom of thought" as " to rescue it from its own suicidal excesses."[1] This may be a good excuse for authority, but it is a bad apology for faith. He who places the rational nature of man on the side of Atheism, that he may the better defend a church, saves the church at the expense of religion and God.

---

[1] *Apol.* 245.

May, 1885.

IV

CATHOLICISM AND HISTORICAL CRITICISM

THE criticism of the intellectual or speculative bases of any institution is criticism of the institution ; the reasons that are thought to justify its existence describe its character. As men conceive God, they conceive Religion ; and as Religion is conceived, so is the Church. Cardinal Newman[1] has affirmed that the ultimate question between Catholicism and Protestantism is not one of history or individual doctrine, but of first principles. He is right, only his principle, whether the Church be or be not a continuous miracle, is not primary enough. A miracle by becoming continuous ceases to be miraculous ; a supernatural which has descended into the bosom of the natural becomes part of its order, and must be handled like the other forces and phenomena of history. Below the question as to the Church lies this other and deeper—What is God ? and what His relations to man and man's to Him ? or, How are we to conceive God, and how represent His rule and redemption of man ? It is this radical issue which

---

[1] *Present Position of Catholics in England,* lect. vii.

gives living interest to ancient controversies, lifting them from the noisy field of ecclesiastical polemics to the serener heights of spiritual and speculative thought.

Now, if the idea of God be conceived as the idea really determinative of our religious controversies, it is evident that the discussion in the preceding essay as to its genesis and proofs, must be incomplete until supplemented by a discussion as to its expression or realization in history. These are parts of a whole, and so absolute is the need of harmony between the parts that we may say this : To determine the idea of God is to fix the standpoint from which history is to be studied and interpreted, while in the interpretation of history we are but explicating and testing our conception of God. If the idea of God in theology be mean, the idea of His action in history cannot be noble ; while, conversely, an adequate notion of His method and movement in history demands a correspondent notion of His character and ends. If we conceive Him as in the same sense and degree the Father and Sovereign of every man, willing good to each, evil to none, equal in His love and care for all, impartial and universal as law, while personal and particular as mercy,—then we cannot allow either Him or His truth to be so much the exclusive possession of a given society, that its history is the history of His mind or revelation, and of His purposes and ways. But if we believe that He has committed His truth, His spirit, and His redemptive agencies to the keeping of a peculiar and pre-eminent church, then we shall regard its history as the history of His special action or providence, all who are without it being judged by and through it, as if it were His visible and articulate sovereignty. Now this, in the very degree that it gives an exalted idea of the church, represents a mean idea of God ; an historical institution is ennobled, but the immensest and most august of human beliefs is narrowed and depraved. In a true sense, therefore, we explicate our theistic idea when we attempt to explain not the mere phenomena of nature, but the immense and complex procession of forces, persons, institutions, and events, which we call the history of man. Our philosophy of history is but our conception of God evolved and articulated.

§ I. *The Ideas of God, Religion, and the Church*

1. This fundamental principle determines the point at which our discussion must be resumed—the Idea of Religion. This idea stands, as it were, intermediate between the ideas of God and the Church, and their mutual relations may be thus described :—Religion is the realization, in the regions of thought, feeling, and action, of the idea of God ; while the Church is the idea of Religion articulated or built into a social organism, whose life is lived on the field of history. What this means will be better understood by-and-by. Meanwhile we note, the three ideas must correspond in character and quality ; the Religion ever is as the God is, and the Church as the Religion. The

radical differences are those of the theistic idea ; it is not the belief, but the conception, of God that most decisively differentiates men. That He is, most men believe ; where they mainly differ is concerning what He is.

In the sphere of thought their differences are expressed in the various theistic philosophies—dualistic, monistic, transcendental, immanent ; but in Religion they are represented by the various churches and societies that embody distinct ideals of life and duty, authority and obedience, worship and conduct. Politics express fundamental beliefs—are, indeed, but those beliefs applied to the regulation of civil life and the organization of society. Men who are of one faith may not be of one Religion ; they may have one name for the object of worship, yet differ in their notion of the object ; and to differ here is to differ radically and throughout. There is a conception of God that makes a great propitiatory and mediatorial church a necessity ; and there is a conception of Him that will not allow any such institution to stand between Him and man. The controversy between these antithetical notions is not of yesterday, but is as old as Religion, dating from the moment when men began to speak of and worship God. In all the ancient faiths the priestly Deity was one, and the Deity of spirit and thought another ; they might agree in name, but they differed in nature and character. In Judaism, the God of the priesthood loved the official sanctities, the temple, the altar, the sacrifice, the incense, the priest and his garments and bells and breastplate, the sabbath, the new moon, the feast, and the solemn assembly. But the God of prophecy loved the moral and spiritual sanctities, the living temple, the whole people constituted a priesthood unto Jehovah, the sacrifices of the broken spirit and the contrite heart, the law written within, the worship expressed in obedience, the obedience that consisted in doing justly, loving mercy, and walking humbly with God. In India the sacerdotal Deity was the ground and cause of caste, and the root of a religion without morality ; while the attempt to transcend so mean a notion produced the philosophies, pantheistic and pessimistic, and provoked the negations which became Buddhism. In Greece the Religion of the temple and the priesthood knew no ethical Deity, and had no ethical spirit, lived by faith in myths and legends, by the practice of mediation, by processions and ceremonial observances, by the grace of the oracle which men consulted when they wished nature helped by the supernatural. But the Deity of the Academy and the Porch was morally beautiful, true, and good ; and their ideal of Religion was so ethical as to be offended and affronted by the myths and customs of the priestly order. Measured by the standard of this order, Socrates was, because of his faith in a purer God, pronounced guilty and worthy of death ; in presence of its moral perversions and impotences Plato was forced to plead for a purged mythology and a new and nobler priesthood and the

Stoic was driven to attempt to translate the ancient beliefs into the symbols of a hidden philosophy. And these are but typical cases, illustrating a conflict every historical Religion has known, and the Christian could not escape. Within it, as within every other, two conceptions of Deity have had to contend for the mastery ; and it is certain that the contest did not begin with the sixteenth century, and will not end with the nineteenth. However much disguised as a question now in philosophy, now in polity, ecclesiastical or civil, here as a controversy of churches, there as a collision of peoples, yet the fundamental and determinative problem has ever remained one and the same —What is God ? and what His relation to man and man's to Him ?

2. The idea of God, then, determines the religious ideal, Religion being but the form in which the idea appears in the sphere of the real, and living, and related. And in Cardinal Newman the two so correspond as to reflect and repeat each other. His religion is as his Theism is : both proceed from conscience and have their qualities determined by it. God appears as Judge, and Religion " is founded in one way or other on the sense of sin."[1] Hence, out of the sense of sin and the fear of the righteous and judicial God, whose absence or estrangement from the world so pierces the soul and bewilders the reason, he educes those mediations, priesthoods, sacrifices, theories of future and even eternal penalties, which he

---

[1] *Grammar of Assent*, p. 392.

holds to be the essential characteristics of all the Natural Religions. Now, his doctrine of Religion is as little true to history as we found his Theism to be true to reason and thought. It is characteristic of Newman that his favourite authority for the qualities and features of Natural Religion is Lucretius, which is very much as if one were to quote Voltaire as our most veracious and trustworthy witness touching the nature and action of Christianity. As a simple matter of fact, the Religion Lucretius so hated, and described as so hateful, was in the highest degree artificial — a product of many and even malign influences, of various and even hostile civilizations. There are cycles of faiths which have sacerdotal ideas and expiatory rites, and there are also cycles of faiths where they can hardly be said to be known ; but even where most emphasized and observed they do not imply such a consciousness of guilt as Cardinal Newman imagines and describes. Indeed, if the history of Religions prove anything, it is that they are not " founded on the sense of sin," and do not regard God, primarily, as the impersonation of " retributive justice." It were truer to say that, as a rule (there are, of course, exceptions), the pre- and extra-Christian Religions are unmoral ; and that the sense of sin is the direct creation of Christianity, including, of course, its historical forerunner. And the older or more natural the Religions, the brighter they are, and the less darkened or oppressed by the consciousness of guilt. The Vedic deities are mainly deities of the light; there is nothing that so little troubles the Homeric gods as the austere duties of justice and judgment. But the inaccurate psychology of the Theism is here reflected in the inaccurate history. Since the reason was released from all duties, and the conscience made " the creative principle," the historical Religions had to be represented as processions or projections from the conscience. This false view of Natural Religion is carried over into Revealed, to the consequent darkening and degradation of both. For Christianity is conceived to be " simply an addition to " the Religion of Nature, the ideas of the one being neither superseded nor contradicted, but recognized and incorporated by the other.[1] Thus as the natural was conceived to be, the spiritual is represented as being ; those features and qualities that have been determined beforehand as essential to Religion are transferred bodily to Christianity, and it is interpreted through them and in their light. The idea is not deduced from the sources, but conveyed into them, with the result that the Religion they contain appears only as the exaggerated shadow of the writer's own ideal.

3. But the idea of Religion is only preliminary, the main matter is its historical realization. Out of many passages, we may select two to illustrate how Cardinal Newman makes the transition from Natural to Revealed Religion, and thence to his doctrine of the Church, or simply to Christianity in history.

---

[1] *Grammar of Assent*, p. 388.

˗ " Revelation begins where Natural Religion fails. The Religion of Nature is a mere inchoation, and needs a complement —it can have but one complement, and that very complement is Christianity." [1]

"Revelation consists in the manifestation of the Invisible Divine Power, or in the substitution of the Voice of a Lawgiver for the Voice of Conscience. The supremacy of conscience is the essence of Natural Religion ; the supremacy of Apostle, or Pope, or Church, or Bishop, is the essence of Revealed ; and when such external authority is taken away, the mind falls back upon that inward guide which it possessed even before Revelation was vouchsafed." [2]

So reason, dismissed from Natural, has no place in Revealed Religion ; authority reigns in both. Religion issues from it and ends in it ; begins in the Divine authority speaking as an internal voice, terminates in the same authority externalized and made visible in an articulate Lawgiver. It is created, so to speak, by legislation ; and the more positive, *i.e.* statutory, forensic, external the legislation is, it is held to be the more excellent, authoritative, and adequate. Religion becomes a matter of precept and rule, casuistry and ritual. Conscience is the prophet and forerunner of the church, which at once fulfils the prophecy and supersedes the prophet. But the

---

[1] *Grammar of Assent,* p. 486. It is curious how completely Deistic is Newman's doctrine both of religion and of the relation of the two religions, the natural and the supernatural. He stands here exactly where the eighteenth century stood and reproduces its .limitations and distinctions with unconscious, perhaps, but most notable accuracy.

[2] *Development of Christian Doctrine,* c. ii. § 2, p. 124 (second edition).

creation of the individual conscience is an individualistic religion, which has its character only the
more emphasized that it appears disguised as a
Catholicism. The false philosophy makes the idea
of Religion defective ; the defective idea of Religion
leads to the misinterpretation of both its nature and
action in history. It is so interpreted that man's
relation to God grows ever less personal and direct,
ever more formal and mediated ; and, as a consequence, the historical process must represent man as
growing into, rather than out of, those symbols and
sanctions and mediations which Lessing conceived to
belong to the childhood rather than the manhood of
the race. The authority of God, with its correlative
in the dependence and obedience of man, is indeed
the essence of Religion ; but this authority, simply
because God's, can never become external, or be
embodied in Pope, or Church, or Bishop. For the
moment it were thus embodied it would be so limited
and conditioned as to cease to be absolute ; it would
have to speak in the terms and work by the methods
of a human institution rather than on the lines and
in the ways of an infinite law. If true Religion be
the worship of the Father in spirit and in truth, then
it is this worship, and not submission to Pope or
Church, that is the primary duty or true characteristic
of the religious man. And the more filial the man
the more perfect the worship ; the purer he is in
spirit the fuller he is of the truth.

§ II. *The Roman as the Catholic Church*

The matter then stands thus :—There are three ideas, God, Religion, and the Church ; and these three are so related that the second and third may be regarded as progressive explications of the first.[1] According to Cardinal Newman, conscience apprehends God as Judge ; Religion is founded on man's consciousness and confession of offence against Him ; and the Church at once embodies God's authority as Judge, and satisfies man's need of expiation. Unless God were so apprehended Religion could not be so defined ; and unless God and Religion were so understood the Church could not be conceived as authoritative and mediatorial. The correspondence between the ideas of God and Religion has thus its counterpart and complement in the correspondence between the ideas of religion and the religious society, the elements held necessary to the one being represented and realized by the other. What the religious idea declares to be needful to the pleasing of God, must exist in the society and be provided for by it ; what is said to be of the essence of Religion must be possessed or affirmed by the Church.

1. Now, if this be true, one thing is evident : the narrower and more exclusive the religious idea, the easier it is to find a society that has realized it ; but the fuller, the richer, and more comprehensive the

---

[1] Cf. ante, p. 17.

idea, the less possible is it to find such a society. A magnificent ideal for a Church may be a mean ideal for a Religion ; what makes a Catholic institution splendid may cover a spiritual and universal faith with shame. The greater indeed ought never to be measured by the less ; the less ought to be studied and valued through the greater. This means: the Church ought to be criticised and judged through the Religion, not the Religion through the Church. The Church is good in the degree that it articulates and realizes the vital elements in the Religion ; bad in the degree that it fails to do so. I freely acknowledge the pre-eminence of Catholicism as an historical institution ; here she is without a rival or a peer. If to be at once the most permanent and extensive, the most plastic and inflexible, ecclesiastical organization, were the same thing as to be the most perfect embodiment and vehicle of Religion, then the claim of Catholicism were simply indisputable. The man in search of an authoritative church may not hesitate ; once let him assume that a visible and audible authority is of the essence of Religion, and he has no choice ; he must become, or get himself reckoned, a Catholic. The Roman church assails his understanding with invincible logic, and appeals to his imagination with irresistible charms. Her sons say proudly to him : " She alone is catholic, continuous, venerable, august, the very Church Christ founded and His Apostles instituted and organized. She possesses all the attributes and notes of catholicity—an unbroken apostolic succession, a constant tradition, an infallible Chair, unity, sanctity, truth, an inviolable priesthood, a holy sacrifice, and efficacious sacraments. The Protestant Churches are but of yesterday, without the authority, the truth, or the ministries that can reconcile man to God ; they are only a multitude of warring sects whose confused voices but protest their own insufficiency, whose impotence almost atones for their sin of schism by the way it sets off the might, the majesty, and the unity of Rome In contrast, she stands where her Master placed her, on the rock, endowed with the prerogatives and powers He gave ; and against her the gates of hell shall not prevail. Supernatural grace is hers and miracle ; it watched over her cradle, has followed her in all her ways through all her centuries, and has not forsaken her even yet. She is not like Protestantism, a concession to the negative spirit, an unholy compromise with naturalism. Everything about her is positive and transcendent ; she is the bearer of Divine truth, the representative of the Divine order, the Supernatural living in the very heart and before the very face of the Natural. The saints, too, are hers, and the man she receives joins their communion, enjoys their goodly fellowship, feels their influence, participates in their merits and the blessings they distribute. Their earthly life made the past of the Church illustrious ; their heavenly activity binds the visible and invisible into unity, and lifts time into eternity.

To honour the saints is to honour sanctity; the
Church which teaches man to love the holy helps
him to love holiness.   And the Fathers are hers;
their labours, sufferings, martyrdoms, were for her
sake; she treasures their words and their works;
her sons alone are able to say, "Athanasius and
Chrysostom, Cyprian and Augustine, Anselm and
Bernard, Thomas Aquinas and Duns Scotus are ours,
their wealth is our inheritance, at their feet we learn
filial reverence and Divine wisdom."   But rich as she
is in persons, she is richer in truth, her worship is a
glorious sacrament, her mysteries are a great deep.
Hidden sanctities and meanings surround man; the
sacramental principle invests the simplest things, acts,
and rites with an awful yet most blissful significance,
turns all worship now into a Divine parable which
speaks the deep things of God, now into a medium
of His gracious and consolatory approach to men and
man's awed and contrite, hopeful and prevailing,
approach to Him.   Symbols are deeper than words,
speak when words become silent, gain where words
lose in meaning; and so in hours of holiest worship
the Church teaches by symbols truths language may
not utter.   And yet she knows better than any other
how to use reasonable speech; the Fathers and
doctors of theology have been hers.   For every
possible difficulty of the reason, or the heart, or
the conscience, she has not one, but a thousand
solutions.   If men are gentle of heart, and do not
like to think that all men without the Church must

be lost, distinctions are made as to the body and soul of the Church, as to kinds and degrees of ignorance, softening stern doctrines into tenderness. If they have difficulties about Infallibility, whether due to papal sins and blunders in the past, or freedom in the present, or progress in the future, they can easily be obviated by methods of interpretation and known and noted constitutional limitations. In the Church alone has casuistry become a science so perfect as to have a law and a cure for every real or possible case of conscience ; in her schools theology has become a completed science, which has systematized her body of truth, explicated her reason, justified her being and her claims. And so the Catholic Church is, in a sense altogether her own, not only an ecclesiastical institution, but a Religion, a system able to guide the conscience, satisfy the heart, regulate the conduct, adjust and determine the relations of God and man."

2. Now this sublime and august Catholicism may well and easily be victorious in its appeal to the pious imagination ; but it is one thing to be sublime and august as an institution, and quite another thing to be true and credible as a Religion. Our concern here is not with the appeal of Catholicism, but with its right to make it ; not with its sufficiency for the men who grant its premisses, but with its relation to the Religion it professes to represent and realize ; whether it be or be not equal to its complete and veracious representation, whether it do or do not

possess energies equal to its realization in man and
society. The Catholic church did not create the
Religion, but was created by it ; and it is the function of historical criticism to discover and determine
the methods and factors of the process which created
the church. The questions involved are many and
intricate, but they may be said to reduce themselves
to two : first, the historical relations of the created
institution or church, and the creative Religion ; and,
secondly, the adequacy of the institution to the interpretation of the Religion and to the fulfilment of its
purposes. The questions are indivisible, but distinct.
If the institution be so related to the Religion as
to be identical or interchangeable with it, the question
of adequacy is, *ipso facto*, settled ; though even then
the adequacy of the church to the work of a Religion
will remain to be discussed. We may distinguish
the questions thus : the one concerns the genesis of
Catholicism, how and by what historical process and
causes it came to be ; but the other concerns its behaviour and action in history—whether it has lived
and acted as a Society which incorporates the mind
and serves the ends of Jesus Christ. The two questions combined relate to what may be termed the
philosophy of Catholicism, but the former alone can
determine whether this must be held identical with a
philosophy of the Christian Religion.

§ III. *Whether it be Possible to Conceive Catholicism as a Development from the Religion of Christ*

The fundamental and decisive question then is as to the relation of Catholicism to the Religion of Christ. The question is at once historical and comparative—historical in so far as the connection of the systems is concerned; comparative in so far as the one supplies the norm by which the other must be measured and criticised. The Religion of Christ must not be judged by Catholicism, but Catholicism by the Religion of Christ.

1. The differences between these relate at once to the form and the matter of faith, both to the political organization of the church and the religious ideal it embodies. What these differences are may appear in the course of the discussion. It is enough to say here that they are too radical to be ignored, and too flagrant to be overlooked. Protestant writers have emphasized them, and Catholic theologians have proposed various theories in explanation. These differences constituted in Newman's earlier period the supreme obstacle to his entering the church of Rome; and the theory by which the obstacle was surmounted and the differences explained is expounded in the book that marks the crisis in his career.[1] The book

---

[1] *An Essay on the Development of Christian Doctrine*, 1846 (second edition). The history of the theory of development in Roman Catholic apologetics is a very interesting one, and well illustrates the obligations of Catholic to what is called

stands in a sort of mediatory relation to his earlier and later works; in it the logic which had hitherto governed his mind reaches its consistent conclusion, and in it the doctrines of the later works are implicit. Studied in their light, sentences that were enigmatical to its contemporary critics become strangely luminous. As in the *Apologia* and the *Grammar*, a natural scepticism forms the basis and justification of a mechanical supernaturalism. Its thesis may be stated thus: to prove how, since reason or nature has forsaken God and been forsaken of Him, a miraculous and infallible church is a necessity to faith. The philosophical scepticism determines the definitions, gives point and force to the arguments, presents the real, though here unformulated, alternative, Atheism or Catholicity. "Corruption" is but a figurative name for the "infallible Protestant succession"; it is "that state of development which undoes its previous advances,' "a process ending in dissolution of the body of thought and usage which was bound up as it were

---

"non-Catholic" thought. I had meant to compare the French, German, and English forms of this theory, and show how these had been affected by the historical and philosophical speculations of their respective countries. De Maistre, Moehler, Goerres, and Newman are well-known names; but Carovè, Gengler, Günther, though he and his school found small favour at Rome, and Staudenmaier no less deserve mention. The comparative neglect that seems to have fallen on a more remarkable man than any of these, Franz Baader, is not creditable to the Church that owned him. The unacknowledged obligations of Newman to French Catholic or neo-Catholic writers, would be an interesting theme for analytic criticism.

in one system," "the destruction of the norm or type."[1] Development is "the germination, growth, and perfection of some living, that is influential, truth, or apparent truth, in the minds of men during a sufficient period."[2] These definitions, which but express the art of the logician who so frames his premisses as to make his conclusion inevitable, mean, of course, simply this: outside Catholicism there reigns corruption, or the tendency to Atheism; inside it, there proceeds development, or there exists a living body of truth, a real and expansive Religion. But the artificiality of the definitions, their unreality as historical doctrines, and their insufficiency for the argument, soon become apparent. For neither the fundamental principle nor the dogmatic purpose can allow growth to be any real or sufficient note of truth; an authority is needed to discover and ratify it. The only healthy growth is one supernaturally conducted and authenticated, and without this authentication the truth could not be known. For unless the development proceeded "under the eye" of the external authority, which is the only sure and unerring judge of what is true and what is false, we should not know what to believe and what to reject. And so infallibility must appear to guarantee the revelation; though, as infallibility can only be conceived as revelation in exercise, the function is rather curious than convincing. And it is still more curious that the idea of infallibility,

[1] pp. 62, 63.   [2] p. 37.

which is the clearest as it is the most recent example
of development within the Roman church, should be
exempted from the operation of the law, and conceived as from the very beginning the duly constituted final authoritative court of appeal in all matters
of faith.   It is thus essentially a " provision " or expedient for retaining God in our knowledge, and was
made necessary by the metaphysical doubt which
would, left alone, have acted as a solvent of faith.
And this simply means that God being lost from
nature and history, an artificial or mechanical, as
distinguished from a supernatural, method has to
be devised for bringing Him back.   Newman holds
" there can be no combination on the basis of truth
without an organ of truth " ; but his organ is an organization, with the natural history, the *modi vivendi et
operandi* proper to one.   He does not say, " There
are no eternal truths " : but he does say, " There are
none sufficiently commanding to be the basis of
public union and action.   The only general persuasive in matters of conduct is authority."[1]   If Religion
is to live, " there is absolute need of a spiritual supremacy," or " a supreme authority ruling and reconciling
individual judgments by a Divine right and a recognized wisdom."[2]   Metaphysical scepticism may seem
a curious basis for belief in what has been called the
most supernatural form of Christianity ; but it is Newman's.[3]

---

[1] p. 128.   [2] p. 127.
[3] For a more detailed exposition and criticism of Newman's

2. But we have had enough of the philosophical question, which is here of interest only as showing the logical coherence and continuity of ideas in Newman's own mind. We must discuss with more care and in fuller detail the historical thesis : How does this infallible Catholic church stand related to the Religion of Jesus Christ ? The reply, as conceived by the Catholic, is, the two are one ; the Church is the Religion. Why, then, do they so differ ? Why do we find so many things in Catholicism that we do not find in the Religion ? The answer of the Catholic is—the differences are those of growth and logical evolution ; they are notes and evidences of life, due to the continuous and divinely guided expansion of the organism that came into being nineteen centuries ago. The theory of development is thus an "hypothesis to account for a difficulty "[1]—the procession or evolution of Catholicism from what was in so many respects radically unlike it, primitive Christianity. But the theory was not simply a method of explaining the differences between the religion which Christ created and the church which the Pope governs; it was, on the one hand, an apology for Catholicism, and on the other, for the man who had been compelled to embrace it. The book was in the strictest possible sense an earlier *Apologia pro vita sua.* But polemical purpose is a serious

doctrine of development, and a more adequate discussion of the subject as a whole, see *The Place of Christ in Modern Theology*, pp. 25 ff. [1] *Development of Christian Doctrine*, p. 27.

obstacle to scientific discussion. History, as Newman handles it, is but dialectic, a method of establishing a dogma or making good a proposition. No man could be less the ideal critic, or constructive historian, than he, or be more deft in the use of historical material for controversial ends. As he conceived the matter, his "Development of Doctrine" ought to have been a philosophy, not only of Catholicism, but of Christianity. But it is too completely without the critical and scientific spirit to be either. What he termed "development" was not what either philosophy or Science means when it uses the word. For he refused to apply the process to the collective result, keeping out of its hands the infallibility, which, as the most abnormal and least intrinsic organ or faculty, had the greatest need to be explained; and he conceived the process in a merely logical rather than a really natural and scientific way. Now, let us "grant the principle of development, but demand that it be philosophically stated and rigorously applied. To speak in the current phraseology, we must have the organism, but also the environment; and these must be studied and exhibited in their mutual intercourse and reciprocal action, the elements they respectively contribute to the result being carefully distinguished and appraised. The organism may modify the environment, but the environment may still more radically modify and even vary the organism. The degree and incidence of change is not to be settled beforehand by a series of purely *a priori* definitions and tests, like Newman's sacred seven,[1] but by actual observation of the process, analysis of its conditions, discovery of its factors, determination of the path and rate of movement."

The problem, then, as to the evolution of the Church, the headship of the Supreme Pontiff, and his *ex Cathedra* infallibility, is historical, and soluble only by the methods of historical research, which does not begin by *a priori* definitions and determinations of one class of growths as "corruptions," and another as "developments," but simply observes the process, the factors, and the results. Hence we must do two things, (*a*) find the germ, viz., the body or system of truth, in its primitive or least developed state, and (β) study the successive conditions under which it lived, their action on it, its action on them. The germ is simple, but the conditions are complex and varied. It is a new Religion: but it lives surrounded by a multitude of ancient Religions, on the soil, within the atmosphere, under the light, amid the customs, memories, manners, associations they had created. It is a body of beliefs: but the beliefs are construed and formulated into doctrines in cities where philosophy had been studied, often by men who had been

---

[1] The "tests of true development" are: "the preservation of the idea"; "continuity of principles"; "power of assimilation"; "early anticipation"; "logical sequence"; "preservative additions"; "chronic continuance" (pp. 64 ff.). These are but so many principles of prejudgment. So independent is he of historical method that he does not condescend to any critical search after "the idea" that was to be preserved.

trained in the schools, or had felt the influence of Hellenic or Hellenistic, Latin or Oriental speculation. The thought of the most catholic Father bears on its face the image of his time, and the superscription of his place. Clement, Origen, and Athanasius are men of Alexandria, with problems that differ according to their differing ages ; but they are as distinctively sons of their city as Philo, Ammonius, or Plotinus. They speak, as it were, in its idiom, and have their minds, methods of exegesis and argument, modes of thought and doctrinal apprehension saturated with its spirit. In the making of Augustine Plato has been as powerful as Paul ; and, if the Kingdom of God suggested his ideal *civitas*, imperial Rome determined its form. Then the Religion could not act and extend without a polity ; but as it grew on the soil of Judaism, lived in Greek cities and within the Roman Empire, first under its ban, and then, in the very moment of its dissolution, in alliance with it, the political type was not uniform, but followed the model which prevailed in its successive homes. Its base was Jewish, its middle stratum Greek ; but its upper and final, imperial and Roman. In its earliest form Christianity might be described as a Religion which had stooped to use the simplest polity ; but in its Roman form it might be more correctly described as a polity which had appropriated the name of a Religion. For after the Church had lived among Jews, Greeks, and Romans, and had affected, and been affected by, their respective faiths, philosophies, and polities, penetrated and

modified as they all were by Oriental elements, it
was no longer the simple and rudimentary structure
known to the Apostles; it had become a highly
developed and skilfully articulated organism, capable
not only of independent political life, but of imperial
or sovereign action. And so when Roman Cæsar
ceased to rule the West, the Roman Bishop became
his substitute and successor. It was as organized by
the spirit and genius of the ancient Empire that Christianity met the newer peoples. It thus appeared to
them the representative at once of the new Religion,
the Roman State, and the old civilization; and so
entered into conditions favourable to further developments, especially of the imperial order. The environment was thus ceaselessly changing, now from internal,
now from external, now from concurrent causes; and
its every change affected and varied the organism.
Movement is complex, development is conditioned;
has its causes, but also its occasions; its laws, but
also its circumstances. The organism cannot be
isolated from its environment, but must be studied in
and through it. The mighty fabric of the Roman
church is a development; no man will question it;
but the significance of the development for the system, for Religion, and for history, must be determined,
not by a series of arbitrary tests, but by the rigorous
methods of historical analysis and criticism.

3. If, then, we follow the historical method, our first
duty will be to find the primary form, the organism
in its aboriginal state. Newman, indeed, does not

trouble himself to discover this form ; but starts with an imaginary picture, marked by manifold inaccuracies, painted without the slightest reference to the sources or what in them is material. The student of development, however, must begin at the beginning—with the New Testament ideal of Religion. Tradition cannot be here trusted ; literature alone can. Tradition is uncertain, unfixed ; its tendency is to grow, to mingle early and late, to throw the emphasis on the most recent, to fuse in the heated crucible of the imagination the marvellous and the unreal with the actual and the real. But the written abides ; its words do not change, do not augment the history with fact or marvel, only become, as men grow critical, more luminous, veracious, graphic, able to set man, however distant in time, like an ear- and eye-witness, face to face with the things he reads. And here our literary sources are clear, credible, truthful. We know the first century as we do not know the second, or even the third. The founding of the Religion is a more legible page of history than the organization of the church ; the earlier throws more light on the later period than the later on the earlier. Indeed, we may say the earlier history is written in lines of living light. If, then, we are to follow the only method valid in historical science, we must begin with our oldest written sources ; on every matter connected with the first or parent form, the real starting - point of the evolutional process, their authority must be held final. This is no dogma of

Protestantism, but a simple necessity of scientific method, which is here, too, the method of nature and assured knowledge. Light lies on the threshold ; it is only after we have crossed it that the shadows begin to thicken.

§ IV. *How the Priesthood came into the Religion*

1. Now, what is the New Testament ideal of Religion ? Its material or determinative conception is, as we have already argued, the doctrine of God. "He appears primarily, not, as Newman so strenuously argued, as a God of judgment and justice, but of mercy and grace, the Father of man, who needs not to be appeased, but is gracious, propitious, finds the Propitiator, provides the propitiation. His own Son is the one Sacrifice, Priest, and Mediator, appointed of God to achieve the reconciliation of man. Men are God's sons ; filial love is their primary duty, fraternal love their common and equal obligation. Worship does not depend on sacred persons, places, or rites, but is a thing of spirit and truth. The best prayer is secret and personal ; the man who best pleases God is not the scrupulous Pharisee, but the penitent publican. Measured by the standard of a sacerdotal Religion, Jesus was not a pious person ; He spoke no word, did no act, that implied a priesthood for His people, He enforced no sacerdotal observance, instituted no sacerdotal order, promulgated no sacerdotal law ; but simply required that His people should be perfect as their Father in

heaven is perfect. And so what He founded was a society to realize His own ideal, a Kingdom of heaven, spiritual, eternal, which came without observation; a realm where the will of God is law, and the law is love, and the citizens are the loving and the obedient." The fact is too remarkable, too characteristic and essential to the mind of Jesus to be described as accidental, or as due to His assumption of these things as understood. On the contrary we have to note His most careful and even scrupulous abstention from the use of all terms that could imply the continuance of any priesthood within His Church. The abstention must have been difficult; indeed, nothing could have been harder than to avoid the use of terms which were on all men's lips when they spoke about religion. Yet the only use He made of the term "temple" was to apply it to His body. He never gave the name of priest either to Himself or to any disciple. The only sacrifice He asked man to offer was the mercy which God loved. These abstentions therefore are express and designed; a priesthood with its offices was no part of His mind and purpose. And as with His own mind, so was it in the Apostolic Church and in the Apostolic epistles. The people the apostles represent and address, the society they describe, may have in its collective being a priestly character, but is without an official priesthood. It has "apostles," "prophets," "overseers" or "bishops," "elders," "pastors," "teachers," "ministers" or "deacons," "evangelists"; but it has no "priests," and no man, or body of men, who bear the name, hold the place, exercise the functions, or fulfil the duties of the priest, or the priesthood, as they were known in ancient Religions. It has no temple, save either the living Saviour or the living man ; it asks from men no sacrifices, save those of the spirit and the life; it has no sensuous sanctities. "Its Founder who, we repeat, never called Himself a priest, stood to the priesthood of His land and time in radical antagonism ; the writers who apply to Him the name High Priest, and describe His work as a sacrifice, carefully deny any similar name to any class of His people, and decline to attach any similar idea to any of their acts or instruments of worship. And this may be said to represent on the negative side the absolutely new and distinctive character of the Religion of Christ. It stood among the ancient faiths as a strange and extraordinary thing—a priestless Religion, without the symbols, sacrifices, ceremonies, officials, hitherto held, save by prophetic Hebraism, to be the religious all in all. And it so stood, because its God did not need to be propitiated, but was propitious, supplying the only Priest and Sacrifice equal to His honour, and the sins and wants of man. In that hour God became a new being to man, and man knew himself to be more than a mere creature and subject—a son of the living God." [1]

2. Here, then, is the aboriginal germ—a Religion without a priesthood, or any provision for it ; as such

---

[1] *The Place of Christ in Modern Theology*, pp. 48, 49.

an exception among the Religions and an anomaly
to men ; and because of its anomalous character, lay-
ing its earliest professors open to the odious charge
of Atheism. But Catholicism is here the precise
opposite of this aboriginal Religion, this Christianity
of Christ and His apostles. The priesthood is essential to it ; without the priesthood it could have no
existence, no Saviour present in its services, no mass,
no sacraments, no confessional ; in a word, no worship
for God, no comfort and no command for man. Here,
then, is the first point for the historic inquirer : How
and whence came the idea and office of the priesthood into Christianity? Was it evolved from within, or
incorporated from without? Was it a latent organ or
capability legitimately evoked in the original, or was it
a foreign or superadded element due to the conditions
under which the organism lived? Without attempting
an exhaustive discussion of these questions, it will be
enough to say that the sacerdotal idea has a perfectly
distinct history of its own ; the date of its first
appearance in the Church can be fixed, its rise can be
traced, its growth measured, its action on the substance and organization of Christianity analyzed and
exhibited. The New Testament did not know it, and
in the second as in the first century it is still unknown ; but the tendencies creative of it are active.
The apologists labour strenuously to explain how
Christianity, though without the sacerdotalism characteristic of all the then licit or recognized worships, is
yet a Religion. In the *Didaché* the prophet has

displaced the Priest.[1] Ignatius may have high episcopal, but he has no sacerdotal ideas ; and of these his friend Polycarp is also free. To Justin Martyr, Christians were the true high-priestly race ; they offer the sacrifices well-pleasing to God.[2] With Irenæus the sacerdotal dignity is the portion of the just ; and the sanctified heart, the holy life, faith, obedience, righteousness, are the sacrifices God loves.[3] The choicest altar was the service of the needy ; to minister to man was to sacrifice to God. There was no order possessed of the exclusive right to officiate in things sacred, exercising their functions by virtue of some inalienable grace. The layman might baptize or celebrate the Eucharist ; there was " liberty of prophesying " ; the individual society or church could exercise discipline, could even institute or depose its officers. But as the second century ended and the third opened, significant signs of change begin to appear. Tertullian in Africa speaks of the " Ordo sacerdotalis " and the " Sacerdotalia munera " ; and describes the bishop as " summus sacerdos " and " pontifex maximus."[4] Hippolytus in Italy claims for himself, as successor of the Apostles, the high-priesthood ;[5] while Origen in Alexandria, though he

---

[1] Chap. xiii. 3 ; cf. Clemens Rom. chapp. xl., xliii., xliv.
[2] *Dial.* chapp. cxiv.–cxvii. ; cf. *Apol. i.* chapp. lxvi., lxvii.
[3] *Adv. Omn. Haeres.* book iv. chapp. viii. 3, xvii. 4 ; bk. v. c. xxxiv. 3.
[4] *De Exh. Cast.* 7 ; *De Praescr. Haer.* 41 ; *De Baptis.* 17 ; *De Pudic.* 1.
[5] *Refut. Omn. Hær.* i. Proem.

holds to the universal priesthood and spiritual sacrifices,[1] also indicates the likeness of the new ministers to the ancient priests and Levites.[2] By the middle of the century the hands of Cyprian have clothed the new clergy in the dignities of the old priesthood, and provided them with appropriate sacrificial functions and intercessory duties. "The development was not complete, but it was begun. The ancient ideal died hard ; reminiscences of it may be found in Augustine, in Leo the Great, even in Aquinas, nay, in the very Catholicism of to-day ; but they only help to illustrate the continuity of the evolutional process and measure the vastness of the change."[3]

Now, why was it that the sacerdotal element appeared so suddenly and grew so rapidly? What were the causes of its so sudden genesis and growth ? In the Religion as instituted by Jesus Christ, taught and practised by His Apostles, received and observed by their disciples, it had no place ; and so its rise could not be due to any process of logical and immanent evolution, of detached and self-regulated development. But what was not possible to the isolated, was necessary to the conditioned organism. The Religion was new, but humanity was old ; and, if the new lived within the bosom of the old, it was by a process of mutual assimilation, the new pervading

---

[1] *Homil. in Lev.* ix. 9, 10 (Ed. Lom. vol. ix. pp. 360-364).
[2] *In Evang. Ioh.* tom. i. 3 (Ed. Lom. vol. i. p. 9).
[3] *The Place of Christ in Modern Theology*, p. 105.

and changing the old, but the old also penetrating and modifying the new. " Men found it easier to adjust the Religion to themselves than themselves to the Religion. Their minds were not sheets of clean white paper on which its truths could be clearly written, but pages crowded with the records, habits, customs, beliefs, of immemorial yesterdays ; and the lines of the new could not but often mingle and blend with those of the ancient writing. A Religion without a priesthood was what no man had known ; a sacred order on earth seemed as necessary to worship as the very being of the gods in heaven. The temple was the centre of the State, but it was idle without a priesthood, and without it the oracle was dumb."[1] How, then, were men, inured by age-long custom and tradition to priestly Religions, able all at once to construe and realize one altogether priestless ? They were helped at first by two things : its very strangeness, its absolute antithesis to the familiar and received ; and, next, by its appearing as a new opinion or belief which spread by teaching and discourse, or as a system of philosophy and social help rather than as an organized worship. But the more its character as a Religion became established and defined, the more men tended to interpret it through the old Religions, seeking in it the elements they had known in them.

And the historical relations of the Christian Faith,

---

[1] *The Place of Christ in Modern Theology*, p. 106.

as child and heir of Judaism, intensified this tendency. It had come to fulfil the Law and the
Prophets; the New Testament did not exist because
of the Old, but the Old had existed for the sake of the
New. Christianity was no accident, was indeed older
than creation, had been designed from eternity, and
appeared as the result and goal of all past history;
but it was no mere continuation of what had been,
was rather as its end, its supersession and fulfilment.
The sub-apostolic Fathers and apologists more or
less consistently maintained this, the apostolic position. They argued with the Jew, that the anticipa-
tions of Christ in the Old Testament were evidences
of His truth; and with the Greek, that the relation of
the New Testament to the Old proved Christianity
to be the result of a Divine purpose running through
the ages. But the parallel of the Testaments easily
became absolute, a forgetfulness of their essential
differences. The use of the Old to authenticate the
New tended to invest the Old with equal or even
greater authority, especially as, alongside the incom-
pleteness of the Christian canon, the Hebrew Scriptures stood canonically complete. They were the
sacred books of Jews and Christians alike, authoritative for both, revered and believed by both, held by
both to be regulative of faith and conduct, affording
to both the one solid common ground of discussion
and argument. And so, as was natural, these Scriptures lost in historical but gained in religious and
ecclesiastical significance; became less a record of

what had been, and more a norm or principle regulative of what ought to be. Indeed, it is the simple truth to say that they were a far more active and efficient factor in the organization of the Church than even the apostolic writings. For these latter were but the memorials of missionaries and missionary churches : but the former exhibited a realized Religion, what was conceived as pre-Christian Christianity. The old Religion had its priesthood, the new had its clergy, and so these two were made parallel. Once they had been made parallel, it was necessary to do the same for the worships ; and once they were assimilated, the New Testament ceased to fulfil the Old, the Old reigned in the New. And this is what Cyprian shows us ; he represents the victory of the older Religions, the rejuvenescence of Judaism, the entrance of the hieratic idea into the Kingdom of Christ, changing it into a kingdom of priests. Inveterate and invariable association demanded and worked the change, but the relation of the Jewish and Christian Scriptures supplied the opportunity and forms for its accomplishment. Without the universal sacerdotalism it would not have been necessary ; without the historical relation it would not have been possible ; the co-existence and co-operation of the two made it not only natural, but inevitable.

§ V. *How the Church Became a Monarchy*

1. The rise and growth of the sacerdotal idea in Christianity can, then, be explained by the principle

of development, but it must be development scientifically interpreted and historically applied. The idea then appears as the creation, not of the isolated or detached, but of the related organism, or simply of the environment within which it lives and moves. Yet this is only the beginning of the evolutionary process. Hand in hand with the change in the idea and functions of the ministry comes a change in its place and in the relation which it bears to the Church. And here, in order to see the process in its completeness, we must study it from within as well as from without ; in other words, in relation to what may be termed the articulation of the organism —or the organization of the Christian society. Catholic polity is one, New Testament polity another; they are not only dissimilars, but opposites. The rise of the monarchical and imperial polity, *i.e.*, the Catholic papacy, within the Christian Church, is explicable on the ground of a conditioned or natural development, but not of one unconditioned or supernatural. Accept the supernaturalism of Catholic dogmatics, and the rise of the infallible headship does not admit of explanation ; but apply to it the scientific analysis of the historical method, and it stands explained. For what on this matter is the testimony of the oldest literature ? There is no evidence that Jesus ever created, or thought of creating, an organized society. There is no idea He so little emphasizes as the idea of the Church. The use of the term is attributed to Him but twice—once it occurs in the local or congregational sense, and once in the universal ; but only so as to define His own sole activity and supremacy. His familiar idea is the Kingdom of God or of heaven ; but this Kingdom is without organization, and incapable of being organized ; indeed, though the ideas may here and there coincide, it is essentially the contrary and contrast of what is now understood as the Catholic church, whether Roman or Anglican. Further, in the Church of the New Testament the politico-monarchical idea does not exist ; there is no shadow, or anticipation, or prophecy of it. The churches are not organized, do not constitute a formal unity, have a fraternal but no corporate relation, have no common or even local hierarchy ; they are divided by differences that preclude the very idea of an official infallible head. Supremacy belongs to no man ; there is no bishop, in the modern sense, over any church, or over the whole Church ; no recognition of Rome as a seat of authority, the only holy or pre-eminent city being Jerusalem. The question as to Peter is very significant. He may be the rock on which the Church is to be built ; the promises made to him may be taken in the highest possible sense ; but what then ? There is no evidence that what was promised to him was assured to his successors, no evidence that he had any successors, least of all that his successors, if he had any, were the bishops of Rome, or that Rome in any way entered into the thought of Jesus. Indeed, so far as the New Testa-

ment is concerned, there is no evidence that Peter
ever was in Rome, or had any relation to it, or held
any office or did any work in connection with the
Roman church. Some things concerning him we
do certainly know—that he was an apostle of the
circumcision; lived and preached many years in
Jerusalem ; was there a man of reputation and a pillar ;
visited Antioch, where he at first befriended the
Gentiles, then withdrew and was publicly rebuked by
Paul. That is our last clear, authentic glimpse of
him. Whether the Babylon, whence he sent an epistle
by no means either cosmopolitan or catholic, but
expressly provincial and particular, was the city really
so named or a metaphor for Rome, is a point on which
scholars have differed ; and is at least too uncertain
to admit of clear and final decision. On the other
hand, Paul's successive homes stand as full in the
light as Peter's retreat into the darkness; from him
we know something of Rome and its church. He
addressed to it his greatest epistle, visited it, suffered
imprisonment in the city, dated from it various
letters ; but never, either in the epistle sent to Rome
or in those sent from it, though he mentions many
persons, most of them mere obscure names to us, does
he either directly or implicitly allude to Peter. This
is a remarkable fact ; no mere conventional argument
from silence ; for Paul was a man scrupulous in his
courtesies, plain-spoken in his polemics, incapable of
omitting from his record what would have been the
most illustrious name of the local church, especially

as it was one he had so expressly used in his controversial epistles. Now, what does all this signify?
Papal infallibility, head and crown as it is of the
Catholic system, is the most tremendous claim ever
made by any man or body of men; and so it, of
all claims, ought to have the most indubitable
historical basis. But an indubitable historical basis
is precisely the thing it wants. From the point of
view of authentic contemporary literature the evidence is altogether against both the primacy and
Roman episcopacy of Peter. The question is capable
of being argued only when tradition is introduced.
And the tradition, though ancient, is neither apostolic
nor primitive—can, indeed, hardly be placed earlier
than a century after the event, though it soon
becomes uniform and general. The case is arguable,
but it is no more. The tradition may be true, but it
must remain doubtful, the reasons that justify the
doubt proving the absolute unimportance of Peter
and his Roman bishopric to New Testament Religion. Doubtful history is a rather insecure foundation for the most awful and august of sovereignties.

2. This point has been selected not for critical discussion, but simply the better to illustrate the fact
that the Catholic system does not lie within the field
of apostolic Christianity. Its rise belongs to the
period when the organism was living within its
environment, and struggling for existence against the
imperial system by following the lines of the imperial
organization. Its history cannot here be written,

though the materials for it exist—it being possible to make every step in the process lie open to the clear light of day. Within the Christian societies various ideals of polity lived, Jewish, Greek, Roman ; ideals derived from the synagogue, the free city, and the school ; the voluntary, the industrial, or the benevolent association ; and these were by-and-by joined by ideals that came of Hebrew, Egyptian, and Syrian asceticism, touched and modified by influences from the further East. The Church was confronted and resisted by an immense organized power ; what unified and directed its energies contributed to its success in the struggle. What conflict made necessary, made conflict easier and victory more possible, if not more sure. Each congregation had its presiding officer, who soon came to represent its unity and embody its authority ; then to act for it ; then to act along with the kindred officers of his province or district ; then along with them to form an order or body ; and, finally, the corporate unity, which the internal growth had made possible, was achieved by the action and influence of the State, the civil unity being the condition procreative both of the ideal and the reality of the ecclesiastical. The more the official order became separate from the non-official, the more sacerdotal it grew in character ; the growth of the clerical idea within the Church prepared the way for the entrance of the priestly, and the coalescence or fusion of the two ideas worked a revolution both in the Church and the Religion. The clergy became the Church; the Church the Religion; and the Religion a transformed Roman empire—with the Pope for emperor, bishops for procurators, and the priesthood for the magistrates and legionaries that levied the taxes, enforced the laws, upheld the unity, and maintained the peace of the civilized world.

3. How it could have happened, why, indeed, it could not but happen, that the Roman State should so organize the Roman church as to change its Cæsar Augustus into the Holy Father, is a question of large import, though capable of a reasonable and accurate solution. The Emperor was Pontifex Maximus, head of the pagan church as well as of the pagan State. The two were identical; the imperial will was as supreme in religious as in civil affairs. If the Emperor decreed that he was divine, and that his statue must receive the honour due to a God, a man could disobey or defy it with impunity as little as he could commit any civil crime. It was, indeed, a serious form of high treason; and this was the justification of the successive persecutions. It was an anomaly, quite unintelligible to the ancient pagan mind, that a man, a citizen of a State, should refuse to do honour to the State's gods in accordance with the State's laws or the will of its head. But this precisely was what the Christian refused to do; and by his refusal he shocked the rulers and judges of the ancient world, provoking them to those penal measures we call martyrdoms, but the Roman called vindications of authority. The system was thus rooted

in immemorial custom and law ; but when the Emperor was converted, a new order of things came to be. The change that happened to the man affected the office. He and his world assumed, though there were noble and notable exceptions, that the imperial power and functions shared in the conversion of the imperial person ; *i.e.* he became in the Christian Church what he had been in the Roman State, a spiritual as well as civil head. He could in the new as in the old act as Pontifex Maximus, call a council, open it, intervene in its affairs, promulgate and enforce its decrees, reward the obedient, punish the disobedient. Hence the man who disagreed with the Emperor was persecuted as much after the conversion of Constantine as he was before it. Patriarchs like Athanasius were banished or recalled, deposed or re-instated, according to the good pleasure of the court. Bishops became courtiers ; intrigued for friends or against foes ; and words such as Tertullian had applied to the severities of a pagan Emperor, were now with more reason applied to those of emperors who professed to be Christian. In the East the system existed in fullest force ; but in the West the imperial was first qualified, then balanced, and finally eclipsed by the ecclesiastical power. In the East the papal was no match for the civil authority ; in the West the civil ceased to be a match for the papal. The more the papal jurisdiction was limited in the East, the higher grew the spiritual claims of the Emperor ; the more the Emperor forsook the

West, the more imperial became the Episcopal Chair of Rome. And so there was a mutual transference of functions : the ecclesiastical was imperialized, the imperial was ecclesiasticized. The Pope represents an older and more august authority than the apostolic ; he is the heir of the men who, from the Eternal City, governed the civilized world. The deity which was ascribed to them has, changed in form but unchanged in essence, descended to him. The apotheosis their State experienced, his has also undergone. For papal infallibility is but imperial supremacy transfigured and spiritualized. Sovereignty is infallibility in the region of law ; infallibility is sovereignty in the region of opinion. The king, who is the source of law, can do no wrong ; the Pope, who defines, sanctions, and proclaims dogma, can commit no error. Infallibility is thus the interpretation, in the terms of forensic jurisprudence or civil monarchy, of a spiritual headship, or supremacy in the realm of belief as distinguished from conduct. It came to the Pope as the successor of Cæsar. The Catholic church thus could not have been without Christianity, but still less could it have been without Roman imperialism. It owes its life to the one, but its distinctive organization it owes to the other. The very forces that disorganized the civil body helped to organize the ecclesiastical. Apart from Rome, and Rome decadent—with the imperial ideal and organism, but without the imperial spirit—Catholicism could never have come to be. If

the Latin church had passed the first five centuries of
its existence under an Oriental despotism or amid free
Greek cities, its structure would have been altogether
different. It seemed to vanquish the empire, but the
empire, by assimilating it, survived in it. The name
that distinguished the dynasty was the name of
Christ: but the form under which its power or
monarchy was constituted was the form of Cæsar.

§ VI. *The Ideas which Organized the System*

1. So far we have been concerned with the conditions and process of outer organization ; but there is
a deeper and more vital question—What were the
organizing ideas? and whence came they? Catholicism is not a mere aggregation of atoms, but the
articulation of an idea, the embodiment of a transcendental ideal. What is termed its supernaturalism
is but this ideal translated into dogma, and then
worked into a reasoned system. Its natural history
is too vast a subject to be here analytically handled,
or even touched, especially as it would involve the
discussion of the relation of Christianity to ancient
thought. The organic doctrines of Christianity and
the organizing ideas of Catholicism are different and
distinct. The former proceed by a synthetic process
from the Religion of Christ, and can be analytically
resolved into it ; but the latter are of foreign, though
not necessarily of alien, origin, taken up into the body
of doctrine and becoming there factors of development and variation. Christianity found the world

expectant; the thought it was to change began by changing it. The philosophy it was able to overcome as an enemy it could not so easily resist as a friend. To forsake an error is not to be purged from it; though Augustine renounced Manicheism, yet his early dualism subtly penetrates all his later thought. And so the heresy that forced the church to formulate its doctrine did not leave it with the old purity of faith or simplicity of polity. Gnosticism was vanquished, but not annihilated; its antithesis of matter and spirit, found a footing in the new society and modified its ideal of life, making it less surely conscious of the unity of the secular and eternal. Ebionitism was defeated, but the mind that cultivated poverty for the increase of Religion lived on, and even gained an ampler and freer field for its exercise. Jewish asceticism, Syrian and Egyptian, did not long survive the Jewish state; but it did not die till its ideas and example had touched and affected the church. Yet these were but incidental influences; the most plastic came from the revived philosophies, the Stoic, Pythagorean, and Platonic. Similar questions were debated in the academies and the catechetical schools, and their ideas and disciplines were also akin. Alexandrian philosophy, as much as Alexandrian theology, had its doctrine of God, of the Trinity, faith, spiritual or allegorical interpretation, bodily mortification, supernatural enlightenment, and final reward; and if the rivals did not copy, they at least stimulated and developed each other. It is

significant that the earlier influence was metaphysical
and theological, but the later ecclesiastical and
mystic, or political and sacramentarian. In the third
and fourth centuries the great questions were those
touching the Godhead ; how God was to be conceived ;
how He was related to the world ; how to man, Christian and heathen; what Father and Son signified, and
what Word and Spirit ; how the One could be the
manifold, and because the manifold, be, while the
One, the All-loving and the All-efficient, the home of
all perfection and the centre of all energy. But in
the fifth and sixth centuries the great questions were
those touching the Church, its idea, orders, people
discipline, sacraments, the mystic allegories of nature
and grace. This change meant many things, but
mainly this :—Ecclesiastical organization had proceeded so far, that it was necessary to find for it a
speculative basis and unifying ideal. With every
change, indeed, in the organism, there had been a
correlative change in the collective consciousness ;
the development of new organs and energies had
developed new ideas and activities ; but what was
now needed was a conception that should unite all
thé parts into an harmonious and homogeneous
system. And to this result Neo-Platonic thought
powerfully contributed. Augustine came to Paul
from the study of Plato, and he more than any man
Platonized the Paul he studied and the ideal of the
Church he depicted and maintained. Synesius had
been a Christian while a Platonist, and remained a

Platonist after he had become a Christian. The Pseudo-Dionysius represents the Neo-Platonic principles and interpretative method applied to the Catholic system : " symbolism reigns in heaven and on earth, a celestial hierarchy holds the approaches to God above, an ecclesiastical hierarchy guards and regulates them below ; and men are graduated according to the degree of their initiation in the holy mysteries which at once reveal and conceal the ineffable Godhead. No book exercised a mightier influence on Catholicism, did more on the one hand to foster its mysticism, on the other to develop its sacerdotalism. It moulded in an equal degree men so dissimilar as Scotus Erigena and Thomas Aquinas, Hugo of St. Victor and Albertus Magnus, Grosseteste and Dante ; and yet it was but Neo-Platonism made to speak with the Catholic tongue." [1]

2. It is therefore due to no mere accident or curious coincidence that so many affinities exist between Plato's Republic and the Roman Church. They differ, indeed, in many respects fundamentally ; the one is philosophical and an ideal, the other is religious and a reality ; but the kinship is manifest enough, especially if the Republic be studied in the Neo-Platonic spirit and method. Each reposes on a transcendentalism that makes the actual exist through and for the ideal ; yet so in opposition to it, that a special order is needed to secure its realization. Each

---

[1] *The Place of Christ*, etc., p. 109.

is an institution founded for the creation of virtue or obedience ; and has as its function and end the making of this life the way to a better, or the discipline of its citizens for a higher and more perfect state of being. Each is possessed with the same sense of the august sanctity of the whole ; the individual is nothing apart from it, has no good save in and through and from it ; he is altogether its, and is to have his whole life regulated by its laws and for its ends. Each has the same need for a sacred or special order : in the Republic the philosopher is king, for he alone knows the idea, or stands in the secret of God, and so is alone able so to organize and administer the laws as to secure its realization ; and in the Church the priest reigns, the man Divinely appointed to speak to men concerning God, and reconcile them to Him. In each the idealism is the basis of a despotism : the authority of the sacred order is absolute, the multitude may not rebel against the custodians of the truth ; they must remain supreme and infallible if the ideal is to be realized. Each has a similar attitude to the home and family ; in the Republic the man must be without a home that he may the better serve the State; in the Church the man who would be its minister must be without family or home. The community of goods in the one has its counterpart in the vows of personal poverty, in alliance with corporate wealth, in the other ; in each the individual derives all his good from the whole, and the whole has command over the all of the individual. These are but the rough outlines of a parallel which might be indefinitely extended and minutely illustrated. But what is significant is this: the differences, so far as ideal— which of course is not to forget that the one system is speculative, while the other is historical—may be described as, in the main, those that distinguished Platonic from Neo-Platonic thought—*i.e.*, differences due to the penetration of the original philosophic ideal with mystic, hierarchic, theurgic, and ascetical elements. The Catholic church is the Platonic kingdom of philosophers transformed into a kingdom of priests.

The conclusion, then, is this:—The principle of development, analytically applied to the catholic system, proves that the parent form or aboriginal germ—the ideal and society of Jesus—was by its environments modified in a twofold direction. First, from the ancient Religions, Jewish and pagan, it received the notion of the priesthood, with all its accessories; and so became sacerdotal. And, secondly, from the Roman empire, working on the material of its primitive Judaeo-Hellenic polity, it received the dream and function of Roman supremacy; and so became catholic, papal, and infallible. Once it had been so modified and developed, it became, largely through current politico-religious speculation, possessed of the organizing ideas needed to give it intellectual consistency and completeness, making an historical system the body of a universal ideal. But this conclusion brings us to our second main ques-

tion—the adequacy of the church or institution to
the Religion and its purposes. Adequacy may be
here interpreted in a double sense, as either historical
efficiency, or as ideal sufficiency ; or, in other words,
as adequacy for work, or adequacy to the spirit and
matter of the Religion. Something must be said as
regards each of these.

§ VII. *Catholicism in History*

1. There is here no desire to question the efficiency
and historical achievements of the Roman Church.
It is to us no creation of craft or subtlety, human or
diabolical, no Man of Sin, Scarlet Woman, or shameless Antichrist, but a veritable creature of God and
manifest minister of His providence. The energies
evolved in the struggle for existence enabled it at
once to survive and be victorious. They were conditions of service, and as such necessary. Thus the
rise of the sacerdotal idea may be conceived as, on
the one hand, a process of interpenetration, and, on
the other, mediation and reconcilement. It is the one
because the other ; the old and the new faiths inter-
penetrate that the new Religion may the better win
and master the ancient mind. Catholicism is the
interpretation of the Christian idea in the terms and
through the associations of the ancient faiths, and as
such represents on the largest scale the continuity of
Religion in history. Its work was a needed work, for
man is incapable of transitions at once sudden and
absolute ; the construction of Christianity through the

media of the older Religions was a necessary prelude to its construction by a spirit and through a consciousness of its own creation. The absolute ideal had, in order to be intelligible, to use constituted and familiar vehicles; but only that it might win the opportunity of fashioning vehicles worthier of its nature and fitter for its end.

The political element, again, especially as dominated and directed by the great organizing ideas, had its own special function; it mediated between the ancient empires of force and the new empires of the spirit. The Pope stood when Cæsar fell; and became, in a sense higher than Cæsar had ever been—master of the world. In those days of anarchy, when the military, legislative, judicial, fiscal, and municipal system of the empire had completely broken down, when the barbarians had seized its provinces and wasted its cities, and were contending with each other at once for plunder and supremacy, the ecclesiastical was the only universal sovereignty possible. And the sovereignty the Roman church was called to exercise, it exercised, on the whole, beneficently; it worked for order, justice, and civilization. Its association with the empire had made it imperial; its religious ideal made it at once authoritative and humane. While it owed its ambition for supremacy to Cæsar, it owed its enthusiasm for humanity to Christ. And so, while it succeeded, it did not repeat the empire; its sovereignty had another basis, and was exercised by other means for other ends.

The church was, in a sense Rome could never be, "the Eternal City"; in it eternity took bodily shape before the eyes of men; and so a vaster meaning came into life, ennobling the men that lived it, dignifying all its affairs. Men were not to it divided into a multitude of alien races; all were to it spirits and immortal, responsible to it, for whom it was responsible to God. It represented, therefore, a new idea of sovereignty, a grander and more awful majesty, an empire that lived by faith in the moral and immortal worth of man, for his good and the glory of God. To say that, out of the chaos Rome left, it created order, is to say a small and inadequate thing; it created a new ideal of government, made man another being to the Sovereign and the Sovereign another being to man. Before it, had been the reign of might; after and through it was to be the reign of the Spirit.

2. It is impossible, then, to regard the history of Catholicism as equal to the history of Christianity; it is at once much more and much less. It is much more: for by many of its ideals, institutions, and associations it represents the continuity of the ancient and modern worlds, their kinship and community in matters of faith and worship; and it is much less, for much of the best work Christianity has done, both in earlier and in later times, has been done without it and in spite of it. There is nothing so little historical as the spirit that identifies Christianity and Catholicism, or that sees in the latter

either the creation of Jesus Christ or the sole vehicle of His truth. It has indeed rendered eminent services to our race and our Religion; these demand and deserve our gratitude. The Catholicism of the Catholic church is large, but there is one still larger, the note and possession of no church, but of all the churches—the Catholicism of the Christian Religion. According to it, the truth preserved by any or each is the property of all; the holiness or beneficence of one is a common heritage, enriching the whole family of the faith. The saints of Catholicism are not Roman, but Christian; the achievements of Protestantism came not of protesting, but of loyalty to conscience and to God. And the right attitude to both is to say:—Since they are due to the inspiration of the one Spirit, they belong to the universalism of Christ, not to the specialism of the churches. From this point of view I claim to be as much as any Catholic, heir to all that is Christian in Catholicism; and the claim is not in any way affected by either absolute negation or qualified assent from the Catholic's side. Whatever is of Christ in his system can be in no respect alien to what is of Christ in me and mine. True Catholicism must be as comprehensive as the action of God; whatever is less, but expresses the particularism of man.

But if Catholicism has served our race and our Religion, it has also done both eminent disservice; and this alike by what it has and what it has not achieved. It has impoverished Christian history, has made it less rich and varied than it ought to have been in ideals of life, faith, and society. The suppression of Montanism was not an unmixed good, indeed in many respects not a good at all; for in it much that was most characteristic and primitive in Christianity died. Donatism had its own right to be; emphasized elements in the Religion, Catholicism had no room for or did no justice to. But a greater evil than the monotony it introduced into the Christian ideal was its failure to realize its own. It was potent in its earlier period, when a necessity to Religion and man; but impotent in its later, when man, having outgrown it, needed Religion presented in a freer form, a nobler and more congenial vehicle. In the hands of Rome Christianity had come so near its death that the Reformation was a necessity to its life. The two centuries before it had been like a desert, studded, indeed, as all who love mysticism thankfully remember, with beautiful oases of faith and devotion. But the main stream of tendency within the Catholic church did not then make for godliness. I do not mean to reproach it with men like the Borgias; all churches have had their share of bad men; and we have heard more than enough of them, though the thing is most pitiful when wicked men become officially infallible. But what I do mean to say is this: Religion in the fifteenth century was the creation of the Roman church, and Italy was then without a Religion, or, worse, had one that aggravated rather than lessened the evil. The Italian states were bad, the church was no better; the moral depravity was encouraged by the intellectual scepticism; the sensuous licence was reflected in the religious. Extenuating circumstances may be discovered; the conflicts with the German emperors, the French kings, and the free cities; the subtle influences of the Renaissance, Moorish philosophy, and Jewish learning. But these neither alter nor explain the facts. Religion was the church's province, in it she had reigned for centuries without a rival; yet her infallibility in doctrine had been so mated with inefficiency in conduct, as to result in the completest breakdown in the matter of faith and morals Christian Europe has ever known. The supernatural and the natural gifts were so ill-assorted that the one did more than neutralize the other; their joint action made the evil of the times more inveterate and acute. The authority of the church forbade the reform of the church, and the act that broke her unity saved our religion.

3. But it is impossible to end here; modern history is as significant as ancient. Catholics reproach Protestants with being blind to the meaning of the centuries that lie between the first and the sixteenth. But there is a Roman counterpart to this Protestant neglect. The centuries that have elapsed since the fifteenth ended, have been without doubt the most eventful, fruitful, momentous in the history of man;

and their history has been the history of Christian
peoples. The record of their material progress has
been a record of marvels. America has been discovered, colonized, peopled; Asia has been opened
up, almost conquered and annexed; Africa has
been explored, and is being pierced and penetrated
on all sides; and in the Australasian continent
and islands the seeds of new States have been
plentifully sown. The European States, with certain
significant exceptions, are mightier than they were
four centuries ago, better ordered, more moral, more
populous, freer, wealthier; and the poorest of the
countries have become rich and full of comforts as
compared with Europe in the days of the Black
Death. But what part has Christianity had in the
making of modern civilization? Not much, if it
and the Catholic church be identical. The conquests
and colonizations effected by Catholic states have,
so far as order, progress, and human well-being are
concerned, been chapters of disaster and failure. The
progressive peoples have been the non-Catholic; from
them have proceeded the noblest of the ameliorative
principles and actions of the period. They have
been the least troubled with revolution; have had
the most happy, well-ordered commonwealths; have
enjoyed most freedom; have most successfully
laboured to temper justice with mercy, to make
judgment remedial, to enlarge the area of rights,
and to raise the ideal of duty. And the same
peoples have been pre-eminent in the realms of

thought and spirit, been most deeply and devoutly exercised by the problems concerning man and his destiny. God has not been sparing of His gifts of great men to those who sit outside Catholicism. The Elizabethan dramatists, greatest of moderns in their own order, were the poets of the English people in the heroic moment of their reaction against Rome. Milton was the poet of a still more radical revolution. Cowper and Burns, Wordsworth and Coleridge, Tennyson and Browning, Scott and Carlyle, represent the inspiration and aspiration of the same people. Herder and Lessing, Schiller and Goethe, were not products of Catholicism. The most splendid cycle of thinkers since the Platonic age in Greece, was that which began with Kant and ended with Hegel, sons of Protestant Germany. It is needless to multiply names. What we wish to know is this—the relation of Christianity to this whole complex movement called progress or modern civilization. Our modern world has had more of God in it than the mediæval, and He is there because of the Religion we call Christianity. But were we to identify the Religion with the Roman church, we should have to regard our world as in progressive apostasy from Him. But its apostasy means His desertion; and a world forsaken of its God would be poorer in its good than ours has been; while a God who could, even in the interests of an infallible church, forsake any part of His World, especially a part that had been so strenuously

feeling after Him that it might know His truth
and do His will, would be less Divine than we
believe our God to be. We will not allow either
the truth or the sufficiency of the religious idea
that would deny God to any man, or make Him the
special possession of any church. For the Atheism
that denies, is less impious than the Atheism that
limits His presence, that dares in its pride to say,
" He is so mine that you must belong to me in
order to belong to Him ; and what you have of
Him is by my grace and through my act." That
vain Atheism God has in these last centuries caused
His very providence to contradict and reprove.
For it were a strange and satirical theodicy that
should exhibit God as working poverty and revolution in the nations that had accepted or been
forced to accept the authority of His own infallible
church ; while sending fulness of life, and grace,
and freedom into those that had deserted and disowned it.

§ VIII. *Catholicism no Sufficient Organ for the Christian Religion*

This brings us to the ideal sufficiency of Catholicism : the question whether it be a vehicle equal to
the spirit and matter of the Christian Religion, the
alone fully qualified interpreter of its truth to our
age. This is the really fundamental question, and
has been so implied in every issue raised, that in
what still remains to be said we must be severely brief.

1. Catholicism claims to present the completest faith in God, and to do the amplest justice to the mysteries of faith and the realities of Religion. The supernaturalism on which it is grounded is indeed marvellous, but it is not mysterious. Cardinal Newman, using the mysteries of nature to justify those of the Church, says,[1] " If I must submit my reason to mysteries, it does not much matter whether it is a mystery more or a mystery less." But it may matter in an infinite degree ; whether it does matter depends on the source and character of the mysteries. The true mystery is a thing of nature ; history neither made it nor can show how it was made ; reason finds it and cannot elude it, for it is bound up with the being of the reason and the system that holds and unfolds it. But a false mystery is only a marvel, a belief with a remarkable history ; without ground in nature or reason in thought ; but bound up with the being of an institution, explicable through it, yet helping to explain it. The mystery is at once immanent and universal ; has its roots in the universe that confronts man, its reason in the man that confronts the universe ; and through it life is invested with all its meaning and all its grandeur. But the marvel is occasional and particular, has no meaning apart from the institution through and for which it exists, while the institution has no majesty apart from it. The mystery exercises reason, but the

---

[1] *Sermons to Mixed Congregations*, p. 275.

marvel taxes faith ; and so, while authority may be based on the mysteries of reason, the marvels of faith must be based on authority. The supernaturalism native to the Christian Religion is mysterious, for in it nature and man may lie embosomed, comprehended, uncomprehending ; but the supernaturalism of Rome is without mystery, for while it is sufficient to the needs of Catholicism, it is inadequate to the idea of God, or the ideals of His providence and kingdom. It has, too, a natural history of its own ; its most transcendent dogmas need but to be studied through their history to be thoroughly intelligible. Belief in them may be the measure of submission to the authority on which they rest ; but it in no way indicates the attitude of the mind to those ultimate beliefs which are the true mysteries of thought and the universe. Nay, a man's faith in the supernatural may be all the less real that his faith in Catholic dogma is strong ; it may be faith in the church and its determinations, not in God and His living Spirit. If God is known and approached through the church, then it is not so much God as the church that is believed ; for its people can know Him only through the terms it approves, and approach Him only on the conditions it prescribes. But to bind God to a church, and distribute and determine His truth through its decrees, is a bad supernaturalism ; it is to bring the Almighty within the limits of an historical institution, and then to argue that the limitation is credible because it makes the institution so divine, justifies its claims, and explains its prerogatives. This, I repeat, may be marvellous, but it is not mysterious; it may make the institution remarkable, but it does not make Religion divine. The more organized authority becomes, the more exigent, imperative, imperious, it grows; in a word, the more it is incorporated in a church, the more the church tends to supersede God, and to become His substitute. The centre of gravity is, as it were, changed; the church experiences a kind of apotheosis, God suffers a sort of political incarnation. It so holds the approaches to Him that it is not so much in His hands as He is in its; and in the very degree that it possesses Him, nature and man are deprived of His presence. The special Theism of the church ends in a more awful Atheism of the universe.

2. Indeed, the radical defect of Catholicism seems to me its want of a true supernaturalism, and even fundamental incompatibility with one. It is throughout conceived in the interests of the church rather than in the interests of Religion and humanity. The Catholic church is built on a conception of Deity that is not Christ's; it dispenses His grace and distributes His truth to those outside its pale on terms, in modes and quantities, that involve the negation of His holiest attributes and divinest qualities—the scholastic distinctions which most incline to charity being but an aggravation of the offence. And even to those within its pale the

representation of Him is imperfect : the church has determined the idea of God ; the idea of God has not been allowed to determine the idea and spirit of the church. There is no Religion so generous as the Religion of the New Testament. God as He appears there is the universal Father, and all men are His sons ; between Him and them no institution or church can be allowed to stand, the only Priest or Mediator being the Christ. The Apostles burn with holy passion against every " middle wall of partition," or whatever would limit the grace and activity of God. He is the God of both Jew and Gentile, " in Him all live and move and have their being," " in every nation he that feareth God and worketh righteousness is accepted of Him." In the early Church this was the doctrine of men like Justin Martyr and Clement of Alexandria ; but, as the idea of the Catholic church rose, the remoter, the more formal and circumscribed, were God's relations to men conceived to be. The greater the emphasis laid on the priesthood and mediation, with their associated ideas and instruments, the less general became His influence and the less immediate intercourse with Him ; and, as He lost, the intermediaries gained in reality to faith. The very notion of Religion was revolutionized, ceased to have the spiritual immediacy, the ethical breadth and intensity, the filial love and peace, the human purity and gentleness, of Jesus ; and became more akin to the ancient sacerdotal and ceremonial worships. The great enemy of God is the idea of the church and its priesthood. Nothing has so estranged men from Him as the claim to be alone able to reconcile Him and them. The most clamant need of our day is to recover the religious idea of Jesus: and the only way to recover it is to think of God as He was declared to be by the only-begotten Son, who is in the bosom of the Father.

But it may be well, before this discussion ends, that we recall its purpose: viz., to inquire concerning, not the truth of rival churches, but the form in which the Christian Faith can best be presented to our age. Religious men are face to face with serious issues, and are burdened with grave responsibilities. The difficulties of belief are great, but the consciousness of them is greater; they spring not so much from the new knowledge as the changed estimate and conditions of life. Men are so possessed and oppressed by the labour needed to win the means of living, that they have not sufficient energy of mind to weigh or to master the deeper mysteries of life, and so are prepared to allow either authority to affirm their faith or criticism to dissolve it. In such an age Catholicism may have its place, and make its converts; and it is no purpose of ours to take it from them or them from it. But if it claims to be the one real, sufficient, and relevant form of the Christian Religion, then the truth must be spoken. Not in and through it, is Religion to be realized in an age of thought, in a world of freedom, progress, order, and activity. Its doctrine of authority and the

church is a direct provocation to scepticism ; its idea
of Religion is an impoverishment of the ideal that
came in the Kingdom of heaven. Faith can come
by its rights only as it fulfils its duties to reason.
And the church that alone has a right to live, is the
church that, by finding in God the most humanity,
most fills humanity with God ; and so works for the
establishment of that Kingdom which was founded
by the Son, and is governed by the Father, of man.

July, 1885.

V

REASON AND RELIGION

[To so much of the criticism in the foregoing essays as referred to his philosophical scepticism, Cardinal Newman replied in a paper entitled, "The Development of Religious Error," in the *Contemporary Review*, for October, 1885. The reply was so characteristic of the writer and of his art and method in controversy that, had it been open to me, I should have liked to reproduce it here; and also a supplement, privately printed later, written in better temper and in a more reasonable vein. The rejoinder, at least so much of it as concerned the Cardinal's substantial criticism, appears in this essay.]

CARDINAL NEWMAN, in his reply to me, has done two things—he has repudiated and denounced what my criticism never affirmed, and he has contributed new material illustrative of the very thesis it maintained. He has represented me as describing him as "a hidden sceptic,"[1] and as "thinking, living, professing, acting upon a wide-stretching, all-reaching platform of religious scepticism."[2] I never did anything of the sort; it would require an energy and irony of invective equal to the Cardinal's own, to describe the fatuous folly of the man who would venture to make any such charge. What he was charged with, and

---

[1] *Contemporary Review*, October, 1885, p. 457.   [2] *Ibid.*, p. 466.

in terms so careful and guarded as ought to have excluded all possible misconception, was " metaphysical" or "philosophical" scepticism. This did not mean that he was other than sincere in word and spirit, especially in all that concerned his religious convictions—his good faith in all his beliefs is, and ever has been, manifest to all honest men ; but it meant what it said, that he so conceived the intellect that its natural attitude to religious truth was sceptical and nescient. Scepticism in philosophy means a system which affirms either, subjectively, the impotence of the reason for the discovery of the truth, or, objectively, the inaccessibility of truth to the reason; and such a scepticism, while it logically involves the completest negation of knowledge, has before now been made the basis of a pseudo-supernaturalism, or plea for an infallible authority, that must reveal and authenticate truth, if truth is ever to become or remain man's. This was the scepticism with which Cardinal Newman was charged, and it was held significant, not simply for his personal history, but also for the movement so inseparably connected with his name. And his last paper is as signal an illustration of its presence and action as is to be found in all his writings.

§ I. *The Philosophical Scepticism of Cardinal Newman*

1. Dr. Newman's reply, then, which relates to the single point of the philosophical scepticism, is so

without relevance to the original criticism, save in the way of illustration and confirmation, that it may be well to attempt to make the real point at issue clear and explicit. He speaks of me as having been " misled by the epithets which he had attached in the *Apologia* to the Reason."[1] The epithets had nothing whatever to do with the matter; all turned on the substantive or material idea. The criticism was simply an endeavour to determine, on the one hand, how Cardinal Newman conceived the Reason and the Conscience in themselves and in relation to the knowledge of God ; and, on the other hand, how these conceptions affected or regulated the movement of his mind from Theism to Catholicism. Stated in another form, the question is this: How is knowledge of religious truth possible? What are the subjective conditions of its genesis and continuance? How and whence does man get those principles which are the bases of all his thinking concerning religion? and in what relations do they and the Reason, at first, and throughout their respective histories, stand to each other? It is the old problem, under its highest and most complex aspect, as to the grounds and conditions of knowledge, how it is ever or any-where possible. The older Empiricism said: All knowledge is resolvable into sensuous impressions and the ideas which are their faint image or copy. There are no ideas in the mind till the senses have

---

[1] *Contemporary Review*, p. 460.

conveyed them in; it is but a sheet of white paper
till the outer universe has by the finger of sense
written on it those mysterious hieroglyphs which
constitute our intelligible world. But the critical
Transcendentalism replied: The impression explains
nothing—must itself be explained : how is it that it
becomes rational, an intelligible thing? The mind
and the sheet of white paper differ thus—the paper
receives the character, but the mind reads it ; indeed
the character would have no being save in and
through the reading of the mind. It is clear, therefore, that we must get before and below the impression to the thought, which is, by its forms and
categories, the interpreter of the impression, the
condition of its being intelligible. Without a constitutive and interpretative Reason, the world that
speaks to the senses would be no reasonable world.

Now, Cardinal Newman may be described as, by
virtue of his doctrine of the Reason, an empiricist in
the province of religious truth. It involves precisely
the same attitude to religion that Hume's philosophy
involved to the reality of the outer world, to causation
and to personal identity. What Hume did by means
of association, Newman does by means of authority.
The reason is, as he is fond of saying, "a mere
instrument," unfurnished by nature, without religious
contents or function, till faith or conscience has conveyed into it the ideas or assumptions which are the
premisses of its processes ; and with religious character
only as these processes are conducted in obedience

to the moral sense or other spiritual authority. It is to him no constitutive or architectonic faculty, with religious truth so in it, that it is bound to seek and to conceive religious truth without it; but it is as regards Religion simply idle or vacant till it has received and accepted the deliverances of conscience, which stand to it much as Hume conceived his "impressions" and their corresponding "ideas" to stand related to mind and knowledge. But, then, to a reason so constituted and construed how is religious knowledge possible? How can religion, as such, have any existence, or religious truth any reality? What works as a mere instrument never handles what it works in; the things remain outside it, and have no place or standing within its being. And hence my contention was, and is, that to conceive reason as Dr. Newman does, is to deny to it the knowledge of God, and so to save faith by the help of a deeper unbelief.

I repeat, then : the doctrine of the reason Cardinal Newman stated in the *Contemporary* for October is precisely the doctrine on which my criticism was based ; and it is essentially, in the philosophical sense, a sceptical doctrine. But let us see how he formulates it. Here is what may be regarded as his earliest statement, with his later notes appended:—[1]

---

[1] *University Sermons*, p. 55. The notes are added : for here, as elsewhere throughout the volume, they are significant by their very limitations. They may qualify the text, explain a term or a phrase, protest against a given inference or result;

"There is no necessary connexion between the intellectual and moral principles of our nature[1]; on religious subjects we may prove anything or overthrow anything, and can arrive at truth but accidentally, if we merely investigate by what is commonly called Reason,[2] which is in such matters but the instrument at best, in the hands of the legitimate judge, spiritual discernment."

Here is his latest statement, which will be found in everything material identical with the earliest:—

"In its versatility, its illimitable range, its subtlety, its power of concentrating many ideas on one point, it (the reason) is for the acquisition of knowledge all-important or rather necessary; with this drawback, however, in its ordinary use, that in every exercise of it, it depends for success upon the assumption of prior acts similar to that which it has itself involved, and therefore is reliable only conditionally. Its process is a passing from an antecedent to a consequent, and according as the start so is the issue. In the province of religion, if it be under the happy guidance of the moral sense, and with teachings which are not only assumptions in form, but certainties, it will arrive at indisputable truth, and then the house is at peace; but if it be in the hands of enemies, who are under the delusion that its arbitrary assumptions are self-evident axioms, the reasoning will start from false premises, and the mind will be in a state of melancholy disorder. But in no case need the reasoning faculty itself be to blame or responsible, except if viewed as identical with the assumptions of which it is the instrument. I

---

but they never either modify or alter the radical doctrine. These notes are needed to elucidate the criticism, for nothing has been more helpful to it than a minute and comparative study of them.

[1] 'That is, as found in individuals, in the concrete.'

[2] 'Because we may be reasoning from wrong principles, principles unsuitable to the subject-matter reasoned upon. Thus, the moral sense or "spiritual discernment" must supply us with the assumptions to be used as premisses in religious inquiry.'

repeat, it is but an instrument ; as such I have viewed it, and no one but Dr. Fairbairn would say as he does—that the bad employment of a faculty was a ' division,' a 'contradiction,' and 'a radical antagonism of nature,' and 'the death of the natural proof' of a God."[1]

2. Now, I do not wish to be minute in my criticism, and argue that if reason, "in every exercise of it, depends for success on the assumption of prior acts similar to that which it has itself involved," then the genesis and very being of reason are inconceivable, for we are landed in the notion of an infinite series. As to Hume man was a succession or series of "impressions and ideas," so to Newman reason, as mere faculty of reasoning, is a series of "antecedents and consequents"; the difficulty in both cases is the same, to find how the series began, and how, having begun, it has developed into what it is. But without resorting to minute analysis, we may begin with the last sentence of the above quotation ; and concerning it, it is enough to say, Dr. Fairbairn never said any such thing, or, meaning what he did and does, could have said it. His criticism referred not to the employment of the faculty, but to the doctrine of the faculty, which determined its use ; and this latest statement seems expressly designed to elucidate and justify the criticism. For reason, as

---

[1] *Contemporary Review*, pp. 459, 460. A few more instances from the *University Sermons*, of Dr. Newman's use of the term Reason, may be added to those he has himself given ; they ought to be studied with the *Catholic Notes*, pp. 58, § 4 ; 60, 61, § 7 ; 65, 67, 70, 73, 88, 179, 194, 195, 214, 215.

here described, is condemned, in all that concerns the higher problems and fundamental verities of thought, to incapacity and impotence. It is emptied of those constitutive and constructive qualities that make it a reason ; and by being reduced to a mere ratiocinative instrument, its very ability to handle religious principles, even in a ratiocinative process, is denied. For the reasoning process, to be valid, must proceed from principles valid to the reason ; but to be so valid they must be more than deliverances or assumptions coming to it *ab extra;* they must have a root in its own nature, and be inseparable from the very being of thought. To use principles truly, one must be able to judge concerning their truth : and how can a reason truly and justly act, even as a mere instrument of inference, on the basis of premisses it neither found, nor framed, nor verified, being indeed so constituted as to be unable to do any one of these things? Reason, then, can be ratiocinative only as it is constitutive ; we must have truth of thought, that we may know or possess truth of being. The getting of principles is a more vital matter than the reasoning concerning them ; and if the constitutive or formulative and determinative factor be made not only distinct from the dialectic and deductive, but independent of it, how can they ever be made to agree, save by the subordination or enslavement of the one to the other ? And even then they will not agree : for the principles cannot signify the same thing to faculties that are not only distinct, but, as realized in the

living person, without "necessary connexion." The
dictate of the conscience changes its nature when it
becomes the axiom of the reason; the "categorical
imperative" ceases to be, the moment it is translated
into a speculative or intellectual truth. It may—nay,
it must—be true that the man who is deaf to the
voice of conscience cannot reason rightly in religious
matters; but it is no less true that the man who
doubts or misuses his reason cannot hear or be enlightened by his conscience. The only justification
of Cardinal Newman's doctrine would have been the
reduction of conscience and reason to a higher unity;
his last condemnation is his distinction and division
of the faculties, for it involves our nature in a dualism
which makes real knowledge of religious truth impossible. There is unity neither in the man who
knows nor in the truth as known. For, make a
present of true premises to a faculty merely ratiocinative, and they will be to it only as algebraic
symbols, not as truths of religion; its deductive
process may be correct, but it will have no religious
character. But to a reason without religious character, unable to construe religious truths for what
they really are, there can be no legitimate reasoning
concerning religion; truth is inaccessible to it, and it
is incompetent to the discovery and determination of
truth. This is philosophical scepticism; and if, to
avoid the logical issue, the truth denied to the reason
is granted to the conscience, and is, on its simple
authority, to be accepted as a "magisterial dictate,"

then a "division," or "radical antagonism of nature,"
is introduced, which is "the death of the natural
proof" for the being of a God, and of all the primary
truths of religion.   This, and no other, was my
original criticism of Cardinal Newman : and this,
confirmed and illustrated by his latest statement, is
my criticism still.

§ II. *Correlation of the Subjective and Objective*
Scepticism

1. Now, this very doctrine of the reason, with its
varied limitations and applications, is the heart and
essence of the whole matter ; it is, in the proper
philosophical sense, both empirical and sceptical.   It
is a doctrine of impotence ; the reason is by its
very nature disqualified from ever attaining the
knowledge of religious truth, as religious.   It is a
doctrine of nescience ; for religious knowledge is, from
its very nature, unable to get within, and be really
assimilated by, a reason which is a mere inferential or syllogistic instrument.   Dr. Newman is very
angry at my speaking of his "ultimate ideas, or the
regulative principles of his thought," or simply his
"underlying philosophy " ; and he declares that from
"leading ideas " and "fundamental principles " he
has "all through his life shrunk, as sophistical and
misleading."[1]   Well, it may be so : and if it is so,
many things that have been a perplexity to people
would be explained.   But it is possible that if Dr.

---

[1] *Contemporary Review*, p. 467.

Newman had been described as a person without "fundamental" or "regulative principles," he would have been angrier still, and with more reason. However, the matter need not be any further disputed; what was meant by his "underlying philosophy" is just this doctrine which he has anew stated and maintained. What was meant by it as a "regulative principle of his thought," was that it exercised over his mind, its dialectic and dialectical method, precisely the sort of influence he has endeavoured to explain and illustrate. Now, what I ventured to say before, I am by the new light the more emboldened to repeat—that this fundamental principle determined, in a way not written in the *Apologia*, his whole inner history. He not only doubted the reason, but he mocked and scorned all who sought to enlist it in the service of religion.[1] It was to him no witness or oracle of God, but simply a servant,

---

[1] See, for example, as applying the principles of the *University Sermons* to contemporary mind and literature, the following Essays :—*Introduction of Rationalistic Principles into Revealed Religion* (1835). This is practically a review, hard and unsympathetic, of Jacob Abbott and Thomas Erskine of Linlathen. *Apostolical Tradition* (1836); *Milman's View of Christianity* (1841), a review of his "most dangerous and insidious" History ; *Private Judgment* (1841). This latter is, in particular, instructive and suggestive. These are reprinted in the *Essays Critical and Historical.* Another, and even more illustrative paper, is "The Tamworth Reading-room," in *Discussions and Arguments,* art. iv. This contains the famous letters of "Catholicus" against Sir Robert Peel and Lord Brougham.

whose duty was to obey, and whose only virtue was obedience. Here, from the critical year 1841, is a significant passage, one out of many, illustrative of how little the empirical and instrumental reason, as he conceived it, had of God, and how little it could find Him in the Nature it was called to interpret :—

"The whole framework of nature is confessedly a tissue of antecedents and consequents ; we may refer all things forward to design, or backwards on a physical cause. Laplace is said to have considered he had a formula which solved all the motions of the solar system ; shall we say that those motions came from this formula or from a Divine Fiat ? Shall we have recourse for our theory to physics or to theology ? Shall we assume Matter and its necessary properties to be eternal, or Mind with its divine attributes ? Does the sun shine to warm the earth, or is the earth warmed because the sun shines ? The one hypothesis will solve the phenomena as well as the other. Say not it is but a puzzle in argument, and no one ever felt it in fact. So far from it, I believe that the study of nature, when religious feeling is away, leads the mind, rightly or wrongly, to acquiesce in the atheistical theory, as the simplest and easiest. It is but parallel to that tendency in anatomical studies, which no one will deny, to solve all the phenomena of the human frame into material elements and powers, and to dispense with the soul. To those who are conscious of matter, but not conscious of mind, it seems more rational to refer all things to one origin, such as they know, than to assume the existence of a second origin, such as they know not. It is religion, then, which suggests to science its true conclusions ; the facts come from knowledge, but the principles come of faith." [1]

---

[1] "The Tamworth Reading-room : " *Discussions and Arguments*, pp. 299, 300 (4th ed.). To this remarkable passage Dr. Newman has appended the following note :—"This is too absolute, if it is to be taken to mean that the legitimate, and what may be called the objective conclusion from the fact of

In this passage, where statement and argument are alike logical results of the implied philosophy of mind, the attitude of the intellectual sceptic is admirably stated ; either alternative is consonant to reason, though the negative is rather the more consonant. If reason stands alone, the conclusion will be nescience. It is all a matter of feeling or faith ; if it be away, "the study of Nature" will lead to acquiescence "in the atheistical theory"; if it be present, the reference will be to the being of God. Dr. Newman elsewhere quotes a doctrine which Hume "has well propounded," though he did it but "in irony" :—"Our most holy religion is founded on *faith*, not on reason."[1] The irony of Hume is the good faith of Newman ; while their creeds so differ, their philosophies so agree, that if the sceptic had ever attempted an apology for religion, he would have made it in the manner and on the lines and with all the implicates and inferences of the Catholic.

2. Nature, then, had not simply to the logical and inferential reason, but even, so far as he allowed it, to the constructive and interpretative, no necessary theistic meaning. As he himself says, "Take the

---

Nature, viewed in the concrete, is not in favour of the Being and Providence of God " (vide *Essay on Assent*, pp. 336, 345, 369 ; and *Univ. Serm.*, p. 194). But this, like the other *Catholic Notes*, changes the doctrine in no material respect ; it simply protests what the author did not wish to mean.

[1] *University Sermons*, p. 60.

system of nature by itself, detached from the axioms of religion, and I am willing to confess—nay, I have been expressly urging—that it does not force us to take it for *more* than a system."[1]   Whence, now, the axioms of religion which were needed to make our view of nature theistic ?   As they had no ground in the reason, they had to be given—*i.e.*, received on the authority either of conscience or of revelation.   If it accepted their *dicta*, it was religious; if it was without or averse to them, it was atheistic. This is the thesis of the most remarkable of his *University Sermons;* it comes out in his account of what he calls the Divinity of Traditionary Religion, which explains what is true in the various faiths, by all men having had " more or less the guidance of tradition, in addition to those internal notions of right and wrong which the Spirit has put into the heart of each individual."[2]   It appears, too, instructively in his doctrine of private judgment, whose province he defines as being to exercise itself upon this simple question, "What and where is the Church?"   We are not to think of gaining religious truth for ourselves by our "private examination," but ought only to ask, "Who is God's prophet, and where?   Who is to be considered the voice of the Holy Catholic and Apostolic Church?"[3]   It ob-

---

[1] *Discussions and Arguments*, p. 302.   The italics are his own.
[2] *The Arians of the Fourth Century*, pp. 79, 80 (4th ed.).
[3] *Private Judgment* (1841).   *Essays Critical and Historical*, vol. ii., pp. 353-355 (5th ed.).

tained its perfect and logical expression in the argument which proved an infallible authority necessary alike to the being of religion and the church :—

" As the essence of all religion is authority and obedience, so the distinction between natural religion and revealed lies in this, that the one has a subjective authority and the other an objective. Revelation consists in the manifestation of the Invisible Divine Power, or in the substitution of the voice of a Lawgiver for the voice of conscience. The supremacy of conscience is the essence of natural religion : the supremacy of Apostle, or Pope, or Church, or Bishop, is the essence of revealed; and when such external authority is taken away, the mind falls back again upon that inward guide which it possessed even before Revelation was vouchsafed. Thus, what conscience is in the system of nature, such is the voice of Scripture, or of the Church, or of the Holy See, as we may determine it, in the system of Revelation. It may be objected, indeed, that conscience is not infallible ; it is true, but still it is ever to be obeyed. And this is just the prerogative which controversialists assign to the See of St. Peter ; it is not in all cases infallible, it may err beyond its special province, but it has ever in all cases a claim on our obedience." [1]

Now, these are only the logical sequences in the process which compelled Dr. Newman to hold Catholicism and Atheism the only real alternatives ; but the compulsion came at every point from what he must allow me to call his " underlying philosophy," or simply, his doctrine, which made the reason a mere ratiocinative faculty or deductive instrument, by nature void of God, and never able to know

---

[1] *The Development of Doctrine*, pp. 124–125 (2nd ed.).

Him directly or for itself.[1] Its knowledge of religion being always indirect and inferential, "on
grounds given," the supreme difficulty was with "the
grounds"; how to get them, then how to have them
accepted, ratified, and obeyed. They were always
giving way beneath analysis, or being departed from,
or being superseded by "false," or "wrong," or "secular" premisses, which indeed ever seemed to be more
easy of acceptance than the religious: in short, his
principles of reasoning had no organic connection
with the principles of knowledge or reason. Reason
to him had so little in it of the truth, that it was
as ready to become the instrument of "the false
prophet" as of the true; to speak for the one was
as congenial to its nature as to speak for the other.
And so its natural inability was the source and basis
of its historical hostility to religion; the more it
was degraded into an instrument, the more it re-
venged its degradation by becoming unstable, intractable, inimical. The more critical, "aggressive,"
or "captious" the reason became, the more imperious
had to become the authority which supplied it with
the "assumptions" or "axioms of religion"; and,
as was inevitable, the more imperious the authority
grew, the more "rebellious" grew the reason. The
result was the one he has so well described in the
now classic passage: "He came to the conclusion

---

[1] "The knowledge of God is the highest function of our
nature, and as regards that knowledge, reason only holds the
place of an instrument." (Note in *University Sermons*, p. 7.)

that there was no medium in true philosophy between Atheism and Catholicity."[1] But it was the philosophy that did it all, and on its truth depends the validity of the conclusion. Where reason is conceived as a mere instrument, so by nature without the knowledge of God that all it ever knows or determines concerning Him must proceed from principles given "on the simple word of the Divine Informant," named now Conscience, now Tradition, and now the Church, then the alternatives—absolute authority or absolute negation—are inexorable. Nay, more, this doctrine, as is so well illustrated by his latest utterance, with its despair of all secular forces and its blind hope in ecclesiastical, is doubly determinative: it yields the theory, on the one hand, of the Church, and on the other of " the False Prophet," or " human society," by whose action " error spreads and becomes an authority." The subjective is reflected in an objective dualism ; the authoritative church has its counterpart and contradiction in the authoritative world ; each succeeds, as it has its premisses or assumptions accepted by the reason as data for reasoning. And thus the notion that loses the immanence of God from the reason, loses the active presence of God from the collective history and society of man. The scepticism of the theory on its subjective side has its correlative in the false supernaturalism of the objective ; to dispossess reason of its divine contents is to deprive man, in his concrete

---

[1] *Apologia*, p. 198.

historical being, of the natural presence and knowledge of God, and to limit God's action and activity to means that are all the more mechanical that they are conceived and described as supernatural.

§ III. *The Dialectical Movement towards Certitude*

1. So far we have been concerned with Newman's doctrine of the reason—first in its intrinsic, and next in what may be termed its biographical significance ; now we must consider whether it has any dialectic or apologetic worth. He has as a matter of course challenged my interpretation of the *Grammar of Assent ;* and another critic of my criticism thinks it "wanting in insight," and "decidedly, though not intentionally, unjust," due to my not having thrown myself "into the spirit of the work," or "viewed it from within." Now, it was because the work was criticised from the most internal of all standpoints, the biographical, that the criticism was what it was. The work cannot be understood alone; it were simply unintelligible to the man who did not know the writer and his history. It is, in a far deeper sense than the book that bears the title, a later—as the "Development" was an earlier [1]—*Apologia pro Vita Sua ;* and is as remarkable for what it does not, as for what it does state and attempt. It holds the place in Newman's collective works that the *Logic* does in Mill's. In the *Logic,* Mill applies his metaphysical doctrine to the discovery and determination of truth ;

---

[1] *Ante,* p. 158.

in the *Grammar*, Newman uses his philosophical doctrine to explain and vindicate the processes that involve and justify religious belief. He explains, indeed, his object as not " to set forth the arguments which issue in the belief" of certain doctrines ; "but to investigate what it is to believe in them, what the mind does, what it contemplates, when it makes an act of faith." [1] But he confesses that to show what it is to believe, is, in a measure, to show "why we believe"; the one problem, indeed, is but the other in its most radical form. Now, the argument from first to last, and in all its stages, reposes on Cardinal Newman's distinctive doctrine of the incompetence of the reason; its inability to be more than a formal instrument is the keynote of the book. Reason is to him individual; "every one who reasons is his own centre, and no expedient for attaining a common measure of minds can reverse this truth." [2] In discussing "first principles," or " the propositions with which we start in reasoning on any given subject-matter," he says :—

"Sometimes our trust in our powers of reasoning and memory —that is, our implicit assent to their telling truly—is treated as a first principle ; but we cannot properly be said to have any trust in them as faculties. At most we trust in particular acts of memory and reasoning. We are sure there was a yesterday, and that we did this or that in it ; we are sure that three times six is eighteen, and that the diagonal of a square is longer than the side. So far as this we may be said to trust the mental act by which the object of our assent is verified ; but in doing so we imply no recognition of a general power or faculty, or of any

---

[1] *Grammar of Assent*, p. 99.   [2] *Ibid.*, p. 345.

capability or affection of our minds, over and above the particular act. We know, indeed, that we have a faculty by which we
remember, as we know we have a faculty by which we breathe;
but we gain this knowledge by abstraction or inference from its
particular acts, not by direct experience. Nor do we trust in
the faculty of memory or reasoning as such, even after that we
have inferred its existence; for its acts are often inaccurate, nor
do we invariably assent to them." [1]

Now, it were a curious point to determine how trust
of a "particular act" is possible without trust of the
faculty that performs it. If we know a given act to
be true, we must have a standard of truth; it is
through the truthfulness of the faculty that we know
the falsity or truth of its "particular acts." But the
significance of the passage does not lie in its inconsistencies, but in its positive doctrine. Reason is
but an instrument, a faculty of reasoning, trustworthy
in particular acts, not trustworthy throughout. Being
so restricted a faculty, we owe to it little, not even
the knowledge "that there are things existing external to ourselves." That is due to "an instinct"
which we have in common with "the brute creation,"
and "the gift of reason is not a condition of its
existence." [2] As with the belief in an external world,
so with the belief in God; reason has nothing to do
with either. "We begin to learn about God from
conscience." [3] "Now certainly the thought of God,
as theists entertain it, is not gained by an instinctive
association of His presence with any sensible pheno-

---

[1] *Grammar of Assent,* pp. 60, 61.
[2] *Ibid.,* pp. 61, 62.	[3] *Ibid.,* p. 63.

mena; but the office which the senses directly fulfil as regards creation, that devolves directly on certain of our mental phenomena as regards the Creator. Those phenomena are found in the sense of moral obligation." [1]

2. Here, then, on the one hand, we have the impotent and instrumental reason, which can never get to God, and is to be trusted only in "particular acts"; and, on the other hand, the capable and authoritative conscience, in which God directly is, and which is to be implicitly obeyed. And this dualism penetrates and pervades the whole book: its argument may be said to be the logical articulation of the doubt which one faculty creates and another faculty corrects. This curious dualism is expressed in the distinctions between "notional and real apprehension," "notional and real assent," and between "inference and assent"; and it underlies the cardinal doctrine of the "illative sense." [2] That doctrine means that religion can never be handled on universal principles by a reason that may truly be termed universal; but must be left to the man so compacted of conscience and imagination as to have a sense for religion and for the determination of religious questions. If the idea of the reason

---

[1] *Grammar of Assent*, pp. 103, 104.

[2] It is impossible to summarize here, or illustrate in needed detail, the significant positions in the chapters on Assent, Certitude, Inference, and the Illative Sense: an opportunity of developing their metaphysical basis, and illustrating its bearing on the argument, may yet be furnished.

had been larger and worthier, or if the relation between the reason and the conscience had been more
organically conceived, so that the two had appeared
as a unity, the whole argumentative structure, and
the principles on which it is built, would have been
different.   As it is, religion never gets inside the
reason, nor the reason inside religion.   They are but
formally related, never really or vitally connected.
Dr. Newman may have a perfect right to limit the
province and define the idea of reason in his own·
way; but then, the exercise of the right has laid him
open to a criticism which apparently he has not understood, and which certainly he has said nothing to
invalidate.   If the reason plays no part in the genesis
of the idea of God, it can play no part in its proof.
But this position involves the converse; the idea of
God and the proofs of His being can never be real
possessions of the reason.   They remain without it,
grounds or premisses for its dialectical exercise; they
do not live within it, principles and laws of its very
life.   The philosophy that so construes the reason as
to involve these consequences, is sceptical; and this
is the philosophy of "The Grammar of Assent."

§ IV. *Reason and Authority in Religion*

1. But what significance has this extended criticism
of Cardinal Newman?   I have been warned not to
identify him with the Catholic church; for it cannot
be identified with "any individual genius however

great."[1] I never did nor ever meant so to identify
him. The Catholic church is greater than any theologian, but a theologian may' also be greater than
the Catholic church. The Fathers do not belong to
Rome, but to Christendom. Rome may have been in
them, but more than Rome was there ; elements larger
and richer than she was able to assimilate. The
earlier Greek Fathers had a nobler catholicity than
she has reached ; the men of the heroic age of the
Greek church had another and more generous an-
thropology, a freer and loftier ecclesiology than hers.
Augustine, too, was greater than Catholicism ; for
while its developments have done the amplest justice
to his ecclesiastical doctrine, they have failed to do

---

[1] Dr. Barry in the *Contemporary Review*, November, 1885,
p. 662. I have expressly wished to avoid making any reference
to this paper, which was notably free from innuendo and in-
tentional misstatements. But in some respects it was open to
the charge of inaccuracy. The writer quite misapprehended
Kant's position, and, as a consequence, the argument which
was based upon it. He also represented me (p. 657) as saying :
—"That religion must be emancipated from the churches,
since these have, on the whole, 'become simply the most
irreligious of institutions, mischievous in the very degree of
their power.'" Now here is the rather tame original of this
rash and atrocious deliverance :—"The churches are the
means, but Religion is the end ; and if they, instead of being
well content to be and to be held means, good in the degree of
their fitness and efficiency, regard and give themselves out as
ends, then they become simply the most irreligious of institutions, mischievous in the very degree of their power." (Cf.
ante, p. 1.)

equal justice to his theological. The official theology
of Rome has more semi-Pelagian than Augustinian
elements; the Augsburg Confession expresses in its
doctrine of sin more truly and nearly the mind of
Augustine, than the Tridentine Canons; and Calvin
is a better and more faithful exponent of him than
either Bellarmine or Petavius. The Schoolmen, too,
are in many ways ours : they are, in the widest sense,
catholic divines : the exclusive property of no church,
but the common possession of all. Nor would I
identify too closely any modern official or apologetic
divine with Catholicism. It has its own history of
variations, as vast and quite as conflicting as those of
Protestantism; and it would be no grateful task to
write it. The distinction between Rome and Cardinal
Newman has been explicit all through this criticism;
is necessary indeed to its force, and was emphasized
by the contrast between the causes of the Catholic
revival in England and on the Continent. But he
was selected as the leader and representative of that
revival in the special form it here assumed ; at once
its real author and true embodiment, the man without
whom it either would not have been, or could not have
been what it was. If it is to be understood and critically appraised, it must be through the man that made
it. The causes and influences that determined his
mind belong, as it were, to its very essence—help us
to see what meaning and worth it has for the spirit
and thought of our time. He has told us by act
and speech, in every variety of subtle argument and

eloquent phrase, that Catholicism is the only secure
and open haven for the doubt-driven and storm-tossed
soul ; that without it the faith and hope of the Christian centuries must be engulphed by the rising tides
of negation and godlessness. But when we examine
the reasons for his act and for his peculiar speech, or
the bases of his argument and apologies, we find that
they proceed from as deep a scepticism as the one he
invites us to escape. He has lost God out of the
reason and the realm of the reasonable, and thinks
He is to be got back only as a *Deus ex machinâ.* To
build a supernatural faith on a natural impotence,
seems to us a suicidal proceeding. We prefer to find
God where he has not found Him, and build faith on
the sanity of a human reason which is full of God
and akin to the divine.

2. But before passing from this subject it may be
as well to allude to a question which has been made
to play a great part in this and similar discussions,
viz., in what relation does authority stand on the one
hand to religion, and on the other to reason ? It was
soberly said, as if it were a true or a relevant thing
to say, that this criticism of Cardinal Newman was an
assault "upon authority itself, considered as the basis
of revealed religion." It is not at all obvious how
even the most mordant criticism of a theory which
made the natural incompetence, or aversion of the
intellect to the knowledge of God, the apology for a
stupendous miraculous mechanism for keeping this
knowledge alive—should be an assault upon either

authority or revealed religion. What is obvious is the exact opposite : that there is no plea for authority like that to be found in an intellect so sane and rational and conscious of its supernatural qualities and relations that it must seek God, feel after if haply it may find Him. But then the authority that corroborates and develops the native godliness of the mind, will be very different from the authority needed to maintain God in the face of the mind's native godlessness. Hence it seems to me mere inconsequence and irrelevance of thought to argue in this fashion : " There is no argument against an infallible Church that may not be directly turned against a visible Christ." " If a dogmatic Church is unreasonable, a dogmatic or inspired Christ is unnecessary." [1] In other words, the argument is in effect this : " If you admit the authority of Christ, you admit in principle the very thing you have been arguing against. Your position, therefore, is illogical, and from it there are only two logical issues : *either*, maintain your polemic against authority as embodied in Rome, and reduce it to consistency and completeness by denying the authority of Christ ; *or*, maintain the authority of Christ, and follow the principle to its legitimate and complete and most august expression in the Church of Rome. "

But this argument is vitiated by two initial assumptions—(*a*) that I have been arguing against authority

---

[1] *Contemporary Review*, Nov., 1885, p. 600.

in religion. On the contrary, what has been argued
against is the paralogism which proved man's need
of authority by an elaborate demonstration of his
inability to see or to use his sight. The blind man
cannot always choose his guides, and so may select
one even blinder than himself, with the result that
both will fall into the inevitable ditch. My argument
has been in behalf of vision, not against authority,
and a vision that can trust all the more completely
that it can see while it believes. But (β) the second
assumption is, that the two authorities—Christ's and
Rome's—are in nature and quality identical and
equivalent. While in both cases the one word is
used, it expresses two distinct and even opposed
notions. There is no sense in which Rome is an
authority that Christ is one; and no sense in which
Christ is an authority that Rome is one. He is an
authority in the sense that conscience is; it is an
authority in the sense that the law and the legislature are authorities. His authority is personal, moral,
living; its is organized, definitive, determinative, administrative. The authority which springs from a
person, and is exercised through conscience, is the
basis of freedom; but the authority of a judicial
tribunal or determinative conclave is its limitation or
even abrogation. The one presents matter for interpretation and belief; but the other decides what is
to be believed, and in what sense. The attribute or
essential characteristic of Christ's authority as exercised and accepted, is Sovereignty; but the attribute

and note of the papal authority is Infallibility. Christ
is not infallible in the papal sense, and the papal
authority is not sovereign in the sense predicated of
Christ. Christ defines no dogma, formulates no *ex
cathedrâ* judgment concerning the mode in which His
own person and the relation of the two natures must
be conceived, or concerning the rank and conception
of His mother, or indeed on any of those things on
which Rome has most authoritatively spoken ; while
the methods of Rome in enforcing her decrees are
those of a legal or judicial or institutional sovereignty.
So absolute is the difference and so emphatic the
contrast between the two authorities, that we may
say, to allow the sovereignty of Christ is to disallow the infallibility of Rome ; and to accept the
latter is to exchange a moral supremacy, which permits no secular expediencies or diplomacies, for one
legal and economical, which must be now rigid and
now elastic, as the public interests or the expediencies of the hour may demand. If, then, there is
to be argument from the principle of authority, it
must conduct to an entirely different conclusion from
the one offered by these crude alternatives. If we
accept authority as embodied in Rome, we cannot
admit it as personalized in Christ ; if we admit it as
personalized in Christ, we cannot accept it as embodied in Rome. That we admit His, is no argument
why we should admit another ; but rather why no
other should be admitted, especially as that other is
entirely distinct in nature, opposite in kind, and

incompatible in action. To seek to supplement Christ's authority by the Church's, is to pass from the freedom of a moral sovereignty to the bondage of a judicial infallibility. And so the most conclusive argument against an infallible church is a sovereign Christ.

There is thus a twofold difference between what we may term spiritual or religious and ecclesiastical or political authority in the matter of faith : (a) subjective, expressed in the agreement or correspondence of authority and thought, rather than in the suppression or contradiction of thought by authority : and (β) objective, the difference between Christ and the church, making them as authorities altogether different. They can be compared only to be contrasted, and are related as the incompatible and the mutually exclusive. And this relation is due not to the antagonism of rival or opposed authorities akin in order or nature, but to the radical difference or essential incompatibility in character and kind of the authorities themselves. Authority as organized, legal, definitive, judicially and officially infallible, embodied in an episcopate or conclave or church, is one thing ; and the authority, personal, moral, religious, which Jesus claimed, is another thing altogether. And the very arguments which proved the former a violation of God's own order, prove the latter its highest expression or manifestation. I cannot allow, indeed, that authority in the Roman sense of the term is " the basis of revealed religion " :

but I hold, on the contrary, that the basis of all religion is Revelation. Without the presence and action of God in nature, through reason and on man, I could not conceive religion as existing at all. That it exists anywhere is to me evidence that God has been active there, seeking man, as man has been seeking Him. Whatever truth is at any place or any moment found, comes from God, and reveals the God from whom it comes. But all His truth comes through persons, and the degree and quality of truth that so comes is the measure of the persons' authority. Belief is not grounded on authority, but authority is realized through belief. Christ's words become authoritative through faith ; faith does not come because His words are authoritative. His sovereignty is felt to be legitimate and absolute, because His absolute truth is recognized ; and to this recognition, authority, in the Roman sense, not only does not contribute, but is through and through opposed. To believe in Christ because of the church's decrees and determinations, is to believe in the church, not in Christ, and to accept its infallibility instead of His sovereignty. The authority based on truth as believed and loved, is in harmony with reason ; the political authority that claims to be the basis and infallible judge of truth, is contrary to it.

And the distinction just drawn holds as much of the Bible and the church, as of Christ and the church. The Bible never was to Protestants an authority in the same or even in a kindred sense with that in which Rome was an authority to Romanists. The difference comes out in its most manifest form in the so-called principle or doctrine of private judgment; which means that the Bible was, by its very nature, not a body of formal *ex cathedrâ* determinations, but, as it were, the home and source of the material that was to be determined by the living Christian spirit, as illumined and guided by the indwelling Spirit of God—the *testimonium Spiritus Sancti externum* sealed by the *testimonium Spiritus Sancti internum*. To this position the exercise of personal thought was a necessity; truth could be authoritative only as it was believed, and belief was possible only as the mind was convinced and satisfied. This does not mean that men must follow an argumentative process before they can believe: but it does mean that it is always their right, and, in certain cases, it may be their manifest duty so to do. In saying this we say that religion is truth, and has as truth nothing to fear from the freest exercise of the reason, though much to fear from the partial or prejudiced or sluggish intellect; that the only authority possible to it, or the persons who bring and realize it, is the sovereignty that comes of its and their imperial and imperative truth. Such an attitude seems to me the only attitude that has living faith either in God or religion, either in Christ or His kingdom. If I read His mind aright, He would rather have His Church live face to face and contend hand to hand with the questioning and critical reason, than see it hedged

round by the most peremptory and invulnerable infallibility. It is too wide and too comprehensive to
be so hedged in: for now, as of old, God does not
leave Himself anywhere without a witness. His
lines have gone out through all the earth, and His
word to the end of the world.

December, 1885.

VI

CARDINAL MANNING AND THE CATHOLIC REVIVAL

§ I. *The Biography*

1. MR. PURCELL'S *Life of Cardinal Manning*[1] is a book which awakens the most opposite feelings, and the most contradictory judgments. Its author has been a sort of inverted Balaam : called in to bless the Cardinal, he has yet, in the view of his admirers and friends, cursed him altogether. Then, his literary offences are too many and too flagrant to allow the mere critic to speak well of his book. He is certainly no master in the craft of letters ; style he knows not ; order, chronology, easy and correct reference, continuity of narrative, consecutiveness of thought, economy in the use of material, coherence and vividness of portraiture, are things to which he has not attained. He is a laborious biographer, but an inaccurate writer, manifestly unacquainted with the religious history of our times, unable on this

---

[1] *Life of Cardinal Manning, Archbishop of Westminster.* By Edmund Sheridan Purcell, Member of the Roman Academy of Letters. London : Macmillan & Co., 1895.

account to interpret many of his own documents or
deal intelligently with the characters, careers, and
opinions of many of the persons who crowd his
pages. The book is thus difficult to read, a sore tax
on one's patience, a continual trial to one's temper,
mocking during perusal all attempts at a fair and
balanced judgment. But when one has finished the
book, and retreated from it far enough to see it in
perspective, and as a whole, some very remarkable
qualities begin to show themselves. It is, perhaps,
rather a frank than an honest book, written by a man
whose lack of insight is redeemed by a sort of blunt
courage, guided by a rather robust common-sense.
He is anxious to be just, yet does not quite foresee
the effects of his justice. His judgments are at once
candid and naïve, the judgments of a man who has
lived in a very narrow circle, has mistaken its whispers for the murmur of the world, and has published,
to the dismay of multitudes, the gossip it likes to
talk but does not love to print. In its light he has
studied his documents, and inquired at his living
sources; and then he has laboriously poured out the
results in this book, which, though a marvel of cumulative and skilled awkwardnesses, yet leaves us with
a distinct and breathing image of its hero, who is
certainly no pallid shadow, but an actual person, all
too concrete and articulate. This is no small merit,
and rare enough in modern biography to deserve
cordial praise.

But the value of the book does not lie in the text

of its author, but in the original documents it contains. The question as to the right or wrong of their publication is not one for me to discuss; what is obvious is that access to first-hand authorities is always a gain to historical knowledge. Cardinal Manning was neither a recluse nor a private citizen, but a man who lived for more than half a century in the full blaze of the public eye. From the first he was a conspicuous figure, the leader of an army; a man of strong loves and intense hates, who handled too many men, fought too many battles both in the dark and in the day—in a word, was too much a force working for change and conflict—to be commemorated in a biography which should be at once innocuous and veracious. If his life had caused no alarm or given no offence, it might have been edifying, but would not have been informing; for it would have told us nothing of the secrets of his character, or the springs of his conduct, or the reasons of his policy. But he was too much the sum of certain great moments and events to be dealt with as a delicate plant, or hidden within the murky atmosphere of circumspect commonplace. More harm is done by the diplomatic suppression of the truth than by its frank publication; the one is the way of wisdom, the other of discretion; and the promise is that wisdom, not discretion, shall be justified of her children.

Of course, I feel that the character of a lost leader is not a thing to be lightly dealt with. While he lives his reputation is his own; but after his death it becomes man's, every blot upon it being a stain, as it were, upon our common good. It can never be to the advantage of religion that any religious man should be dispraised. The heroes of Protestantism are no reproach to Catholicism ; the saints, the Catholic Church reveres, the Protestant Church grows better by admiring. There is nothing that so proves poverty of soul as the tendency, so common in ecclesiastical controversy, to make our own plain features look comely by darkening the fairer features of another face. Mr. Gladstone, addressing Manning in his Anglican days, says : " Your character is a part of the property of the Church and of the truth in the Church, and must be husbanded for the sake of the association with that truth."[1] This is even more true to-day than it was then, and in a larger sense than was at first intended. In his good name all churches share ; and any shadow of reproach that falls on him will send a chill through the heart of all our good. But then, to attempt an analysis of his character in relation to his work is to do him no dishonour ; what the man did, depended upon what he was ; and so we study him only that we may the better watch the evolution of a movement in which he was a potent factor.

2. What is here termed the Catholic Revival began with three men, whose spirit it may be said to have incarnated :—Hurrell Froude, who was its impulsive

force; John Henry Newman, who embodied its intellectual and ethical energy; and John Keble, who created the atmosphere of emotion or sentiment within which it lived and by which it was nourished. But while these men presided over its birth, its later fortunes were shaped within the Anglican Church mainly by Dr. Pusey, and within the Roman Church mainly by Cardinal Manning. The significance of the personal factor has been recognized by every serious student of the movement, and most of all by its leaders themselves. The earliest expression of this feeling is Hurrell Froude's *Remains*; the most classical is Newman's *Apologia*; the largest is the recently finished *Life of Pusey*; and the latest, this *Life of Cardinal Manning*, which is, in its original documents, so largely the work of his own hands. Of these, the *Apologia* has the greatest personal value, but the least historical worth. It is neither a biography nor an autobiography, but simply what it professes to be, a dialectical apology for a life by the man who had lived it. The real history is not there, but only a history idealized—all the more completely that the ideal represents a reality seen in retrospect, and under the transfiguring light of a superlative ratiocinative genius, whose imagination made his successive experiences like steps in the logical process which led him from a dubious to an assured and infallible faith. But a man's history is too complex a thing to be done into any dialectic, even though it be the supreme feat of the most dexterous

16

dialectician of his age. The mistakes, the falterings, the lapses, the blind gropings, the ignorances, the confusions, the unreasoning likes and dislikes which marked the actual way of the man are lost sight of, forgotten, or softened out of all significance; the end being made to illuminate the beginning rather than the beginning to explain the end. Froude's *Remains*, on the other hand, have even more historical than personal worth. Here we see the man as he actually lived, the circle he lived in, how they thought and spoke, believed and acted. The men are intensely sincere, but curiously superficial; where most thoroughly in earnest, there most audaciously ignorant, full of the inconsiderate speech which came of hatreds they were too impatient to justify and too prejudiced to be ashamed of. In the *Remains*, in the *Tracts*, and in the private correspondence, when we can get it unexpurgated, the real men live; and history must know the real man before it can construe the man idealized. Now this Life of Manning is full of the same sort of documents as Froude's *Remains*. We have not all we could wish, but we have enough to be grateful for. We have the man in his every-day habit, in the flesh-and-blood reality of his ecclesiastical being; and we can interpret him in terms we owe altogether to himself, or to the men he worked with, and for, and through. We are admitted into his secret soul, we hear his solemn confessions or astute suggestions to the men he trusted; and then we have the records of the public policy which now contradicted and now carried out his inner mind. What this biography does, no other and later biography can ever undo ; for what gives it character is not what the author writes, but what he publishes. The picture is not, indeed, quite complete ; some of Manning's most characteristic letters, written at the crisis of his career, perished under his own hand. By the same hand certain of his diaries and memoranda have, as a rule at the most critical places or in connection with the most decisive events, been expurgated, amended, adjusted to reminiscence, adapted to history ; but, happily, the untouched originals reflect the living man. And it is the man as he lived, and not the man apologetically idealized, which explains the history he contributed to make.

§ II. *The Character of the Man*

In attempting an estimate and analysis of Manning's character in relation to his work, we shall, as far as possible, confine ourselves to the documents our author has published. We cannot, indeed, entirely dismiss the author from our minds, nor would it be just to do so. His very attitude is significant, and has been assumed not according to his original bias, but against it. It is apparent that he began as an admirer, that he did not mean to be unfriendly, and that he believes, in the heart of him, that his hero could stand being painted as he really was, warts and all. If he is to be held responsible for the use of the materials entrusted to him, we ought also to remember that the responsibility for much in his tone of mind and for many of his judgments, lies with the materials themselves.

1. Well, then, looked at in the light of the documents here published and the inner history they unfold, we may say Manning's character seems, though strong, neither subtle nor complex. Subtlety was too little the note of his mind to be the distinction of his conduct. His ends were clearly and eagerly conceived : and his means, though often underhand, were, as a rule, obvious and simple, their efficiency lying in the strength of his will rather than in their delicate fitness. While fond of intrigue, he was too self-conscious to hide his designs from the observant. His characteristic qualities appear very early in his career. As a boy he was averse to real and serious study[1] and, happily, without the curse of precocity; but he had ambition, claiming as his motto *Aut Cæsar aut Nullus*,[2] only his ambitions were as yet neither intellectual nor academic. He found fame at Oxford in the Union, and once he became famous, men said, " Manning is self-conscious even in his nightcap." [3] He " drew into his orbit a certain number of satellites," assumed " omniscience," and " spoke as one having authority," now and then to the disaster of his claims.[4] His reminiscences seem to show that, even in later life, he had

---

[1] i. 27.   [2] i. 28, 48.   [3] i. 30.
[4] The words of Sir Francis Doyle, i. 46-7.

more interest in himself than in any of his school-fellows.[1] These were, in a boy, natural traits; they indicate a nature which by attempting to conceal only the more revealed itself; but the traits natural in a boy may grow into much less innocuous qualities in a man. Possibly Manning suffered through his whole career from the want of an early period of storm and stress, especially those higher and more tragic religious experiences which do so much to purify the character. Accident, rather than necessity, drove him into the church; compulsion of circumstances more than the vocation which will not hear a "Nay."[2] He knew nothing of the fierce intellectual conflicts which vexed the reason of Newman, and made his sermons, lectures, and tracts like the cries of a soul in travail. He did not enter the ministry by the way of sorrow, and so was not redeemed and made fit for it by suffering. Comfort surrounded him from the first; he glided easily into high position; even death was kindly, and removed obstacles from his path; but, while his tact is excellent, his intellect remains unawakened. He was a churchman whose conduct was guided by policy, rather than a thinker mastered by convictions. His biographer notes with satisfaction that he served under four bishops, and, while he agreed with none,

---

[1] i. 18.

[2] On this point there was a good deal of romancing later, but the contemporary evidence justifies the statement in the text. See i. 86–97.

he made himself agreeable to all, and as nearly as possible indispensable. He behaved as one who sympathized with the Tractarians, not as one who believed with them ; but in the day of trial it is the man who believes, not the man who sympathizes, that endures. Hence came those early relations to Newman which left no memories Newman cared to record. Hence came those extraordinary vacillations of policy, resented by many as duplicities of conduct, represented by his High Church professions and strongly Protestant charges; his Fifth of November sermon, and private, though rejected, visit to Newman at Littlemore; his studied neutrality as to the professorship of poetry, and his uneasy and, for awhile, anxiously uncertain action on Ward's degradation. To the same cause may be traced a series of incidents less easily explained or defended. There is his concern about the trivial personal matters of the sub-almonership and the preachership at Lincoln's Inn, in contrast with his unconcern about the loss of Newman and the grave disasters it threatened to the English church.[1] But his judgment as to the character and motives of the seceders was more extraordinary than even his unconcern. Mr. Gladstone asked Manning, amid the consternation caused by the many conversions to Catholicism, what he considered " the common bond of union, the common principle, which led men of intellect so different, of such opposite characters, acting under circumstances so various, to come to one and the same conclusion."[1] Manning's answer, which "surprised beyond measure and startled" his interlocutor, was this: "Their common bond is their want of truth." The one common characteristic of the men was surely their passionate sincerity, witnessed by the sacrifices they made to conviction and conscience; but Manning's answer shows not so much a want of honesty or charity as of insight and intelligence—his complete puzzlement of mind as he faced conduct which nothing in his own experience could as yet interpret. And the same bewildered and ineffective mind is reflected in all the correspondence of this period. Nor, as we shall yet see, did he ever escape from this inability. The timidity which is the mark of certain intellectual limitations governed even his most audacious policies. He was a political craftsman in the arena of faith and reason, and his trust in machinery was as great as his distrust of mind. This was the root of his lifelong antagonism not only to Newman, but to all Newman's name stood for Catholicism never meant to the two men the same thing; they never were Catholics in the same sense; their relations were not simply those of contraries, but of antipathies based on intellectual differences. Their feud was not a thing of policy, or even of principle, but of nature and character.

---

[1] i. 318.

2. These mental and ethical qualities are well illustrated in what we may term the diplomacy of his
conversion—*i.e.*, the policy which made his outer
history in the years which preceded it so strange a
contrast to his inner or spiritual history. It is, on
any construction we may please to put upon it,
melancholy as well as "startling" to find Manning,
as his biographer says, "speaking concurrently for
years with a double voice";[1] but it was by no means
out of keeping with his character, as some of those
who had good occasion to know him understood it.
The facts stand out in the clear language of his own
diaries and letters, and in those of his correspondents.
In August, 1846, he wrote to Mr. Gladstone: "I
have a fear, amounting to a belief, that the Church
of England must split asunder."[2] Entries in his
diary of the same date show what he means: the
Church of England is organically diseased, because
separated from the Church Universal and from the
chair of Peter, and is, for certain specified reasons,
functionally diseased as well.[3] In an earlier month—
May—he had confessed to himself "an extensively
changed feeling towards the Church of Rome," and
most serious doubts as to the Church of England.[4]
In 1847 his doubts became more positive, and so do
the beliefs which look to Rome; two things which
it alone can satisfy, seem to him necessary to the
church—infallibility and the unity of the episcopate.[5]

---

[1] i. 463.   [2] i. 317.   [3] i. 483.   [4] i. 485.   [5] i. 467-73.

In the pathetic letters, under the seal, from this time onward to his conversion in 1851, confession of his inward mind is made to Laprimaudaye and Robert Wilberforce. Now, no man can handle these letters otherwise than tenderly; to the man who has known a great intellectual and spiritual crisis they will be sacred epistles, the record of a soul's tragedy, still agitated with sorrow and damp with the sweat as of blood. But, unhappily, they are profaned and shamed by the position in which they are made to stand; yet they must stand there if history is to speak the truth. It was no reproach to Manning that he should hesitate; it would have been a real reproach had he been precipitate. The issues were too grave, the possibilities of mistake too many and serious, the feelings, the hopes, the fears involved too high and solemn, to allow a sensitive and honourable man to be other than painfully and laboriously deliberate. But this on one condition : that he be silent and use no public speech that contradicted his private thoughts or mocked his own personal experiences. And this condition Manning did not observe, nay, he flagrantly violated. While confessing under the seal of secrecy his utter disbeliefs, he yet in his charges and sermons, in his letters to penitents and friends, spoke or wrote like a man who never knew a doubt. While he openly, as it were in the ecclesiastical forum, argued in July, 1848, as to Hampden, that "no man is a heretic to us who is not a heretic to the Church"; that to the Church Hampden was no heretic, for it had not tried and judged him ; and that his " public subscription of the Catholic creeds," as a bishop, had purged him from the charge of heresy [1]— he had yet, in the March of the same year, privately written to Robert Wilberforce : " I do believe Hampden to be heretical in substance and in principle. It makes it worse to me to find that fact palliated or doubted." [2]   His public attitude was well represented by an answer he gave earlier to Mrs. Lockhart : " But, Mr. Archdeacon, are you quite sure of the validity of Anglican orders ? "   " Am I sure of the existence of God ? " he replied. [3]   Even more significant was his conduct to Mr. Gladstone.   The two had been intimate, even confidential friends ; he had, in the phrase quoted above, hinted his doubts, but had found no sympathetic response, had received instead an emphatic contradiction ; and was thereafter, throughout what seemed the frankest correspondence and intercourse, silent as to his secret mind till the Gorham Judgment made a convenient season for speech.   These letters of his were returned to him, and " had, so far as could be ascertained, been destroyed by the Cardinal not long before his death." Mr. Gladstone is reported to have said, when he heard of the correspondence, so unlike that with himself, with Robert Wilberforce, and the destruction of his own : " I won't say Manning was insincere, God forbid !   But he was not simple and straightforward " [4]

---

[1] i. 478-9.   [2] i. 514.   [3] i. 449.   [4] i. 569.

—a judgment which cannot be called in any sense uncharitable.

3. It would be a radical misapprehension to regard this diplomacy as an accident, an exception to his normal character, due simply to the bewilderment of a perturbed and distracted mind. The conduct represented a real and permanent quality, as it were a grain or bent of nature, which came out on critical occasions, and made intimacy with him to many difficult, to some impossible. Thus Canon Oakeley, who knew him both as Anglican and as Catholic, wrote of him when appointed Archbishop of Westminster: "I wish I could confide in him as much as I like him."[1] So, too, Newman writes to Oakeley: "The only serious cause of any distance which may exist between the Archbishop and myself is the difficulty I have in implicitly confiding in him."[2] And this feeling receives new meaning in the characteristic colour and phrasing of Newman's answer, declining Manning's request for an interview in order to mutual explanations, and, if possible, reconciliation :—

"I say frankly, then, and as a duty of friendship, that it [*i.e.*, my feeling to you] is a distressing mistrust, which now for four years past I have been unable in prudence to dismiss from my mind, and which is but my own share of a general feeling (though men are slow to express it, especially to your immediate friends) that you are difficult to understand. I wish I could get myself to believe that the fault was my own, and that your words, your bearing, and your implications ought (to have),

---

[1] ii. 256.   [2] ii. 327.

though they have not, served to prepare me for your acts.
. . .

"No explanations offered by you at present in such a meeting could go to the root of the difficulty, as I have suggested it.
. . . It is only as time goes on that new deeds can reverse
the old. There is no short cut to a restoration of confidence,
when confidence has been seriously damaged." [1]

No one will say that these are lightly used or
malicious words; they evidently express a judgment
at once well weighed and reluctant. And it was a
judgment in which many shared. Soon after his
conversion, in the year 1853 or 1854, while he was
studying theology in Rome, the very man who later
became his serviceable friend at the Vatican inquired,
with evident reference to him, "half in jest, half in
earnest," "whether a man who was already manœuvring for a mitre would make any the worse a bishop
for that?" [2]   After he had returned to England and
begun work as a Catholic priest, the then President
of Ushaw is reported as saying of him: "I hate that
man, he is such a forward piece," [3] meaning that he
was already seeking to thrust himself through and
past his brother pawns to an important and commanding place on the ecclesiastical chessboard.
During the Vatican Council it was said of him:
"There is no better hand than Manning's at draw-
ing the long bow." [4]   It was characteristic of him,
too, to seek relief at the hands of the Pope from
the oath of secrecy, that he might coach Mr. Odo

---

[1] ii. 305–6 : see also 329–30.   [2] ii. 17 *note.*

Russell in the version of the Council's affairs which he wished to reach the English Government and public.[1] The man is the same man under all these conditions, whether it be in ecclesiastical or personal matters : the management of Wiseman, the policy of the Holy See, the displacement of Errington, the control of the Chapter, or the deliberations of the bishops : the way of Providence is made smoother and more sure by the help of a little human diplomacy. Diplomacy is always double-voiced : and the ear addressed has to learn how to discern by accent which voice speaks the more truly, or rather the less falsely. And there are regions and affairs where it is in place, and there are others where it is not; and one would think that the least suitable of all regions was the church, and the least appropriate of all affairs the decrees and policies of the infallible Chair. Yet here we are made to see it prevail, with all its hateful accessories of intrigue and cajolery, flattery of hopes and play upon fears. And the curious thing is, that while the diplomacy and the agent were known, the result was accepted with a public silence and submission which speaks of the most wonderful discipline in the world.

§ III. *His Conversion: its Process and Reasons*

1. But, of course, this analysis of Manning's methods or executive policies does not carry us very

---

[1] ii. 433.

far ; the man had deeper and better things in him than can be thus reached and revealed. We must, if possible, get down to his ultimate convictions or fundamental beliefs, and discover both the attitude of his mind to them and the conditions of their validity to his mind. It is only in this region that we can find the motives that governed him, and the forms under which duty appeared to his conscience. That duty did appear to him in a most imperious form, is a point too obvious to need to be argued. Only beliefs and motives of irresistible potency could have forced him out of the church of England. Every inferior motive, all that could be compre-hended under the world and the flesh, was on the side of his staying. By going he had almost every-thing to lose, and there was no certain promise of any compensating gain. It could not be said that he was attracted to Rome by friendships ; for the men who had gone before him he had no peculiar affection, with them he had no special affinity, and their conversion had not been a very manifest suc-cess. We must believe, therefore, that he changed under intellectual and moral compulsion ; like Luther, he could do no other. But this only the more em-phasizes the problem : What, then, were his reasons, his motives ? We have no cause to doubt the truth of his own statement—it was the ideas of the unity and the infallibility of the church ; and the conviction that these could be found in the Roman, but not in the Anglican communion. But we have, in consequence, a twofold problem : How did he come by these ideas ? And what did they mean to him ?

He said that the idea of unity began to take possession of him about 1835, infallibility about 1837–38 :[1] but, at first, he conceived both under forms which upheld against Rome. The idea of unity seemed to follow from the Apostolic Ministry and its necessity to the Church ; where the one was, the other could not but be. And because the Anglican Ministry was apostolic, the Church was the same, and so its unity was assured. The idea of infallibility followed from the perpetual presence and office of the Holy Spirit in the Church ; where He abode in the plenitude of His illuminative power error could not be, the truth must be absolute. These two ideas seemed, then, to him ultimate ; but they involved as their necessary consequence the independence and autonomy of the Church. If its unity lived in an apostolical episcopate, and was realized through it, then the episcopate must be a self-perpetuating body, deriving its being from its Apostolic Source, and holding its authority directly under its Spiritual ·Head. If the infallibility was real, then the Church must be free ; for if it could not use its own voice, but must either be silent at the bidding of the State, or speak in terms the State prescribed, it would have but a dumb infallibility, which were of all things the most fatuous and impotent. But a series of incidents

---

[1] i. 470.

forced upon Manning the unwelcome conclusion that
there was within the English church no room for
the realization or exercise of his two fundamental
ideas. If there was any man both the High and
the Low Church regarded as heretical, it was Hampden ; but while both had the most ample will to
convict him of heresy both were powerless to do it ;
the strong hand of the State shut their mouths, and
placed him where it willed. If there was anything
more capable than another of disproving at one and
the same time the apostolicity of the ministry, which
was the condition of unity, and the infallibility of the
church as the home of the Holy Ghost, it was the
act of the State in putting a man so unanimously
adjudged heretical into the episcopate. The confusion and controversies of the time did not allow
Manning for a moment to feel free from this ubi-
quitous and inexorable civil power, whose violent
hands reached everywhere, and touched at every
point his most sacred convictions. If he thought of
the episcopate as the *sine quâ non* of unity, the State
mocked his faith by co-operating with a schismatical
body in founding a Jerusalem bishopric, and frocking
its new bishop. If he argued that the church had
the power to interpret its own creed and enforce its
own discipline, the State was at hand with the
Gorham Judgment to prove his whole elaborate
argument a series of logical illusions. By slow degrees he found himself deprived of every alternative,
and reluctantly forced to the conclusion that if these

two ideas, as he had conceived and defined them, were notes of the true Church, he must seek it elsewhere than in the church of England.

2. Such seems to have been the process, stated in its most naked and simple form, by which Manning's conversion was effected ; but of course it was a much more complex process than this. It did not move in a straight line, but was zigzag and circuitous, deflected by fresh currents of thought and emotion, by new views of policy, and by the changes incident to an agitated and distressful day. Vacillations are not duplicities ; variations of mood are not changes of part. There is, in the English mind, no deeper, or more common and characteristic conviction than the belief in the sanity of the State ; the belief in the sanctity of the Church is not so distinctive and inveterate. The Churchman acquires the one, but the Englishman is born with the other. It is the instinctive basis of his jealous guardianship of the supremacy of the Crown which, in its essential idea, represents the place and function of the laity in the church. It means that, in the view of the English people, it is they, and neither the priesthood nor the episcopate, singly or combined, who constitute the English church, and are the guarantees of both its unity and continuity. And we can well believe that this idea, though in a blind way, now and then seized Manning, and explains some of his most strenuous Protestant utterances, which were visions of a larger and more historical Church than the ecclesiastical

17

mind of his day had conceived. But these were contradicted by experiences of another order. Civil action in the religious sphere seems, to the ecclesiastical mind, harsh and insolent; and, in troublous times, sensitive are imperious consciences. And Manning's conscience was here sensitive, for his deepest convictions were on the side of freedom for the church, and they were quickened in suffering. Then, again, his Continental wanderings, and long residence at Rome, counted for much. He was, when in a most susceptible mood, isolated from England with all the coercive force of its traditions, social customs, and ambitions; and set in the very heart of new and potent influences, which made him feel what it was to live and worship in a Church-state as distinguished from a State-church. The end of it all was that change became inevitable; he waited but a fit occasion, and this the Gorham Judgment supplied; under the shadow it so conveniently cast, he passed from the Anglican to the Roman church.

If this analysis of the logical process of his conversion be even approximately correct, it places us in a position to appraise its significance. Within its limits the process was one of marked logical cogency; but the limits were marvellously narrow. The thing it most nearly resembles is a procession of the blind between two blank walls. The man argued his way to his conclusion with the very slenderest intellectual outfit, if, indeed, considering the problems at issue, he could be said to have had any such outfit at all. There was a wealth of reasoning, but a paucity of reasons ; and it is reasons that justify, and make a great thing mean or a mean thing great. There is no evidence that he had even conceived what infallibility meant ; how it had ever come to be the attribute of one church ; what the claim to it involved ; or how the claim harmonized with its history. In his charges and sermons, and in the letters and memoranda here published, there are the usual current commonplaces, now of the Protestant, now of the Anglican, and now of the Roman order ; but there are no signs of an awakened intelligence, of a man thinking in grim earnest, challenging commonplaces, getting behind them, resolving them into their component parts, compelling them to give up the reason of their existence, to tell why they claim to be believed. For this man scholars have lived and inquired in vain ; for him problems which touch the very heart of the formulæ he plays with, have no being. He does not know of their existence, he cannot understand the men who do know that they are and what they mean. As a consequence, his whole conception of religion is formal ; emptiness and shallowness mark it from first to last. There never was a biography of a great Father of the church—so full of letters written in supreme crises of his own and his church's history—that is yet so void of mystery, so vacant of awe, so without the traces of struggle after the everlasting rock on which truth stands, so without the infinite yearning to-

wards the light, which is as the face of God. And
this is due to no defect in the biographer, but to
the character of the original documents he publishes.
These things are not written in the mere love of
being severe, but in wonder and regret, and out of
deep conviction. The logic of Manning's conversion
was the logic of an unawakened intellect; and as
it was, so also was his policy as a father and prince
of the church.

§ IV. *His Policy within the Roman Church*

1. But now we must proceed to an even more
delicate and difficult question—his policy and career
within the Roman church. And here we may be
allowed to remark that in those days a conversion
was a critical event both for the convert and the
society he entered; and the more eminent the
convert the more critical the event, for it was the
fuller of dangerous possibilities. The Anglicans who
reasoned themselves into Catholicism knew nothing
of it as an actual and operative system. It was to
many, in a sense, a mere algebraic symbol; they had
assigned to it a definite value, and reasoned convinc-
ingly from it as a fixed quantity or stable standard.
And the danger was that the convert might find the
actual Catholicism a contradiction of his ideal, and, in
the despair of disillusionment, take some rash and
irreparable step. It is a matter of history that some
entered only to return; it is an open secret that many
remained, among whom we may number the greatest

convert of them all, in discomfort, disappointment, and despondency, even while cherishing the faith they had embraced. But the dangers to Catholicism were as real as those to the converts. They were, as a whole, personalities of no ordinary kind, men to be reckoned with. They were all men who had lived in controversy, and been convinced by it. Some were men of strong characters; a few were men of fine intellects and ripe scholarship ; one was a man of real talent, of strong will, and exceptional angularity ; another was a man of rare genius. They had been nursed in a proud and aristocratic church, had been trained in an exclusive and conservative university ; they were accustomed to a society which did homage to their culture, and they bore themselves as men who took life seriously and knew that they were seriously taken. And it was by no means certain that the men who had defied the authorities of their mother church would submit to those of their adopted communion. For within it there was much to offend and even shock. The culture was not so fine, the tone was the tone of a sect, with the feeling at its heart that in the eye of English law it was mere Dissent, and that it had lived its life apart, separated by the penal legislation of centuries from the main stream of the nation. To find themselves within a society of this kind was no small trial to the Oxford Tractarians ; to find it a society as much divided by jealousies and feuds as the one they had left, was a sorer trial still. It was a question whether the new men would transform the

old society, or the society subdue the men. What is
certain to-day is that the possibilities of good which
entered with the men were, if at all, in a very doubtful degree realized ; while the possibilities of evil,
thanks to the men mainly concerned, were in no
small degree averted.

2. If now we continue from this point our study
of Manning, we must note two things—the mind he
brought into Catholicism and the mind he found
there. His mind we have seen in part : it was formal
rather than creative, more rhetorical than speculative,
more political than philosophical, convinced that the
cardinal notes and necessities of the church were a
political unity and an official infallibility. He was,
indeed, one of the least intellectual of men ; and so his
rational interests were always subordinate to his
social or political, using these terms in their proper
rather than their conventional sense. He could
understand enthusiasm for institutions, but not for
ideas. He could never have written *The Idea of a
University*, or *The Present Position of Catholics in
England*, or the *Apologia pro Vitâ Suâ*, or *The
Grammar of Assent*. He could not understand the
man who wrote these books ; or why they should have
such an extraordinary influence ; or why multitudes
of men who had no belief in Catholicism should so
admire their author. It all seemed to him evidence
of an "anti-Roman" spirit in Newman,[1] of a proud

intellect, unfaithful to the Holy See, exercising itself in dialectical gymnastics to the delectation of English Rationalism! His eyes looked for help in an entirely opposite quarter. The church he had entered was the Roman, and Rome meant the Pope; and his supremacy was the infallibility which he was in search of, and without which he conceived the church could not be. In practical working a complaisant Pope was to prove a very convenient tool, and the actual infallibility a very different thing from the ideal.

The mind within English Catholicism was very unlike what he had anticipated. It was by no means a united or harmonious mind, or distinguished by anything really catholic or large. He found a laity "without Catholic instincts," worldly, selfish, and self-indulgent, all they cared about being "the key to Grosvenor Square"; yet this is not surprising, considering Monsignor Talbot's definition of their proper function. "What is the province of the laity? To hunt, to shoot, to entertain? These matters they understand, but to meddle with ecclesiastical matters they have no right at all."[1] And the clergy were even as the laity; "malcontent bishops, insubordinate chapters," everywhere "disloyalty to the Holy See," and "the taint of Gallicanism." The "Old Catholics" were not inspired by "zeal for religion, for the greater glory of God, and the salvation of souls," but by

---

[1] ii. 318.

"jealousy and prejudice against the converts." The candidates for Holy Orders were "a shifting and discordant body, living under no rule." He and his principal Roman correspondent agree in the belief that "until the old generation of bishops and priests is removed no great progress of religion can be expected in England." It was no wonder that, as his biographer says, "Manning took a pessimist view of the state of Catholicism in England," and "was at that time a pessimist of the deepest dye."[1] It would have been almost a miracle if he had been anything else; but much of his discontent was no doubt disillusionment. He may have expected to find a Catholicism which corresponded to his ideal of an infallible church; and he had found instead one which corresponded to the ideas of a provincial sect, which had suffered much from penal laws, but more from the narrow and insulated life it had been compelled to live. It was now that Manning's character showed itself as it had never shown itself before. It was not in him to submit and obey as Newman had done, to go where he was sent, lecture where he was told, teach or preach under humble or under public conditions as he was required, and redeem himself from the neglect of the community he had sacrificed so much to enter by commanding the respect of those that were without. Manning, on the contrary, knew his strength, and resolved to rule, that

[1] ii. 88-9.

he might reorganize what he called the " Church in England." Catholicism was not to him, as to Newman, an ideal system, full of mystic meanings, to be loved for the truth's sake, to be accepted as it was for the peace it gave to the intellect, and as God's own contrivance for keeping His truth alive in the world. It was to him, rather, a practical system, a machine to be worked, an agency to be made efficient and effective, an army to be ordered and officered, drilled and disciplined, for the conquest of England. With splendid courage, he turned himself to this work ; and with no less splendid audacity and the political skill which results from a fine blending of direct strength and adroit diplomacy, he proceeded to do it. And, great as his success undoubtedly was, it would have been infinitely greater if Catholicism, and if Christianity, had not both been more and different from what he conceived them to be.

§ V. *Manning as Roman Churchman under
Pius IX*

Manning's Catholic career may be said to fall into two periods, marked by two distinct tendencies, if not governed by two very different ideals : the period under the pontificate of Pius IX., from 1851 to 1878, and the period under the pontificate of Leo XIII., from 1878 to 1892. All that our space permits is to indicate the respects in which these tendencies differed and their significance.

1. Manning's policy, or method of dealing with the

emergency which we have just described, admirably
expressed his mind, and was adapted to the situation
as he saw it.   In English Catholicism and the minds
that ruled it he had no faith.   He said, its spirit is
"anti-Roman and anti-Papal," and so divided that
"our work is hindered by domestic strife." [1]   His cure
was to increase the authority of the Holy See, to
deepen the respect for it, to make the Pope, not in
name only, but in deed and in truth, sovereign in
English Catholicism.   What this meant he well knew;
it meant the success of the man who could best
please the Vatican, or who had most influence with
the men who shaped its policy.   I do not say that
Manning put it to himself in this bald form; on the
contrary, it was with him a matter of both conscience
and faith.   He did believe not so much in an infallible
Church as in an infallible Papacy; and he thought
that this signified a Pope who did not simply reign,
but governed.   Also as a practical statesman he
could not but see that the one chance of making
English Catholicism cease to be local and provincial,
was by penetrating and commanding it by the mind
which dwelt at the heart of Catholic Christendom.
But the reality as he found it and as he used it was
an ironical counterfeit of the ideal; and the marvellous thing in the correspondence now before us, is that
the ideal is nowhere, the ironical counterfeit everywhere; and it walks abroad naked and unashamed.

-----

[1] ii. 81.

We see Propaganda sitting in council, its decisions anticipated, prejudiced, prejudged by its individual members being got at, primed, and prepossessed. We see the old Pope, potent yet feeble, shrewd and humorous, obstinate and self-willed, yet easily susceptible to influence by those about his person and in the secret of his character and foibles. We see the chamberlain, Monsignor Talbot, a willing and astute go-between, avid of gossip, violent in his judgments and dislikes, jealous for the papal autocracy, yet feeling the need of manipulating the autocrat in a very common human way ; keeping his correspondent informed of all that passed at the Vatican—who came, who went, what was said, and whether doubted or believed, or how taken ; very anxious to hear what was going on in England that he might put things in their proper light and proportions before the pontifical patient. Then we see his English correspondent, Manning himself, playing many parts, always deft, pointed, impressive, full of schemes and suggestions ; telling who helped and who hindered ; how this bishop or that chapter was to be circumvented or induced to do things they did not mean to do. It is, under certain aspects, a deplorable correspondence : for it unfolds a tale of sordid backstairs intrigues, is full of hinted hates and unjustified suspicions, and the stratagems and policies devised and followed by those who would use the authorities at the centre as instruments for effecting their own will at the circumference. I do not wonder that the successor

of Manning has stigmatized the publication of the
book which contains this correspondence as a crime.
To one sitting in his seat and burdened with his
responsibilities it could seem nothing else. But it can
hardly be described as private correspondence ; on the
contrary, the letters have all the value and function of
public despatches. They were written by men who
were not simply friends, but officials in a great church.
They affected the policy of a famous court ; they
determined vexed ecclesiastical questions ; and decided
matters affecting the happiness, the status, the character of some eminent and many influential men. I do
not see how they could have been suppressed, if the
biography was to have any veracity or historical
value whatever. For here we see Manning at work
on the Catholic revival ; and are led to the sources of
events which puzzled many, though they might be
open secrets to the initiated. Mr. Purcell says :
" Monsignor Talbot played no mean part in the
management of Catholic affairs in England." It
was easy " to a man of such infinite tact and skill as
Manning to gain supreme influence over Mgr. Talbot.
If Mgr. Talbot had the ear of the Pope, the tongue
which spoke in whispers was not Talbot's."[1] Of
course not ; Talbot persuaded the Pope, Manning
persuaded Talbot ; and so the papal policy which
he carried out in England was, while nominally
the Pope's, yet really his own.

---

[1] ii. 87.

2. Into the forms, incidents, and developments of this policy I will not enter : for to analyze and describe it would be a piece of work too utterly distasteful to be done justly or well. Any one who wants to know how chapters were counter-worked or superseded, how a coadjutor and designated successor to Wiseman was, in spite of powerful connections and the sanctions of order and custom, unseated and set aside by the direct act of the Pope, or as he himself, according to Manning, described it, "Il colpo di stato di Dominiddio";[1] how bishops were sketched, discounted, outwitted; how the Catholic press was handled and judged when unfriendly, and how the more important organs were got possession of and made to speak as the potent cardinal willed—such a one has but to study the correspondence now published, and he will see the whole system in operation. But there is one event too significant to be thus passed over—the treatment of Newman and his Oxford scheme. Into the relations between the two men it is not necessary to enter. Their tempers were incompatible, their minds dissimilar, their characters different; in a word, they were so unlike as to be mutually unintelligible, with a sort of innate capability of inter-despising each other. This was intensified by the similarities of their histories, but the dissimilarities of their fortunes. If any one man was the cause

---

[1] ii. 95.

of the movement to Rome, it was Newman. His logic made it seem to many inevitable; and then with a proud but reluctant humility, which, whatever we may think of his reasons, we can only admire, he bowed his own lordly head, and submitted to enter the church of Rome by the lowliest door. And the places assigned him, and the duties laid upon him, were such as became his submission rather than his eminence. Manning followed six years later, and within fourteen years he was Archbishop of Westminster and head of the English Catholics; while Newman was to the chamberlain who had the ear of the Pope "the most dangerous man in England,"[1] a man who had never "acquired the Catholic instincts."[2]   Manning, too, thought him dangerous, the type of "a worldly Catholicism," which would "have the world on its side"; he considered the friends who grew enthusiastic over the *Apologia* as "literally playing the fool";[3] and said that "the Anglicans regarded it as a plea for remaining as they are."[4]

But these are not the significant things. Almost as good a case could be made out against Newman for his attitude to Manning, as against Manning for his attitude to Newman. Neither shows well, especially when they fall into amenities of the feline order.[5] What is significant is their alternative

---

[1] ii. 318.   [2] ii. 323, *note.*   [3] ii. 206.   [4] ii. 323.

[5] Newman ends his correspondence relative to the proposed interview thus : "I purpose to say seven Masses for

policies as to Oxford and the Universities. Newman proposed to found a Catholic Hall or Oratory at Oxford, secured land for this purpose, and got the provisional approval of his ecclesiastical superior. He may have been guided by his instincts. He must have yearned for Oxford as the thirsty traveller for the well-watered oasis. There he had lived a life he could never forget; influence had there been his, and honour; there he had found the friends who were bound to him by hoops of steel; his spirit had quickened theirs and they had quickened his spirit in return, making his blood run warmer and his pulse beat faster; in a sense, all his friendships then and always, were made either in or through Oxford. It was then, by a necessity of nature, interpreted by experience, that he turned to his old home, possessed of the feeling that where the passion of his life had been suffered, and its sacrifice accomplished, there, if only his church would send him, he could most victoriously do the work of conciliation and conversion. And among the wise and powerful in his church a cognate feeling prevailed. The Anglican converts had made obvious the need of

---

your intention amid the difficulties and anxieties of your ecclesiastical duties." But Manning, not to be outdone in ironical innuendo, retorts: "I shall have great pleasure in saying one Mass every month for your intention during the present year." So have we heard arrogant and self-conscious superiority, mistaking itself for piety, threaten to pray for the soul of a meek and saintly man.

English culture to the success of Catholicism in England. It was too alien, too foreign to flourish on our insular soil; it wanted the sentiment, the taste, the attitude to public and domestic questions; in a word, the consciousness which makes a man English, a person capable of understanding and being understood of the people. The wiser and larger Catholics felt, too, that the more public life and high careers in the State opened to their sons, the more was it necessary that they should be educated and disciplined in the schools and universities of the nation; and they no doubt also believed that, in their freer and fuller contact with the centres of living thought, Catholicism would give while it got, and influence all the more that it was being influenced. Indeed, considering the man they had, his name and his history, it seemed as if the very voice of God called them to go where he was ready to lead. But this was not the view of the man who was then shaping the public policy of Catholicism. The question rose in the last year of Wiseman's life, indeed only four or five months before his death, when the ruling mind was the mind that was to reign after him. Manning threw his whole weight into the opposition, used all his skill to defeat Newman. The common and characteristic method was pursued. Rome was fully informed of Newman's defects; his anti-Roman tendencies; the danger of sending him to Oxford; the danger of indulging those who wanted him to go; the certainty if he went, that he would attract the sons of rich Catholics after him, and they would be "protestantized," "de-catholicized," in a word, made more English and less Roman. Propaganda deliberated. Cardinal Reisach came and investigated; was taken to Oxford, shown over the ground by an opponent of the scheme; was taken to Birmingham, interviewed various persons, some young and quite inexperienced, but was not allowed to see Newman,[1] who complained that he, "who had certainly as great a claim as any one to have an opinion, had not been allowed to give one." And so the well-informed Cardinal was sent off, while a following letter vouched for his competency, saying that he had seen and understood all that was going on in England. The affair ended in the only way possible; but what is even more significant to us than the method of the victors, is their reasons. They are reasons of alarm, of fear of both light and freedom. They imply the most amazing distrust of Catholicism, of its ability to hold its own in the face of a university which it does not itself control. There is no sense of any special mission to the science and education, to the intellect and culture, of England. There is no feeling that it is possible so to teach their youth as to enable them to brave the fierce light which the living academic mind casts upon all creeds; or that it is better for

---

[1] ii. 314.

a man to know what his opponent believes than
to grow up in ignorance of it; or that the man
who has not understood another church has not
believed his own. The reasons are all of the
narrowest order, and where most emphasized, show
the essential uncatholicity of this Catholicism. It
must be Roman; cannot be allowed to become
English lest it cease to be papal. Yet a system
which has no place in it for the most distinctive
and preservative characteristics of a people and a
state, is the last system that can claim catholicity
as its special attribute.

3. The event that is by many considered the
crowning success of Manning's career is the part
he played in the Vatican Council. That is a larger
question than we can here discuss. But there are
a few things that may be said concerning it. His
advocacy of the Council and its decree was typical
of his whole attitude of mind. It epitomized, as
it were, his intellectual and spiritual defects. His
religion was more political than reasonable, more
legal than ethical, more a creation of positive law
than a thing of spirit and truth. It shows, as almost
nothing else did, the extraordinary limitations of
his thought. He never saw the decree of Infallibility
as it seemed to other minds, more capable and
more learned. He rather gloried that the ignorant
and foolish had prevailed over the wise and prudent.
Here, on the one side, was he, a comparatively
recent convert to Catholicism, no scholar in the

proper sense of the term, no theologian, not well acquainted with the history of the church or its thought, quite without the scientific spirit, or the ability to read with critical insight the events and forces which had created the church he adorned; and with him a host of bishops from the more backward regions of Catholicism, though, of course, not unrelieved with some of another sort. And, on the other side, were a multitude of great scholars, learned theologians, lifelong devout Catholics who knew, as he did not, the genius, the career, the achievements, the possibilities, and the claims of Rome. And yet their differences never appear for a moment to start within him a doubt of his position or policy; and he goes forward, manœuvring in his own gay fashion, as if the gravest and most tremendous of all possible questions could be settled in the same way as the affairs of his own diocese. And his alarmist pleas as to the need of arresting revolution by the decree of Infallibility are, alike in principle and in policy, exactly on the level of his arguments against going to Oxford. The thought or the religion that is afraid to go into the universities of a country will never convince its reason or command its conscience. The church that expects to stop the revolution by passing a decree which declares its head infallible, is like the child who stands on his castle of sand and defies the tide to rise above the rampart he has built.

§ VI. *Manning under Leo XIII., more English, less Roman*

1. But his life was not destined to end in the moment of victory. Nemesis had in store for him something more tragic, yet better. The second period of his catholic life came, and with it came another mind and policy. His correspondent at Rome passed away; the old Pope died, and another filled his place. With the changed men came changed relations in Italy and in England. A new spirit reigned at the Vatican, and the forces he had long commanded from Westminster began to break from his control. The change was signified by the honour which came to Newman, connected with which is a tale we would rather not attempt to tell. But the effect on Manning was remarkable; he became less Roman and more English. He threw himself with extraordinary energy and enthusiasm into public and social movements. He became more of a zealot in temperance, more of a social reformer, more of an English states-man, forward in every public question and work of beneficence. And he became jealous of the very power he had once so loved to invoke and use, saying that " I hardly know in Rome a man, high or low, who understands the con-dition of the church in the British Empire." [1] And as there, so here. He complained that he was

---

[1] ü. 743.

left alone, that "Catholics took no interest in Catholic affairs of a public character";[1] that the Catholic clergy were "mischievously wanting" in attempts "to share and promote the civil life of the people." And he said that they failed because they did not take the work of preaching seriously; because they had in their midst a reaction against the popular use of "the Holy Scriptures"; because they had no "perception or consciousness" of the reality in the spiritual life of England, or the meaning of the fact that "all the great works of charity in England have had their beginning out of the Church"; because they laid too much stress on "Sacramentalism," priests being in "danger of becoming Mass-priests, or Sacrament-mongers"; because the clergy are too official and have the vanity and weakness of officialism; and because they are too controversial and forget the truth that "destruction builds up nothing."[2] I have found his *Hindrances to the Spread of Catholicism in England*, from which the above points are taken, impressive and pathetic reading. They were written in the summer of 1890, and show how the old man was feeling as he neared the end. The mind is more childlike, more wistful, more alive to natural good, less strenuous for ecclesiastical pre-eminence, full of the great conviction that the church can conquer only through the love and service of her sons. I am happy to find these notes standing where they do. They show that to the old man had come a saner and

---

[1] ii. 714.   [2] ii. 773.

a nobler mind. He does not now rage at his own people as anti-Roman and anti-Papal; he speaks no more of infallibility, looks no more to Italy for light and salvation; but feels that Catholicism has much to learn of England, and must know and love her virtues better before it can hope to win her faith. We must not call the events that worked this change tragic; rather let us say they were the fruits of the Spirit of grace.

2. The writing of this essay has not been a pleasant task. Deep as is the difference which divides the writer from Manning and his church, it would have been infinitely more agreeable to write of him in another strain. But the study of the documents published in this book left him no option but to write as he has done, or not to write at all. He is grateful therefore to be able to strike at the end a note of cordial admiration. Manning was a vigorous administrator, a man of policies and methods, who was determined to have work done in his own way; but he was not always as careful as he ought to have been about the means he used. His early inclination to politics was a real expression of nature; for his aptitudes were for the service of the State rather than the Church, and he loved and served the Church as if it were a State. He had the ambition that place satisfied, and that could not be happy without place; power he loved more than fame, and if he sometimes gained it by ignoble arts, he yet used it for more noble ends. He was a man success improved; and when the temptations which appealed to his lower

instincts were removed, he showed in his age some of those finer qualities of nature and character which we miss in his strong and aggressive manhood.

With the passing of Manning the time has come for gathering up the lessons of what is called the Oxford Movement and the Catholic Revival which it is said to have effected. That cannot be attempted here and now; but one or two things are obvious enough. It has not done, at least as yet, for the Roman Catholic church all that was either feared or hoped. It has made the English people kindlier to Catholics, but not to Roman Catholicism. For this Catholicism has itself greatly to blame. It did not know the time of its visitation. It doubted where it ought to have believed, and believed where it ought to have doubted. It sacrificed the Church to the Papacy, and lost England through its belief in Rome and its use of Roman methods. This book is full of evidence that a Catholicism seated at Rome, or, indeed, with a head localized anywhere, can never again govern the world. To rule the Middle Ages was a relatively simple thing; Europe, Southern and Western, was but a little place, homogeneous, with all its parts easily reached, and all its forces so concentrated as to be easily controlled. But the Christian world to-day is another matter; vast, populous, diversified, full of many minds, and of minds touched with a freedom that ecclesiastical authority cannot bind. Government of such a world from a single centre has ceased to be any longer possible : all that survives of it is appearance and make-believe. For the centre

must be got to do as the circumference requires ; and
so the authorities in the provinces negotiate and
intrigue at the capital, that their will may be done
there, in order that what seems its will may be done
within their borders.   Then, the attitude of Catholicism to thought is a radical weakness.   The less
it can mingle with the world in the free marts of
knowledge, the less will the world mind what it says.
The authority that does not speak reasonable things,
reason will not hear.   And Catholic thought taken as
a whole is a peculiarly sectional thing, apologetical,
polemical, standing outside the large movements of
modern literature and science.   Within Catholicism
itself, then, there seems to us no promise of victory
over the mind, or control over the destinies, of our
people.   But it is possible that forces outside the
Catholic ranks may repeat by-and-by the story of fifty
years ago.   As the danger of the Low Church party
was its affinity with Dissent, the danger of the High
Church is its affinity with Rome : and affinity has a
trick of turning into identity.   But one thing is certain.
The English people are, and intend to remain, masters
of their own religion in their own churches ; and they,
and not the clergy, will be the arbiters of our destinies.   Manning found the English Catholic laity too
strong even for him, and in the other churches the
laity are—well, the English people ; and in religion,
as in other things, they are a people who have, when
the need arises, a masterful way of settling matters
according to their own mind.

VII

ANGLO-CATHOLICISM—THE OLD AND THE NEW

THE book[1] which has suggested this discussion may be described as a new series of "Tracts for the Times"; but the "Times" have changed, and with them the "Tracts." The noise of battle is not in the new as in the old; the writers have been born in the age of "sweet reasonableness"; they do not indignantly address an apostate church, or an impious State, but seek gently to succour a "distressed faith," loving the faith and pitying its distress. They believe that "the epoch in which we live is one of profound transformation, intellectual and social, abounding in new needs, new points of view, new questions, and certain therefore to involve great changes in the outlying departments of theology." The qualification is careful, but more easily made than applied; a change in the circumference of a circle changes the circle all the same. "Theology," it is confessed, "must take a new development"; but

---

[1] *Lux Mundi. A Series of Studies in the Religion of the Incarnation.* Edited by Charles Gore, M.A., Principal of Pusey House, Fellow of Trinity College, Oxford. London: John Murray.

" a new development," though it be of but a single
organ, affects the whole organism, all its parts in all
their relations, internal and external. "To such a
development these studies attempt to be a contribution." The writers are men of learning, piety,
and sincerity, "servants of the Catholic Creed and
Church"; but they are also believers in evolution and
in theology as a living science. The combination is
excellent. "The Creed and Church" are the organism, the men are its living energies, the forces and
conditions of the time are the environment; and if
the thoughts generated in the environment penetrate,
quicken and modify the energies of the organism, we
may contentedly leave the new life to reckon with the
old restrictions.

A book like this is suggestive of many things,
especially of the changes that have happened within
the last sixty years. In 1833 the first issue of the
" Tracts " began, breathing the courage, defiance, and
furious despair of a forlorn hope; in 1890, the men
who have replaced the old leaders are within the
citadel, victorious, proposing their own terms of peace.
The revolution has come full cycle round, which
means the counter-revolution is at hand. It were a
curious question, why, in what is fancied to be a
critical and sceptical age, so extraordinary a revolution has been achieved. Perhaps this very critical
scepticism has helped to achieve it. Sceptical are
always credulous ages; the more radical the disbelief
in things fundamental, the easier the belief in things

accidental; where faith in God is hardly possible, acceptance of an ancient historical church may be as agreeable as it is convenient. It belongs to the region of the phenomenal, it lives in the field of experience; and so men who think God too transcendental for belief, may conceive the church as real enough to be deferentially treated. · The thing is perfectly natural: what has died to the reason may live all the more tenderly in reminiscence. Make a thing beautiful to such persons, and it becomes attractive, which is an altogether different matter from its being true or credible. But one thing is clear, the real cause of success has been faith; for victories are won only by men of convinced minds. In this case they have been mocked, ridiculed, and have looked ridiculous; but they have been in earnest, and have prevailed. Over them our modern Samuel Butlers have made merry, collecting the materials for a new *Hudibras*, richer than the old in the grotesqueries of sartorial pietism, and the too consciously conscientious scrupulosities of the well-applauded martyr for a rite or a robe; only in this case the robe is not the livery of " the scarlet woman," or the deadly splendours of the " Babylonish garment," but the very garniture, the sacred and seemly vestments of the truth of God. The situation is full of exquisite irony; the delusion of the old hyper-Calvinist, who was sure only of two things, his own election and the reprobation of the immense multitude, becomes seemly and sane beside its modern parallel—the superb egotism

which enables many excellent but most commonplace
men to believe that their order, whose constituents
are often selected and formed in a most perfunctory
way, is necessary to the Church of God, and has command over the channels and the instruments of His
grace. If Englishmen had their old sense of humour,
the notion could not live for a single hour; and where
humour fails, so coarse a thing as ridicule has no
chance of success. For ridicule is the test of truth
only to men who fear laughter more than God. Men
like Samuel Butler see a very little way into the heart
of things—nay, do not see the things that lie on the
surface as they really are. The man who has a genius
for caricature has a bad eye for character ; he who is
always in search of the ridiculous never finds the
truth. So Anglo-Catholicism, if it is to be understood,
must be studied from within as well as from without ;
in relation indeed to the forces that created its opportunity and conditioned its progress, but also as it lives
in the minds and to the imaginations of the men who
have been its chiefs and spokesmen.

§ I.   *The Outer Factors of the Revival*

The Anglo-Catholic revival may be said to have
been in its origin the product or three main factors :
Liberalism, the inadequacy of the old church parties
to the new situation, and the spirit of Romanticism in
religion. The political conditions supplied the provocative or occasional cause ; the inability of the existing ecclesiastical parties to deal with the emergency

supplied the opportunity ; while the Romanticist tendency in literature supplied the new temper, method, standpoint, and order of ideas. Our remarks on these points must be of the briefest.

1. It is usual to make 1833, the year when the issue of the Tracts began, the beginning also of the ecclesiastical revival, though for a few years before then the waters had been gathering underground. Liberalism just then seemed victorious all along the line, and had effected changes that were as to the English State constitutional, but as to the English Church revolutional. The Deists of the eighteenth century had died, though only to return to life as Philosophical Radicals, learned in economics, in education, in theoretical politics, in methods to promote the greatest happiness of the greatest number, though the greatest number was largely middle class, and the happiness was more akin to social comfort than moral beatitude. The Roman Catholics, just emancipated, were still suffering from the social proscription which in England is the worst sort of religious disability ; and seemed a people with memories but without hopes, with illustrious names but without leaders, enfeebled by having lived so long as aliens amid their own flesh and blood. The Dissenters, strengthened by their recent enfranchisement, and as it were legitimated by the State, were demanding still ampler rights, freer education, and universities that knew no church, and were also mustering and marshalling the energies that were largely to determine the march of

reform. The Episcopal Church was the grand bulwark against Rome, and stood in very different relations to the two forms of dissent, the Catholic and the Protestant: to the one it stood as became a bulwark, absolutely opposed ; but to the other its relation was rather mixed. One church party was, for theological reasons, sympathetic ; but another was, for ecclesiastical reasons, at once tolerant and disdainful— feeling as to a superfluous auxiliary, which would exist and assist without either its existence or assistance being wanted.

The effect, then, of the political changes had been twofold. They had, on the one hand, broadened the basis of the English State, made the terms of citizenship distinctively civil, and incorporated or affiliated classes that had hitherto been dealt with as aliens. But, on the other hand, they had worked for the English church what can only be described as a revolution. For up till now it had been, and indeed still is, more easy to distinguish Church and State ideally than actually ; the English constitution may be said to have recognized their formal difference, but to have affirmed their material identity. Parliament is, in theory, the English people assembled for purposes of legislation ; the English church is, in idea, the same people associated for the purpose of worship. The supreme legislative authority for both Church and State is one and the same. Our great ecclesiastical laws are, as regards source and sanction, civil ; our civil authorities appoint the men who fill our great ecclesiastical offices. Civil penalties follow the violation of ecclesiastical laws, and our ultimate ecclesiastical tribunals are all civil. The Act of Uniformity was passed and enforced by the civil power, and under it dissent was a civil offence punished by civil and political penalties. The same power determined at once the books to be subscribed, the persons who were to subscribe them, and the terms of the subscription. The practice was intelligible and logical enough on the theory that Church and State were, though formally different, materially identical ; each was the same thing viewed under a different aspect, the civil legislature being at the same time in its own right also the ecclesiastical. So long as the theory even tolerably corresponded with fact, the system could be made to work ; but once Church and State ceased to be, and to be considered as being, co-extensive, the system became at once illogical, unreal, and impracticable. Now, the Acts which emancipated the Catholics and abolished the Tests, declared that for the State dissent, whether Catholic or Protestant, had ceased to exist ; that to a man as a citizen, it could no longer apply the categories of Conformist or Nonconformist ; in other words, it might be a State with a Church, but had ceased to be a State that was, or tried to be, a Church. Nor did this change stand alone ; it involved another more flagrant, if not so radical. Dissenters, Catholic and Protestant, had not only by the State been abolished for the State ; but they could sit in Parliament, and perform all the functions of legislators

without any irritating condition of occasional conformity, or pledge to respect what they did not believe.
And as Parliament was the supreme Legislature for
the Church as well as for the State, it happened that
men whose distinctive note was dissent from the
church, were, by a constitutional change which enlarged and benefited the State, invested with legislative authority over the church they dissented from;
and men the church could not truthfully recognize as
fully or adequately Christian, became, by civil action
and on civil grounds, lawgivers for the very church
that refused them recognition. The anomalies in the
situation were many; but to the State they were only
such as were inseparable from its progress out of a
mixed civil and ecclesiastical society into a society
purely and simply civil; though to the church they
were fundamental contradictions of its very idea as
national, and as such ought to have been felt intoler-
able. And the inexorable logic of the situation soon
became manifest. The Whigs were in the ascendant,
with ample opportunity to gratify their traditional
disbelief in church claims and their hereditary love
of church lands, especially as a means of creating a
patriotic aristocracy. The Royal Commission on
Ecclesiastical Revenues was appointed, the bishops
were advised to set their house in order, and almost
the half of the Irish Sees were suppressed. The outlook was not hopeful, and in the church camp there
was rage not unmingled with despair.

2. Within the English church the old varieties

of thought and policy prevailed, but all were charac-
terized by the same unfitness for the new circumstances. The High Church was at its driest; the old
chivalrous loyalties had become impossible; and,
unexalted by any new ideal, its character had deteri-
orated. It was like an ancient dame whose pride is
sustained by inveterate prejudices and the recollection
of conquests in a time too remote to be pleasantly
remembered. Its original theory had been built on
the royal prerogative : the divine right of the king
had defined and determined the right of his church
to be the church of his people; its authority within
the State was a form of his, and men could not secede
from the church without being disloyal to the king.
It was a perfectly intelligible theory, and as coherent
as it was intelligible, but then its primary premiss
was the king's divine right; once the premiss had
been disproved or made impossible by events, the
theory ceased to be either intelligible or coherent.
And disproof had come in the most cogent form: first,
and most disastrously in the revolution of 1688; next,
and permanently, in the Hanoverian succession.
But a life without reason is never a happy life : what
obstinacy keeps alive demoralizes the obstinacy by
which it lives ; and so throughout a good half of the
eighteenth century the High Church party hated the
reigning dynasty, plotted treason in its heart, and was
depraved by the treason it plotted. And when the
reconciliation came, it came not by the theory being
so modified as to suit a constitutional king, but by an

19

attempted adaptation of the king to the theory. Now, a party out of harmony with the fundamental tendencies and principles of a State, can never so live within the State as to be either an efficient or a beneficent factor in its development. The forces that make for change are forces it does not understand, and so cannot control. And so it happened that with the utmost will to resist, the High Church party was without either the strength or the faculty for resistance.

Of the Broad Church, only this need here be said : it was inchoate, perplexed, struggling out of its old formal latitudinarian policy into the new spirit, without, however, having found for its idea a form suitable to the century. The Evangelicals, on the other hand, seemed fuller of energy and promise, represented what might then have been termed the type of religion most characteristic of the English people. On the intellectual side it was timid, *borné*, formal, closed. Its hatred of rationalism turned into fear of reason ; it lived within its narrow tidy garden, cut its trees of knowledge into Dutch figures, arranged its flower-beds on geometrical lines, but was careful never to look over the hedge or allow any fresh seeds from the outer world to take root within its borders. Yet by a curious necessity the spirit of an age lives even in the strongest reaction against it ; and to the formal rationalism of the eighteenth century the Evangelical revival owed its violently conventional theology, the foolhardiness which could represent the relations of

God and man by a series of formulated and reasoned abstractions. But whatever may be said of its theology, the heart of its piety was sound ; it might be narrow, but it was deep and genuine. Men who did not know it, took offence at its manner of speech touching the more awful mysteries of being, and sneered at it as *other*-worldliness. But no piety was ever more healthily and actively humane. Face to face with a corruption that might appal even the society of to-day, it pleaded for purity of manners and created a social conscience and moral shame where for centuries they had been asleep. In an age which knew no duty of rich to poor, or of educated to ignorant—save the duty of standing as far off as possible and leaving them in their vice and filth, passions and poverty—it awakened an enthusiasm for their souls and a love for their outcast children, which yet was so blended with love of their bodies and their homes as to coin the now familiar proverb, so characteristic of the then Evangelical faith, "Cleanliness is next to godliness." In a time when humanity was unknown in the prison, and a merciless law became even criminal in its dealings with the guilty, Evangelical, and indeed specifically Dissenting piety (John Howard was an Independent, Mr. Fry was a Friend) began the more than Herculean work of reforming the prisons and Christianizing the law. In a period when the less civilized races were regarded only as chattels, or as a means of replenishing the coffers or gratifying the ambitions or even the

passions of the more civilized, the same piety—in spite
of the mockery of clerical wits, and the scorn of the
New Anglicans, who could not love the wretched
" niggers," because they "concentrated in themselves
all the whiggery, dissent, cant, and abomination that
had been ranged on their side," [1] in spite, too, of the
antagonism of statesmen and of all interested classes—
taught the English people to consider the conquered
Hindu, the enslaved negro, the savage African or
South Sea Islander, as a soul to be saved. And so it
created in England and America the enthusiasm that
emancipated the slave and helped to form the rudi-
ments of a conscience, if not a heart, in the callous
bosom of English politics, and even in the still harder
and emptier bosom of English commerce. Nay,
Evangelical piety must not be defamed in the home of
its birth ; it was the very reverse of *other*-worldly,
intensely practical, brotherly, benevolent, beneficent,
though somewhat prudential in the means it used to
gain its most magnanimous ends. He who speaks
in its dispraise, either does not know it or feels no
gratitude for good achieved. Happy will it be for
Anglo-Catholicism, which we may, in contradistinction
to the Evangelical, term the ritual and sacerdotal
revival, if, once it has run its inevitable course, men
can trace but half as much of human good to its
inspiration. Great are the things it has aehieved for
the idea of the church, for the restoration, which too
often means the desecration, of churches, for the

---

[1] Hurrell Froude, *Remains*, part i. vol. i. p. 382.

elaboration of worship and the adornment of the priest ; but the final measure of its efficiency will be what it accomplishes for the souls and lives of men.

But two things disqualified the Evangelicals for adequate dealing with the emergency—their intellectual timidity and their want of any sufficient idea of the church. These two were intimately related ; their theology was too narrowly individualistic, too much a reasoned method of saving single souls, to admit easily, or without fracture, those larger views of God, the universe and man, needed to guide a great society in a crisis, or, as it were, in the very article of revolution. They did not sufficiently feel that the Church was a sort of spiritual Fatherland, within which they had been born, through which they lived, for whose very dust they could love to die. The Evangelicals have often been described as the successors and representatives of the Puritans within the Anglican church, but here they were their very opposites. The Puritan theology was remarkable for its high and catholic doctrine of the Church, so conceiving the sovereignty of the Redeemer that the body in which he lived and over which He reigned could never be dependent on any State or subordinate to any civil power whatever. The high Anglican rather than the Evangelical has here been the Puritan's heir, though the Anglican has lowered the splendid idea he inherited by giving it a less noble and a less catholic expression. It was the want of such a vivifying and commanding idea that lost the

Evangelical the leadership of the Church in its hour of storm and crisis.

3. So far, then, it seemed as if the battle against vigorous and victorious Liberalism must be fought on the lines so abhorred of the old High Church, the lines of the latitudinarian utilities. Church and State were allies, their union was due to a contract or compact, by which the Church received so much pay and privilege, and the State so much service and sanction. To argue the question on this ground was to be defeated; there was no principle in it, only the meanest expediences, profits to be determined by the utilitarian calculus, with contract broken when profits ended. It was at this moment that Romanticism assumed an ecclesiastical form, and emerged, changed in name, but unchanged in essence, as Anglo-Catholicism.

Romanticism may be described as the literary spirit which, born partly in the frenzy of the Revolution, and partly in the recoil from it, executed in the early decades of this century summary vengeance upon the rationalism of the last. It was not English merely, but European; it had achieved great things on the Continent before it took shape here. In France it produced Chateaubriand, whose rhapsodical *Génie* was at once a *coup de théâtre et d'autel*; Joseph de Maistre and the hierocratic school, with their idealization of the Papacy. In Germany, it blossomed into the Stolbergs and the Schlegels, who preached the duty of a flight from the present to the past, and believed that they preserved faith by indulging imagination.

Through the philosophical theologians and critical historians in the Catholic faculties of schools like Tübingen and Munich, as represented by Moehler and Döllinger, it entered theology, furnishing Roman Catholicism with a new and potent apologetic, and the Anglican with a no less potent source of inspiration and guidance. Its characteristic was an imaginative handling of its material, especially mediævalism and its survivals, with a view to a richer and happier whole of life. Rationalism was an optimism which glorified its own enlightened age, and pitied the ignorance and superstition of the earlier men; but Romanticism was an idealism which wished to transcend the present it disliked, by returning, either with Wordsworth to a severe simplicity, all the more refined that it was so rustic and natural, or, as with Scott, to the gallant days of chivalry and the rule of the highly born and bred. All were subjective, each used a different medium for the expression of himself; but the characteristic thing was the self that was expressed, not the medium employed. The Lake poets sang in praise of Nature, but it was the Nature of the poet's dream, sleeping in the light that never was on sea or shore. Scott loved to picture the past, but his was the past of the poet's fancy ; not the hard, grim world, where men struggled with existence and for it, but an idealized arena, where noble birth meant noble being ; and only a villain or a hypocrite could lift a hand, even for freedom, against a head that was crowned. In this use of the imagination there was

more truth, but less reality, than there had been in the
cold and analytic methods of the previous century.
Rationalism, for want of the historical imagination,
sacrificed the past to theory. Romanticism, for want
of the critical faculty, sacrificed history to the past.
What one finds in the elegant yet careless pages of
Hume, is a record of events that once happened,
written by a man who has never conceived so as to
realize the events he describes; what one finds in the
vivid pages of Scott is a living picture of the past,
but of a past that had never lived. This is the very
essence of Romanticism, the imaginative interpretation of nature or history: but it is only the form
that is natural or historical, the substance or spirit is
altogether the interpreter's own.

§ II.   *The Makers of the Revival*

1. Now it was this Romanticist tendency that was
the positive factor of Anglo-Catholicism. While the
other two sets of circumstances supplied respectively
the occasion and the opportunity, this gave the creative impulse; it was the spirit that quickened. The
men in whom it took shape and found speech were
three—Keble, Newman, Pusey. Perhaps we ought
to name a fourth, Hurrell Froude; but he lives in
Newman. He was the swiftest, most daring spirit of
them all; his thought is hot, as it were, with the
fever that shortened his days; his words are suffused
as with a hectic flush, and we must judge him rather
as one who moved men to achieve than by his own

actual achievements. The three we have named were in a rare degree complementary of each other; they were respectively poet, thinker, and scholar, and each contributed to the movement according to his kind. Keble was a splendid instance of the truth that a man who makes the songs of a people does more than the man who makes their laws. His hymns are a perfect lyric expression of the Romanticist tendency; in them the mood of the moment speaks its devoutest feelings in fittest form. This was the secret of their power. They are without the passion of the mystic, the infinite hunger of the soul that would live for God, after the God it cannot live without, the desire to transcend all media, win the immediate divine vision, and lose self in its supreme bliss; rather are they the sweet and mellow fruit of "pious meditation fancy-fed," which loves means as means, feels joy in their use, in reading their meaning, in being subdued by their gentle discipline; and which loves God all the better for the seemliness and stateliness of the way we get to Him. Keble learned of Wordsworth to love nature, to read it as a veiled parable, or embodied allegory, spoken by God and heard by the soul; he learned of Scott to love the past, and seek in it his ideals. His love of God became love of his own church, of what she had been, what she was, and, above all, of what she ought to be; of her ancient monuments, her venerable institutions, her stately ceremonial, her saints and her saints' days. And by his sweet, meditative, poetic gift he made what he loved seem lovely. What ecclesiastical polemics, parochial activity, and sacerdotal ritual never could have accomplished, his hymns achieved; indeed, they not only made those others possible, but even necessary, creating for them that disposition, that readiness to receive, to learn, and to trust, which is, according to Newman, the greater part of faith. It is by sure instinct that the name of Keble has been seized as the name most typical of the Anglo-Catholic revival. He caught the prevailing sentiment, and translated it into a form at once poetic and religious; and by so doing he turned a rising tide or tendency into the service of his party and his church. But the secret of his strength may become the source of their weakness. The man of pious and meditative fancy may evoke the historical spirit, and make the present beautiful in the light of an idealized past; but when the appeal is to history, scientific criticism becomes the ultimate judge, and, though its judgments are slow, they are inexorable as those of God.

2. Newman was more rarely gifted than Keble, but his gifts, though of a rarer and higher order, were less pure in quality. He had in a far higher degree the poet's temper, and more of his insight, creative genius and passion. It was his misfortune to be an ecclesiastic in a stormy crisis, and indeed to be of the crisis the foremost and characteristic polemic. He had a subtle and analytic intellect; but dialectical rather than speculative, discursive and critical rather than synthetic and constructive. He had more of the

mystic's nature and intensity than Keble; the passion for God burned in his spirit like a fire, impelled him as by an awful necessity to the Infinite, yet divided him from it by a still more awful distance. He loved to seek everywhere for symbols of the divine, which would at once assure him of the Eternal Presence, and help him to gain more conscious access to it; yet he had the genuine mystic's feeling that all means were inadequate, and so divisive; as mediative they held the spirit out of the immediate Presence, and not only shaded but obscured its glory. Hence he had none of Keble's love of means as means; he had too much imagination to be satisfied with the sensuous seemliness, the Laudian "beauty of holiness," which pleased Keble's fine and fastidious, but feebler fancy; what he wanted was to stand face to face with God himself, and to find a way to Him as sure as his own need for Him was deep and real. But to find such a way, never an easy thing, was to one situated and constituted like Newman peculiarly hard. For as deep and ineradicable as his passion for God was his scepticism of reason, which is, in the last analysis, the subtlest of all scepticisms as to God.[1] And it is the least toler-

---

[1] This interpretation of Newman is admirably illustrated by Mr. Hutton, *Modern Guides of English Thought in Matters of Faith*, pp. 78 ff. The conclusion was not intended, but is only on that account the more significant. "It is, I think, profound pity for the restlessness and insatiability of human reason which has made him a Roman Catholic." But the "pity" is

able, because the most paralysing, to the man with
the spirit and temper of the mystic. To believe in
God, yet to doubt His real presence in the reason, is
to be impelled to imagine that what in man has most
of God is also remotest from Him, and most completely out of His control; and so the inexorable
logic of the situation forces the man, if he does not
surrender his doubt of the reason, either to surrender
all certainty and all reality in his knowledge of God,
or to end the conflict by calling in some violent
mechanical expedient, such indeed as Newman was
slowly but irresistibly driven to adopt. Whence this
sceptical tendency came in Newman's case is a
question we have already in part discussed; but
here we may say he owed it, partly, perhaps mainly,
to native intellectual qualities, partly, to his place in
the reaction against Rationalism, and, partly, to an
author he greatly loves to praise, who possibly represents the greatest mental influence he came under,
Butler. The reaction against Rationalism was in
Newman more a matter of imagination than of
reason; and he hated and disowned its results without transcending its philosophy. As a consequence,
he shared in the common inheritance of our modern
English thought, that doubt of the reason which has
become in the more consistent philosophies either a
reasoned doubt, or, what is the same thing adapted

---

only the superficial expression of the deeper scepticism, which
so doubts " God's Spirit as revealed in conscience and reason,"
as to require an infallible institution for their control.

to a positive and scientific age, a reasoned nescience. And to the difficulties or antinomies of his thought Butler more than any man awoke him. The underlying or material idea of the *Analogy*, what may be termed the theory of the correspendence of the physical and spiritual realms, especially when further qualified by the influence of Keble, gave indeed to Newman his grand constructive principle, the notion of the sacramental symbolism of Nature ; but its formal and regulative maxim, " Probability is the guide of life," was more creative of disturbance and perplexity. For to a man of his temper, mental integrity, and theistic passion, as sure of God's being as of his own, it must have seemed a sort of irony to make such a maxim the judicial and determinative principle in a religious argument. It may be said to have formulated his master problem—How is it possible to build on probable evidence the certitude of faith? or, How, by a method of probabilities, can the existence, if not of necessary, yet of infallible truth, be proved? Indeed, Butler's probability, which was not without similar tendencies in his own case, determined the search which landed Newman in Papal infallibility.

We have, then, to imagine Newman, with his mystic passion, his philosophical scepticism, and his apologetical maxim, called to face the disintegrative and aggressive forces of his time. He could face them in strength only by maintaining his intellectual integrity ; and from the antinomies of his thought there were

only two possible ways of escape, either by a higher
philosophy or a higher authority. And of these two
each was exclusive of the other. If the way by
philosophy had been chosen, then the process of reconciliation would have been immanent and natural;
the antitheses of the formal understanding would have
been overcome by the synthesis of the transcendental
reason. But to choose the way of authority was to
deny that any natural process of reconciliation was
possible, and to seek to silence the inward dissonances
by the sound of an outward voice; and, of course,
the deeper the dissonances grew, the more authoritative had the voice to be made. For many reasons—
constitutional, educational, circumstantial, social—the
philosophical way was not selected; and Newman began his wonderful polemical career a mystic in faith,
a sceptic in philosophy, a seeker after an authority
able to subdue the scepticism and vindicate the faith.
His power, studied in connection with his marvellous
literary faculty and intense religious sincerity, is explicable enough; but, regarded as a question in philosophical criticism, it is more complex and difficult of
analysis. No man has more thoroughly understood
the men of his age; no man of genius ever less comprehended the problems of his time, or contributed
less to their solution. It is remarkable, considering
his immense productivity, and the range and kind of
subjects he has handled, how few constructive principles, speculative and historical, can be found in his
works. The critical philosophy he does not seem to

have cared to understand. Modern criticism, as regards both principles and methods, he never tried to master, or even, objectively, to conceive. The scientific treatment of history is too alien to his spirit and aims to be comprehended by him. His one considerable historical work [1] is but an overgrown polemical pamphlet—a treatise on the controversies of his own times disguised as a history. His *Doctrine of Development* [2] is not original ; and its thesis, so far from being the equivalent of evolution, is its antithesis and contradiction. It may be logic applied to dogma, but is not science applied to history. His most considerable, at once philosophical and apologetical work, [3] may be described as a treatise on the necessity of the personal equation in religion : it ignores what is primary and universal in the reason, that it may build on what is specific and acquired in the individual. But it is no paradox to say, those very elements of his philosophical weakness have been sources of his literary and controversial strength. The very severity of the conflict in his own spirit has given him the profoundest sense of any thinker in our day of the perplexities of living man — the bewilderments of thought, motive, and conscience that come of limited and passionful being, bound by law yet in revolt against the law that binds it. Convictions the more strenuous that they were formulated in conflict and

[1] *The Arians of the Fourth Century* (1833).
[2] *An Essay on the Development of Christian Doctrine* (1845).
[3] *The Grammar of Assent* (1870).

have been held amid controversies, internal and external; a piety that is nothing less than a genius for religion; an intense imagination, using the instruments of subtle dialectic, and clothing argument in speech of wondrous grace and force, have enabled him to address with unequalled, often irresistible, power, men who could be reached most easily through the conscience or imagination. Such men he has awed, subdued, converted, though by a process that silenced or overpowered rather than convinced the reason. And the process he has pursued without, is but the counterpart of the process he had before pursued within. Truth has never been to him so much an object for quest or question as for acceptance. Intellectual difference has been a sort of moral offence, and he has reasoned as if the men who held the principles he hated must themselves be odious. Hence came what Blanco White called his "deceiving pride," and his resolute sacrifice of old friends to new views. Hence, too, the temper I will not call intolerant, but so severely and logically authoritative that, to quote Blanco White again, "he would, as sure as he lives, persecute to the death, if he had the direction of the civil power for a dozen years." These are the invariable characteristics of the man who bases a faith of authority on a scepticism of the reason. Newman, with all that he stands for, represents the struggle of English empiricism to remain empirical, and yet become imaginative and religious.

3. But the scholar of the band was as notable in

his own order as the poet and thinker were in theirs. Pusey, indeed, was less a scholar than a schoolman, these two being distinguishable thus: the scholar loves learning, and uses it as an instrument for the discovery of truth, while the schoolman is a learned man who uses his learning as a means of proving an assumed or formulated position. The scholar studies that he may cultivate mind, develop and exercise the humanities : but the schoolman searches that he may find authorities to verify his axioms and justify his definitions. The scholar aims at objectivity, seeing things as they really were, how and why they happened, whither tended, and what achieved ; but the schoolman is throughout governed by subjectivity, brings his system to history, and pursues his researches that history may be made to furnish evidence of the system he brings. Now Pusey had the making of a scholar in him, though he never became what he could have been. He had a susceptible, sympathetic, assimilative mind, combined with a certain largeness of nature that at once qualified him to understand man and distinguished him as a man men could trust. His famous *Inquiry into the Probable Causes of German Rationalism* admirably illustrates his mental qualities, especially the susceptible and assimilative. It is full of his German teachers,[1] their spirit, method, materials, though all has passed through

---

[1] For what the *Inquiry* owed to Tholuck, and his judgment on the use made of his material, see Witte's *Das Leben Tholuck's* vol. ii., pp. 242, 243.

a conservative English mind, wise and honest enough to defend a cause by being just to the cause it opposed. But in Oxford, Keble and Newman superseded Tholuck, and Pusey passed from the scientific to a local and insular standpoint, the scholar became the schoolman. What he was to the new movement Newman has testified; he brought to it the dignity of high academic office and social rank, weight of character, counsel, judicial faculty and speech, the service of vast erudition, and reverence for the sources his erudition explored. He had precisely the qualities most needed to consolidate and guide the party. Keble's fancy had idealized the church and its past, had made its worship poetical, had touched its services with fine and well-ordered emotion. Newman's genius had filled the church with new meaning and new ideals, his eloquence had pealed through it like the notes of a mighty organ waking long silent echoes, . and had kindled in men a new enthusiasm for their transfigured church. And now Pusey's erudition came to search the Fathers and the Anglican divines for evidence that the new was the old, and based on venerable and invariable tradition. Keble was loved, Newman admired, but Pusey trusted. Keble moved in an atmosphere of reverence and emotion; difference in his case did not breed dislike; the very men who most disagreed with his theology were most subdued by his hymns. Newman was even more feared than admired; the men who followed doubted, uncertain whither he might lead; the men who resisted disliked, certain that he tended with increasing momentum whither they did not mean to go. But Pusey had Newman's strength of conviction without his dangerous genius; he was conservative not because sceptical, but because convinced; he loved his church in the concrete, and he lived to prove that she embodied the "quod semper, quod ubique, quod ab omnibus creditum est." On any dubious or questioned point he was ready to bring determinative evidence from his recondite lore; on any critical occasion he was no less ready to use the pulpit of St. Mary's as a platform for the issue of a manifesto. And so the movement others created, Pusey controlled; and in his hands its character became fixed as a creation or Renaissance of Romanticism conditioned and tempered by scholasticism.

§ III. *The Anglo-Catholic Theory*

1. To these men, then, the progress of events in literature and philosophy on the one hand, and in Church and State on the other, combined to set the problem: How can the Church be rescued from the hands of a State penetrated and commanded by "Liberalism," and be elevated into an authority able to regulate faith and conscience, to control reason and society? What Newman named "Liberalism" was a single force disguised in many forms, rationalism in religion, revolution or reform in politics, Erastianism and latitudinarianism in church. It was the spirit of change, negation, disintegration, destruction.

The church must destroy it, or it would destroy the church, and with it faith in God, godliness, religion. To save the church, two things were necessary—to invest it with divine authority and all the rights flowing from it ; and to set it strong in its authority and rights over against the apostate State on the one hand, and the rebellious reason on the other. With sure instinct the New Anglicans began by assailing the Reformation. The Puritans had disapproved and opposed the royal authority, because it arrested and restrained the Reformation ; but the Anglican hated the Reformation, because it had been effected by the royal authority. In the old days, when the king reigned by the grace of God and through the zealous spirits of the Episcopal bench, the Anglican had loved the royal supremacy, and soundly punished the Puritan for denying it : but when, in the process of constitutional change, the royal supremacy became only the form or mask of parliamentary power and control, which in its turn was but the instrument of the hated " Liberalism," —then the Anglican became as convinced as the Puritan of the excellence of independency.[1]　The

---

[1] It is instructive to see how similar ideas under similar conditions demand for their expression similar terms. Thus the earliest treatise from the High Church point of view on this subject is Charles Leslie's ; the title runs : " The case of the Regale and of the Pontificate stated, in a Conference concerning the Independency of the Church upon any power on earth, in the exercise of her purely Spiritual power and authority." This exactly reproduces the very idea, in what is almost exactly

secular arm in touching had wronged the church; and while the men who did it, and those who suffered it to be done, were alike reproached, she was pictured as the gracious mother of peoples, with her heroic yet saintly sons, and clinging yet stately daughters about her, creating literature, civilization, art, and whatever made life rich and beautiful, and remaining benignant, though forlorn, in the midst of a greedy and graceless posterity, blind to her beauty, and forgetful of her beneficence. But Newman touched a higher strain; his genius scorned to ask aid from sentiment; he called upon the church to become militant and equip herself in the armour of her divine attributes. The State might suppress bishoprics, but bishops were independent of the State; they were before it, existed by a higher right, were of apostolical descent and authority, stood in a divine order which the State had not made and could not unmake. And as with the bishops, so with the clergy; their orders were sacred, inalienable, instituted of God, and upheld by Him. And their functions corresponded to their authority; to them had been committed the keys of the kingdom; they could bind and loose, and were by their commission empowered to act in their Master's name. In their

their own phraseology, as to the relation of Church and State held by those who were the ancestors of the later " Independents." Indeed, the Anglican "autonomy of the Church" is but the Puritan independency, or rather a single aspect of it, and the Presbyterian " Crown rights of the Redeemer."

hands too, and in theirs only, were the sacraments, and "the sacraments, not preaching, are the sources of divine grace." The sacred order was the condition of the church's being, and the factor of its efficiency; where the authorized priest was not, the sacraments could not be; and no sacraments meant no church, no life communicated by Baptism and maintained by the Eucharist. And the church which ministered life by her sacraments, guarded, defined, and interpreted truth by her authority; for to the being and belief of the truth, an authoritative interpreter was even more necessary than an inspired source. And this was to be found in tradition, not indeed as collected and preserved by Rome, but as contained in the Fathers, and as gathered from them by Anglican scholars and divines. Rome was corrupt, but catholic; the Protestant churches were corrupt and sectarian; but the church of the Fathers was catholic and pure; and after it the Anglican was fashioned, and tried to walk in its light and read the truth with its eyes. And so a proud, coherent, and courageous theory of the Church stood up to confront and dare the State; to rebuke it as of the earth, to speak to it as with the voice of heaven, to command it to revere and obey where it had thought it could compel and rule.

2. It is no part of my purpose to criticize the Anglican theory; it was the work of men who made an impassioned appeal to history, but were utterly void of the historical spirit. The past they loved

and studied was a past of detached fragments, violent divisions, broken and delimited in the most arbitrary way. Their canon, "quod semper, quod ubique, quod ab omnibus creditum est," they honoured in speech rather than observance; the "semper" did not mean "always," or the "ubique" everywhere, or the "ab omnibus" by all; but only such times, places and men, or even such parts and sections of times, places and men, as could be made to suit or prove the theory. Then, for an authority to be of any use in the region of truth, it must be authoritative, accessible, self-consistent and explicit; but this authority was not one of these things—it was only the voice of these very simple, very positive, unscientific, and often mistaken men. Their supreme difficulty, which broke down the transcendent genius of the party, was to get their own church to speak their mind; and they were even less successful with the Fathers than with their church. There is no more splendid example anywhere of how completely a professedly historical movement can be independent of historical truth. The Tractarians in this respect present a remarkable contrast to the Reformers. Calvin in his treatment of doctrine was nothing if not historical; the Tractarians in their treatment of history were nothing if not dogmatic. They were traditional but not historical, while the Reformers were historical but not traditional. The Reformers courageously, if not always thoroughly, rejected tradition and authority that they might reach the mind and realize the ideal of the Christ of history ; but the Tractarians, with no less courage, tried to adapt the historical mind and bend the historical ideal to authority and tradition. Truth is patient, and suffers much at the hands of sincere men ; but she always comes by her own at last.

§ IV. *The Anglo-Catholics and Literature*

1. What has been the result of the Anglo-Catholic revival? If the success of a religious movement is to be measured by its power to penetrate with its own spirit, to persuade and reconcile to religion the best intellects of a country, then even its most devoted advocates can hardly say that Anglo-Catholicism has succeeded. While at first championed by the greatest literary genius and master of dialectic who has in this century concerned himself with theology, it is marvellous how little it has touched our characteristic and creative minds ; with these neither Roman nor Anglican Catholicism has accomplished anything. Take the poets, who alike as regards period and place ought to have been most accessible and susceptible to the Catholic spirit and influence. Arthur Hugh Clough was educated at Balliol, and elected to a Fellowship at Oriel in the days when Newman reigned in St. Mary's ; and he is considered by the most competent of our critics to be " the truest expression in verse of the moral and intellectual tendencies of the period in which he lived." He is fascinated by Newman and held by

him for a while, but only that he may learn how
little there is behind the subtle and persuasive eloquence to satisfy a mind possessed with the passion
for veracity ; and he is driven by the recoil into the
anxious uncertainties where " the music of his rustic
lute " lost " its happy country tone,"

> " And learnt a stormy note
> Of men contention-tost, of men who groan."

Matthew Arnold, son of a father who made England love breadth of view and truth in history,
studied, learned, and suffered with the Thyrsis he so
deeply yet so sweetly mourned ; like him he became
a poet, jealous of truth in thought and word, and
like him, too, faced the problem and the men of the
hour ; but he did not dare to trust as guides for the
present men too credulous of the past to read its
truths aright.   Too well he learned the bitter moral
of all their arguing, and concluded : " If authority be
necessary to faith, then an impossible authority
makes faith impossible " ; and he turned from Oxford
to learn of Weimar—

> " The end is everywhere,
> Art still has truth, take refuge there."

William Morris, formed in the Oxford of a later
day, when in the calm that follows conflict Anglo-
Catholicism reigned, could find in it no satisfying
veracious ideal of truth, of art or of life; and he went
instead to the wild Scandinavian and distant Greek
mythologies for the forms in which to impersonate

his faith and hope. Swinburne, who had the hot imagination that easily kindled to noble dreams of liberty and human good, could find no promise in the crimson sunset glories which Anglo-Catholicism loved ; and he turned passionately towards what seemed to him the east and the sunrise. But it was not only those younger sons of Oxford who had in a measure "the vision and the faculty divine," that the new Catholicism failed to touch ; it touched as little the maturer and richer imaginations of the two men who will ever remain the representative poets of the Victorian era. Tennyson has been essentially a religious genius ; the doubts, the fears, the thought perplexed by evil, by suffering, by a nature cruel in her very harmonies, by the presence of wicked men and the distance of a helpful God, the faith victorious in the very face of sin and death, certain that some-how "good will be the final goal of ill," have all received from him rich and musical expression. But his ideals are not those of mediæval or modern Catholicism ; they may be clothed in forms borrowed from a far-off world of mythical chivalry ; but it is not a priest's world ; it is one of men all the more saintly that they are kings, warriors, statesmen, a world of fair women and goodly men. Browning, who was as essentially a religious poet as Tennyson, and indeed, though no writer of hymns, as a poet more profoundly, penetratively, and comprehensively religious than Keble, bears throughout in his sym-pathies—in his love of liberty, in his hopeful trust in man, in his belief in God as the All-loving as well as the All-great, who through the thunder speaks with human voice—the marks and fruits of his Puritan birth and breeding. But the sensuous seemliness of Anglo-Catholicism had no charms for him ; it had too little spiritual sublimity, stood too remote from the heart of things, had too little fellowship with the whole truth of God, and all the infinite needs and aspirations of man. He had seen, too, the outworking of its ideas ; had studied their action and character in history ; and his curious lore and large experience helped him to many a fit yet quaint form in which to embody what he had discovered or observed. Browning more than any man has deepened the faith of our age in the Eternal ; but he has also, more than any man, made us conscious of the evil of fancying that we can transmute our ephemeral polities and shallow symbols into the infallible and unchangeable speech of God.

2. This failure of Anglo-Catholicism to touch our higher literature is both remarkable and instructive. It has had and has its minor poets, a goodly multitude ; but even their poetry has been mainly reminiscent and sentimental, not spontaneous and imaginative. Indeed, this has been its characteristic in all periods of its being ; writers of hymns, quaint, devout, beautiful, melodious, it has always had, but never poets of the imagination ; if it has ever taken possession of such, it has paralyzed the poet in them, as witness Wordsworth and his ecclesiastical sonnets.

In this stands expressed some of its essential characteristics. Within the rich and complicated and splendidly dight folds of the Spenserian allegories, there lives much of the brawny Puritan mind and purpose. The same mind, and the faith it lived by, made the noblest epic and the most perfect classical drama in the speech of our English people. No man will claim John Dryden as a religious poet, though he forced poetry into the ignoble strife of ecclesiastical politics, and made it the mean apologist of royal and papal designs. Deism lisped in numbers through the lips of Catholic Pope; and the Evangelical Revival inspired the gentle soul of Cowper to verse, always genial and graceful, and often gay. But Anglo-Catholic poetry, measured by the Puritan, is remarkable for nothing so much as its imaginative poverty, its inability to create a literature that shall adequately embody the true and the sublime. And this has its parallel in the theology of the past half-century. Newman, of course, stands alone—Catholic still, but Anglican no more. Apart from him, what names represent the most potent forces in theology and the higher religious thought? Of all preachers, Frederick Robertson has most moved the mind and conscience of this generation; but though an Oxford man of the time when the Tracts were at their mightiest, he escaped from their toils with a rare love of reality, an abhorrence of all false sanctities, a dread of all violence offered in the name of authority to reason.

Frederick Maurice was a personality of rare charm, with a soul ever turned towards the light, with a large range of vision, and a love of love and light that makes him the most mystical thinker of our century; yet his whole life was one sustained protest against the attempt to incorporate the religion of Christ in a sentimental and sacramental symbolism. There has been in our generation no writer in religious history so picturesque, no churchman so bold in speech and in action, so possessed of a broad and inclusive ideal of the national church as Arthur Stanley; but he lived and died as the resolute antagonist of those Catholic schemes that so laboured to sectionalize the church he loved. Of another, though lower, order was Charles Kingsley; but he was in his earlier period full of generous impulses, philanthropies, socialisms, quick and fertile at embodying his ameliorative dreams in attractive fiction; and he was possessed with what can only be described as a great terror lest the rising tide of sacerdotalism should drown what was most ethical and historical in the life of the English people. If Oxford has had within this period a scholar who could be named a Humanist, it was Mark Pattison. But, though he fell under the spell of Newman—and indeed for him the spell was never broken—yet to him the Catholic theory became ever more incredible and false, and the system ever more mischievous in its working, fatal to freedom, learning, and all the fair humanities. It may, too, be allowed to me

to allude to one, though the grass above his grave
is not yet green, who, of all recent Oxford men,
most fulfilled the ideal of the scholar in theology ;
and applied in a spirit as reverent as it was
thorough the scientific method to the history of
ecclesiastical institutions.   But there was no man
who so strongly believed, or was so armed with
proofs to support his belief, that Anglo-Catholicism
was utterly unhistorical, as Edwin Hatch.   It is
needless to multiply names; it is not in literature
nor yet in theology that the movement has hitherto
achieved success.[1]   Perhaps success here is not
possible to it; the signal of victory would be the
sign of decease.

§ V. *The Anglican and the Broad Church*

But this has brought us face to face with another
and no less interesting problem, or rather series of
problems.   How does it happen that the party that
has been so active and so eminent in literature has
accomplished so little in religion, while the party
that has accomplished most in religion has been less
eminent in literature?   For two things seem manifest and beyond dispute—the decay, pointing to

---

[1] We do not forget distinguished names in connection with
the Anglo-Catholic school.   It has had, and still has, learned
historians and men of fine literary gifts ; but to have noticed
these would have taken us beyond the limits defined by our
problem.   What was intended was to measure influence by the
major rather than the minor intellects.

approaching extinction, of the Broad Church, and the revival and growing dominancy of the High. It may seem more dubious to say, a main condition of the success achieved by the High Church has been the literary activity and efficiency of the Broad; but, paradoxical though it may sound, this represents the sober historical truth. Why it has so happened is a question we must discuss in order to get a fuller view of the situation.

1. The same events that had occasioned the rise of Anglo-Catholicism determined the being of the modern Broad Church. The latter was due to an attempt to adapt the Church to the new conditions by broadening it as the State had been broadened. Its fundamental notion was not their ideal difference, but their material identity. The Broad Church has throughout its history been dominated, though not always clearly or consciously, by Arnold's idea, which was also Hooker's, of the coincidence and co-extension of Church and State. The idea is at once English and historical; it implies a far deeper sense than the other party possesses, of the continuity of history and the unity of the institutions created and mantained by the English people both before and since the Reformation. The idea underlying the old legislation was right, but the legislation was in spirit and method wrong, calculated to defeat rather than fulfil its idea. What was necessary was to realize the idea by changing the legislation. Parliament had made civil rights independent of ecclesias-

tical tests; tests ought now to be so construed as to guard rather than invade religious freedom and ecclesiastical privilege. The Act of Uniformity had but created division and established variety ; it was time to attempt, by an Act of comprehension, to legalize variety and create unity. The idea was thus, through the State to reconstitute and reunite the church, as by the State the church had been broken and divided. Comprehension and relaxed subscription were to undo what uniformity and enforced subscription had done. The Broad Church was thus the very opposite of the Anglo-Catholic ; while the one emphasized difference till it became independency, the other accentuated coincidence and relation till they became identity. The primary element in the one idea was,—the English people constitute the English church ; the primary element in the other idea was,—the Anglican church constitutes the religion the English people are bound to confess and obey. The one conceived the church as national, able to be, only as it included and was realized by the nation ; the other conceived the church as of divine authority, because of divine institution, able to fulfil its mission only by enforcing its claims. In the one case, not establishment, but incorporation with the State or in the civil constitution was of the very essence of the church as English and national ; in the other case, control of the church by the State was held to be alien to its very idea as a society divinely founded and ruled. The parties differed in their conception of the church, but still more in their notion of religion. To the Anglican, in a very real sense, church was religion, that without which religion could not be acceptable to God, or sufficient for man; to the Broad Churchman the two were separable, religion being inward, spiritual, a matter of heart or conscience, while church was a means for its cultivation, good in proportion to its suitability and efficiency. In polity and dogma, ritual and symbol, the Anglican could hardly distinguish between accidental and essential—all was of God, and all was sacred; but in all these things his opponent saw the creations of custom or law, to be upheld or dismissed as expediency or advantage might determine. In a word, to the one the church was a creation of God, instituting religion; but to the other the church was an institution of man, though religion was an inspiration of God.

2. Now these differences were radical, and determined in each case the mental attitude and action on all religious questions. The Broad Church attitude tended to become critical, acutely conscious of the inconvenience of a too positive mind and institutions too authoritative to be capable of adaptation to the new conditions of thought and policy. Civil legislation was conceived as able to accomplish what was impossible to it; while the differences that divided, the agreements or affinities that united men, were conceived more from without than from within, from the standpoint of the State rather than of the Church.

21

Hence, there was superabundant criticism of things positive, the dogmas which authority had formulated and enforced, the institutions it created and upheld. The criticism struck the Evangelical most heavily, for his faith was of the fixed and frigid type that most invites criticism.   The Pauline Epistles were translated into a speech and resolved into ideas that were not his; his theories of justification and atonement were assailed at once from the historical, exegetical, and speculative points of view; his doctrine of inspiration was discredited and made untenable, and his conception of the church dismissed as arbitrary and insufficient.   But to hit the Evangelical so hard was to do the utmost possible service to the Anglican.   It disabled, pre-occupied, paralyzed his most resolute adversary, thinned his ranks, blunted his weapons, deprived him of the convictions that give courage.   Then the Broad Church criticism, while making no impression on the Anglican, appealed to the sort of minds the Evangelicals had been most able to influence, surrounded them with an atmosphere, begot in them a tendency within and before which the old Evangelical formulæ could not vigorously live; and yet it did nothing to provide new homes or agencies for the generation and direction of religious life.   The Broad Church is only the name of a tendency, but the Anglo-Catholic denotes a party, well officered, well led, disciplined, organized, and inspired by a great idea.   The representative men within the former have all been marked by a certain severe individúalism; they have attracted disciples, but have not formed schools. Arnold was a man of intense ethical passion, and to it he owed what we may call the most transcendent personal influence of our century; Maurice was a thinker seeking to translate Christian ideas into the terms of a Neo-Platonic idealism; Arthur Stanley was a charming irenical personality, fertile of schemes for reconciling our divided religious society; but neither they nor any of their allies had the enthusiasm of the sect. They loved a church as broad and as varied as the English people, but would neither do nor attempt anything that threatened to narrow its breadth or harass it into a prosaic uniformity. And their positive qualities helped the Anglican even more than their negative. They loved liberty, used the liberty they loved, but preached toleration even of the intolerant. They were impatient of formulæ, but patient of aggressive difference; they resisted every attempt to restrict freedom, but encouraged attempts at its extension and exercise. Hence they helped at once to create room for Anglo - Catholic developments and to lessen the forces of resistance. Their intellectual activity made the English mind tolerant to the most varied forms of belief and worship; which means that they prepared the way and the opportunity for the men who believed that theirs was the only form of divine sufficiency and authority.

§ VI. *The Theological Idea in the Anglican Mind*

1. But while the Broad Church was thus securing for it an easier path and a freer field, the Anglo-Catholics were gathering momentum and growing more missionary and theological. The Tracts had been mainly historical and ecclesiastical; only in a very minor degree doctrinal and religious. They had been more concerned with the archæology than the theology of the church; but the work of Archdeacon Wilberforce on the Incarnation forced theology to the front with most significant results. This work is an expansion of a section in Moehler's *Symbolik*, which, in its turn, is an application of the Hegelian idea to the Catholic church. The idea, indeed, is much older than Hegel, but its modern form is due to him. Schelling formulated the notion: the incarnation of God is an incarnation from eternity. Hegel expressed the notion in the terms of the philosophy of history; Moehler translated it into a philosophy of Catholicism; and apparently its changeful career is not yet ended. It was said of Petavius, that he so penetrated Catholicism with the Protestant spirit that his very apology for the Catholic system was a victory for Protestantism; at least this much is true, that in handling dogma he was the liberal, and Bull, his great Anglican opponent, the conservative. Now if we substitute Hegelian for Protestant, we may say much the same of Moehler. It is curious that the fundamental idea of Moehler

was also the fundamental idea of Strauss,[1] with this difference : Strauss universalized, but Moehler sectionalized the idea. Strauss transferred the predicates of Christ to Man, conceived humanity as the Son of God, born of the invisible Father and visible Mother ; as eternal, sinless, feeble, suffering, dying in its members, but in its collective being risen, reigning, immortal, infallible, and divine. But Moehler restricted the divine predicates to the Catholic church ; it was the abiding incarnation of Christ, the Son of God continuously appearing in human form among men, with an existence ever renewed, a being eternally rejuvenescent. Strauss' notion expressed a consistent Pantheism ; humanity was the incarnation of the divine, represented the process by which the impersonal All created persons, passed from subjective to objective being, and was realized in the realm of conscious existence. But Moehler's expressed what we may term an ecclesio-theism, which represented the church as the form in which God existed for the world, and through which the world could reach God. The church was thus conceived as arrayed in all the attributes and possessed of all the functions of the Son of God. The notion was audacious, and destined to achieve victories in a field Moehler had never dreamed of; it was adopted by Wilberforce, though stated without the sharp precision which dis-

---

[1] Moehler, of course, was the elder and earlier. The *Symbolik* was published in 1832, the *Leben Jesu* in 1835.

tinguished Moehler. The incarnation is the central
dogma of Christianity; Christ as incarnate is, on one
side, the pattern and representative of humanity; on
the other, the mediator between God and man—at
once the one sacrifice for sin and the one channel of
divine grace. The church is His body mystical; to
be united to it is to be united to Him. It is, as it
were, His organized presence, exercising His functions
as Mediator and Saviour. It is impossible to tell
"whether men are joined to Christ by being joined
to His Church, or joined to His Church by being
joined to Him. The two relations hang inseparably
together." Hence the value of the sacraments:
they "bind to Him," make us "participate in His
presence," communicate to us His man's nature, incorporate us in His body mystical, "the renewed
race" which He "has been pleased to identify
with Himself." They are, therefore, the primary and
essential means of grace on which all others depend;
they work our unity with the incarnate Son of God,
and through Him with the Father.

2. Now the significance of this work lies here; it
supplied the Anglo-Catholic movement with a dogmatic basis; placed it, as it were, under the control
of a defining and determining idea. Most of the
positions had been maintained before; what Wilberforce gave was a co-ordinating and unifying principle.
This changed the whole outlook; the question did
not need to be debated as one of Patristic or Anglican archæology; it had a philosophy; its reason was

one with the reason of the incarnation. The church
was, as it were, the Son of God articulated in sacraments, explicated in symbols, organized into a visible
body politic for the exercise of His mediation on
earth. This dogmatic idea created the new Ritualism
as distinguished from the old Tractarianism; and
changed the centre of gravity from a dubious question in ecclesiastical history, discussed with learning,
but without science, to a fact of faith or living religious belief. Ritualism may be described as the
evangelical idea done into the institutions and rites
of a sacerdotal Church. The idea remains, and is
the same, but its vehicle is changed. To speak with
Hegel, the *Begriff* is translated back into the *Vor-
stellung*, the spiritual truth is rendered into a sensuous picture. Ritual is dogma in symbol; dogma is
articulated ritual. Justification is as necessary as
ever, but it is conditioned on the sacraments rather
than on faith. Regeneration is still held, but it is
worked by an outward act rather than an inward
process. Where the pure preaching of the word
once stood, the due administration of the sacraments
now stands. To it an authorized priesthood is necessary; without it there can be no Eucharist, in other
hands the Supper is no sacrament or efficacious
means of grace. In order to a valid priesthood there
must be a constitutive authority—the bishops who
stand in the apostolical succession; and a constitutive
act—ordination at their hands. The chain is complete: without the apostolical authority no bishop;

without the bishop no priest; without the priest no sacrament; without the sacraments no church; without the church no means of grace, no mediation or reconciliation through Christ of man with God. Two things are essential to the church, the clergy and the sacraments; and of these the clergy are the greater, for without them the full sacraments cannot be, while the sacraments cannot but be where they are. They are therefore in a most real sense of the essence of the church, while the people are but an accident; the clergy represent its formal or normative authority—*i.e.*, they are the regulative principle of its being, give status to the people, do not find in them the condition and warrant of their own existence. But, so construed, the theory is less a doctrine of the church than of its officers; it is not the Christian Society or people or commonwealth constituting its officers or priesthood, but the priesthood constituting the people. In its Anglican form the Apostolical Succession of the clergy, or the bishops who ordain the clergy, is a denial of the Apostolical descent of the Church. And so, it is not too much to say, the greater the emphasis which is thrown upon the idea of the clergy, the meaner becomes the idea of the Church; and so we may add, that here the Broad Church has a nobler idea than the Anglo-Catholic. To resolve the English church into the Christian people of England is to show a right conception of the place of the people within it; but to resolve it into a hierarchy or hierocracy, with its instruments and dependencies, is utterly to misconceive the relation of the society and its organs.

Yet even under these conditions the evangelical idea has proved its energy ; the men who have construed their church and their order through their Christology, have been of another spirit than the men who construed them through Patristic and Anglican tradition as interpreted by an impossible canon. The change is so marked, that, did we know only the first stage of the process and the last, we could not believe that they were moments in the life of the same party. Ritualism, while the most superficial, is the least characteristic sign of the change ; one deeper and more real, is the supersession of the old aristocratic spirit by one humaner and more democratic. The new men are possessed, as the old were not, by missionary zeal, by the passion to reach and reclaim the masses, by the endeavour to make the church the attractive home of the people, and the people the obedient sons of the church. The religious polemics of the older men were often inspired by the intensest political antipathy to " Liberalism " and all its works, even when these were philanthropic or remedial. But the new men are distinguished by a progressive spirit, which has tempted the more forward to grapple, in the interests of the poor, with our graver social problems, and even to help in their practical solution. Of course the country has changed at once with the party and because of it ; while common tendencies have been at work in both, shaping their respective activities, and modifying their mutual relations. The sense of responsibility to the people, which is a tribute levied by their accession to power, has, of course, penetrated what used to be called the governing.classes; the men who serve the State live under a more jealous criticism, and the men who minister in the Church have become more conscious of duties, parochial and national. But, for the clergy, the Anglo-Catholic revival has given at once form and sanction to this new consciousness of duty; it has made them, while more priestly, more evangelical, ministers of a more ornate service, studiously seeking to help worship by a richer symbolism, and to teach dogma by a more elaborate ceremonial. Under their hands the church has become a new institution, more active, more aggressive, making claims that would have bewildered or amused the men of fifty years ago. But while merely academic claims are heard with scorn, claims supported by devoted lives, and illustrated by fulfilled duties, are, even when doubted, patiently endured. The clergy believe that in their hands are the instruments of life; and they multiply symbols and administer sacraments as men who possess and distribute the grace that saves.

§ VII. *The Theological Idea in the Church*

1. But we must now attempt to discover and define in what respects the theological idea has affected and changed the conception of the church in the

newer Anglo-Catholicism, so as to distinguish it from the older. We may say, then, that the new men are less Anglican and more catholic than the old, using the term catholic in its proper and not in the Roman sense. Their church, while no less political or institutional, is more ideal; they conceive it more through a dogma or a philosophy than through a fixed and provincial, or limited, tradition. The old and the new agree in identifying what may be described as a given framework of the church with its essence; they agree as to its polity, the value and function of its sacraments, the origin, necessity, gradation, and succession of its orders. These things must be, that the church may be; whatever may be changed or transcended, they must stand. In all its forms Anglo-Catholicism is a theory as to the necessity of a specific ministry to the church, not of the church to any ministry. But these points of agreement only emphasize the point of difference, with all that follows from it. This point may be stated thus : the determinative principle of the older men was historical—tradition ; but the determinative principle of the younger men is metaphysical—a doctrine. What we may term the immanent idea is in each case different ; in the one it was an objective model, or specific authority—certain Fathers as interpreted by certain Anglican divines ; but in the other it is an underlying philosophy or theology, which penetrates and modifies the whole conception of the Church, and governs the methods and use of historical proof.

This philosophy or theology may be conveniently described, though by a species of synecdoche, as the notion of the church in its Catholic or Anglican sense as "naturally of a piece with the Incarnation";[1] in other words, the church is so construed through the Incarnation as to experience a kind of apotheosis, or to become "a new and higher mode" of the profoundest mystery known to the Christian Faith. The poetry in the sublime and beautiful image of Paul,—the Church is the body of Christ,—is, for the benefit of an institution, turned into the most prosaic of prose. Truths that relate to the theanthropic Person, His sanctity, His sovereignty over mind, His authority over conscience through belief, become predicable of a church with a specific organization, which, as continuing the work of the Founder, is the only recognised way of man reaching God or God reaching man. "Access to God" is free to a man, provided he belongs to the one body ; "fellowship with God" is possible "only through membership in the one body and by dependence on social sacraments," "of which ordained ministers are the appointed instruments."[2] And so the church, taken as strictly an episcopal and sacerdotal institution, becomes the mystical and "Spirit-bearing" body,[3] created and inhabited by Christ, and possessed of all

---

[1] Gore, *The Church and the Ministry*, p. 64 ; *Lux Mundi*, p. 367.
[2] Gore, *The Church and the Ministry*, pp. 93, 94.
[3] *Lux Mundi*, p. 321.

the energies, capabilities, and functions of a living organism. It may be conceived as a colossal individual, whose years are centuries, whose life is continuous, and who alone is able, by virtue of its apostolic descent and proper administration of sacraments, to articulate and realize Christ's presence on earth.

2. So much for the determinative idea translated into an ecclesiastical and institutional form ; now a word or two as to its action on Anglo-Catholicism. For one thing, the point of emphasis was changed ; it passed from the Patristic period to the church as a unity, living, catholic, continuous. The change was, as it were, from the idea of the law that ruled the body, to the idea of the body that made the law. The church in a sense superseded the Fathers, and though Apostolic and Patristic voices are still heard with reverence, it is less as independent authorities and more as organs through which the society has spoken ; they must be canonized that they may have authority. But this change involves another. The authority the older men appealed to was specific and concrete, —antiquity as understood by recognized Anglican scholars ; but the authority of the younger men is more general and ideal, either a composite abstraction spoken of in historical terms as "the Catholic Church," or a series of selected opinions called "the Catholic Tradition." By the very terms of the appeal and the logical necessities of the situation, the authority appealed to is masked and made but an

echo of the appealing voice ; for an eclectic Catholicism is the most arbitrary of individualisms. It is but
subjective tendencies or judgments done into œcumenical formulæ. The man who speaks is for the
time being "the Catholic Church"; the thing he
believes is "the Catholic Tradition." And under the
use of concrete terms he hides a pure abstraction,
which has nothing corresponding to it in the whole
field of history. If the usage and connotation be
carefully analyzed, we shall find that what it really
denotes is the merest "private judgment" enunciating
its own deliverances and definitions as decrees of the
catholic church. And this involves another difference : the older men defended dogma by institutions,
the younger defend institutions by dogma; which
means that the attitude of the mind to the ideal contents of religion and to the intellectual tendencies of
the age has changed. The old attitude to reason was
hostile, the new is friendly ; the older men had the
idea of an authority that must be obeyed, but the
younger have the idea of an authority that must be
adapted to living thought. The "Anglicans" laboured
so to organize the church after a definite ideal, that
it might the more effectually resist the modern spirit:
but the new "Catholics" endeavour so to construe
the traditional creed as to make it incorporate the
ideas of the age. The "Anglican" idea of the
church was more concrete, and its conception of
authority more defined ; while the "Catholic" idea
of authority is more elastic, and of the church, on the

intellectual side, more flexible—so much so, that it is conceived as able to assimilate all new material, to welcome and give place to all new knowledge.[1] In a word, a new philosophy, and, as a consequence, a new theology, has penetrated the Anglican system : and, though old terms and positions survive, the philosophy has just to be allowed to do its work, and the new will not be as the old.

§ VIII. *The Church and the Age*

My purpose has been analytical and historical rather than critical ; and I shall not here attempt a criticism, either philosophical or historical, of the theory whose growth has been described.[2] But I may venture, in conclusion, to raise two practical points which seem to deserve discussion.

1. The church may have a message to the age, but the age has also a message to the church. And it is possible that in the age's message there may be most of the voice of God. To the being and character of the age the church has contributed ; and has therefore its own share of responsibility for what the age is. In every period its one clear duty is this—to turn for living men the idealities of religion into the realities of being. Hence the question which our age addresses to the church may be stated thus :—Is there any power within you that can make the Chris-

---

[1] *Lux Mundi*, Preface, p. ix.

[2] But see *ante*, pp. 167 ff. ; and the concluding chapters of the *Place of Christ*, etc.

tian Faith credible to the living reason and authoritative to the living conscience? Are you able to make it so to pervade the atmosphere we breathe, and impregnate the soil on which we grow, as to be, as if by a natural process, incorporated into our being, or as to become the determinative factor of our personal characters, ideals, ends, and of our collective customs, institutions, laws? To have such a problem so stated is to feel rebuked and humbled. We are in the nineteenth century of the Christian era ; for almost all these centuries Christianity has lived on our soil, for the greater part of them we have been formally and ostensibly Christian. Yet we are faced by problems which imply that there are whole provinces of our national and social life where Christianity as a religion has little place and less power, and a multitude of minds for whom it has as a Faith no reality, no credibility, and no authority. At such a moment to profess pessimism were to confess to defeat ; but to cultivate optimism were to prepare for extinction. No man who believes in the Christian religion can despair of its success ; no man who loves his people can be satisfied with their state, or persuade himself that it proves the sufficiency of the church or churches which have been charged with the realization of the religion. Class interests, passions, prejudices, still reign untempered by love ; they have grown more bitter and dangerous since they have come to contend hand to hand, foot to foot, for the seat of sovereignty. The rebellion arms can quell may be easily ended ; but the slow revolution worked by inexorable law mocks at arms or dynastic forces, and can be changed into a beneficent process only by the gracious energies of religion. Such a revolution is even now in process ; but has religion so penetrated the people by whom it is being accomplished that the church can watch its completion with a light heart and an easy conscience? Our political problems are grave, but our economical are graver, and still more grave are our social. Towards the solution of the economical many natural factors are co-operating ; the intellects and energies engaged in the industries are, by combinations, councils, arbitrations, and enlarged education, by securing the more equal and equitable distribution of wealth, contributing to the creation of happier conditions. But in the solution of our social problems the supreme factor is the religious, the factor that fashions upright, honourable, beneficent men, that substitutes the reign of ordering love for Rousseau's social contract or the iron hand of Hobbes' strong man. Of all States, a democratic most needs virtue, integrity, disinterestedness of motive, sanity of intellect, and inflexibility of moral will in its governors and guides ; but while we cultivate politics with passion, do we not leave the creation of the politician to chance? Have our people been constrained to conceive that the office of the statesman is not less sacred than the office of the churchman, and demands, because of its greater perils and more manifold temptations, a more enlightened con-

science and a larger endowment of grace? Few
things are more disastrous to a society than the substitution of conventional for moral standards of
judgment ; and is it too much to say that the society
most purely ecclesiastical is also the most thoroughly
conventional? Immoralities live as they have never
lived before in the public eye, and the scandals of the
West End do more to debauch the national conscience than all the sordid vice and gaunt poverty of
the East. We seem to have reached a state where
evil has more solidarity than good : rich and poor
meet together and understand each other more in
their vices than in their religion, which ought to have
destroyed their vices, root and branch. But within
the community there lives this difference : the rich
have the gift of oblivion in a higher degree than the
poor. The easy conscience of society sweetly forgives the man who has sown his wild oats, but the
retentive memory of the people does not so readily
forget the ruin he may have worked in the process.
These, and things like these, formulate grave problems
for the church. How have they come to be? How
is their being to be ended? The higher the theory
of the church the deeper ought to be the notion of
its responsibility ; the greater our idea of its power
and its function, the more sternly must we judge its
failure. ˙Wisdom is justified by her works : but if
the works are not there, or there in an altogether
inadequate degree, what becomes of the justification?

But the deepest and most pathetic appeal which

our age can make to the church concerns the question of what it is to believe. The living intellect and
the historical faith have somehow drifted, if not
asunder, yet out of relation: and where truth does not
live to the reason it can have no authority for the
conscience. The characteristic of the age is here
not so much unbelief as a want of belief, so extensively and uniformly diffused as to represent a
common tendency rather than specific causes. It is
distributed through all classes, and is peculiar to
none, though it receives in each characteristic expression. Among the less skilled labourers it is simply
indifference; poverty shows no mercy to ideals,
thinking that what brings no amelioration is entitled
to no reverence. The man who with hungry mouths
to feed struggles with failing strength to feed them,
will not long continue to find comfort in contem-
plating the beauty and sufficiency of abstract truth.
The response of the poor to a religion which has no
concern or cure for poverty, is neglect of the religion.
Again, the hard-headed artisan has difficulties of
another and more varied order, and they grow with
his rather moody and defiant independence. He is
proud, sensitive to small things, especially if touched
with affront or condescension or disdain, and conscious of a manhood too honourable to brook those
class and caste distinctions that are often only the
more emphasized by the circumstances and conven-
tions of common worship. Or he brings a vigorous
intellect, all the severer in its logic for being without

formal culture, to bear on formulæ that have survived their occasion or lost their original sense, and yet have in his mind continued to be identified with the essence of religion ; and he forthwith resolves the formulæ and the religion into a series of fantastic absurdities, which only folly or knavery or the blindest self-interest can tempt men to believe. The parson or preacher he regards with lofty scorn as the mercenary impersonation of all the superstitions he most despises ; and his most effective and offensive weapons of assault he draws from the Old Testament Scriptures, conceived as so inspired that every word, character, and event is due to the direct action of the Almighty. In the educated classes similar types of unbelief, often in still cruder forms, are represented ; only here fashion and current tendencies account for more. The fleshly materialism of our gilded youth, too gross to care for any intellectual justification, is an utterly vile thing ; while noble purposes may live within and speak through the reason and conscience of the secularist artisan. The doubt that is too indolent to reason or to be reasoned with, or that is indulged as a private intellectual luxury, or that is used to give point and flavour to an otherwise vacuous cynicism ; the agnosticism that speaks the language of one set, and the pessimism that repeats the formulæ of another ; the cultivated indifference that treats as bad form every allusion to religion ; the culture that believes in translating dogma into the language of the club or the coterie ; the scientific temper that despises religion, or benevolently deals with it as if it were a thing for weak or dishonest intellects, because it does not follow the processes or attain the results of some science misdescribed as exact—these and many similar phases of floating opinion may be found in society and in literature. They are easily over-estimated, easily under-estimated, and still more easily misconceived. Singly they may be insignificant, but collectively their significance is immense. They mean that the unsettlement of belief is general; that men cannot think, or speak, in the society of the thoughtful, without feeling it; that in religious matters it is true courtesy to assume difference, and avoid speech: and that it is only reasonable to suppose that every new science will be in conflict with the old faith. But the fateful agitation is not the superficial; it is rather the deeper movement of thought that throws up and throws out the bubbles and eddies of the surface. The old conception of nature and man, of the universe and its history, is breaking up; a new conception is making its way into the collective consciousness and becoming the regulative principle of all its thinking; with the inevitable result that religious beliefs, if they are to live, must undergo a correspondent transformation. Our most real and radical scientific enquiries raise questions as to creation, the Creator and His mode of working, as to man and his origin, the being of sin, the birth of religion, the reality of progress; our most rigorous and fruitful historical enquiries deal with the genesis of social and religious institutions, the evolution of thought, the formation and growth, now of mythologies, now of theologies ; the place and composition of religious books, the appearance and action of religious personalities ; and these in the most inexorable way compel men, if they would be reasonable while religious, to ask how the new methods affect their own beliefs. The scientific temper of to-day may be described as a passion to explore and explain origins, and to find out the reason and method of a thing's becoming ; and it is so universal that no belief or institution can escape the enquiry, how, when, and why it came to be. This means that the ultimate problem of a church is not to explain the faith it has authoritatively defined, but to vindicate the process by which it became possessed of the authority to define it, the competence to enforce what it has defined. Hence the final word of our age to Anglo-Catholicism, and ail modes of verifying theology or realizing religion by authoritative institutions is this : What claims to authenticate our most fundamental beliefs must have nothing dubious about its own title deeds.

It is possible to speak in this way, simply because above all other facts this fact is evident : that the Christian religion has not been so interpreted by the societies or churches in England whose mission it is to realize it, as to have penetrated, possessed and commanded the English people. We are still far from the kingdom of heaven; and of all evidences of truth, alike as regards a man and a society, the most infallible is the ancient canon, " By their fruits ye shall know them." This is not to be construed as a word of reproach against the English church as a church. The writer feels that there is nothing less noble or more despicable than the mutual reproaches of religious men and societies, or the memory too mindful of past faults, and too forgetful of present duties, especially those of charity and truth. But what he means is this, that those who claim that a given church is the one and only divinely created and guided church of Christ for the English people, are not dealt with seriously unless their church be required to have lived up to its character, and have proved it through its works. There is no tribute to a man or institution like the demand that he or it be no less or no worse than his or its claims. Now, it is not too much to say, in the face of what has been said, that the church has not made its supernatural character obvious by its works; and for an institution that must be supernatural to be anything at all, this is certainly a serious circumstance. If its character and claims are things that have still, after all these centuries of opportunity and endeavour, to be proved by an argumentative and evidential process, then the process must be cogent indeed, sufficient at least to satisfy a reason both scientific and reverent. An age which deeply reveres good

things well done, but is dubious and slow of conviction as to high abstract claims, is a trying age
for a system or a society whose claims are mainly
abstract, and whose evidences are not very apparent
in the realm of the real.

2. If the church is to serve the age, it must be by
embodying more of the mind and ideal of the Master.
It must be the church in His sense and for His ends.
We have already seen something of the claims made
by the Anglo-Catholics on behalf of the church as
they conceive it. It is Christ's Spirit-bearing body,
"the special and covenanted sphere of His regular
and uniform operations."[1] The Church has a finality
which belongs to its very essence, "expressed in the
once for all delivered faith, in the fulness of the once
for all given grace, in the Visible Society once for all
instituted," "and in a once for all empowered and
commissioned ministry."[2] By virtue of the first it is
the custodian and interpreter of the truth ; by virtue
of the second it possesses the Sacraments, which are
instruments for the communication of grace ; because
of the third the Church is a political unity into which
man must be incorporated to be truly and effectually
saved ; in the fourth "the instrument of unity" is supplied, "and no man can share her (the Church's)
fellowship except in acceptance of the offices of her
ministry."[3] Now, of these the last is the greatest and

---

[1] *Lux Mundi*, pp. 312, 322.
[2] *The Church and the Ministry*, pp. 64, 65.
[3] *Ibid.* p. 86.

most essential. Though it may be argued, all are alike necessary and distinction between necessities cannot be drawn ; yet here this distinction exists, the apostolic ministry is the condition through which the other things are ; it is primary, they are secondary and sequent ; without it there can be no unity, no sacramental grace, no authoritative transmission and definition of truth ; with it these things cannot but be.

Now, into this question I will not enter further than to say : the divine right of a clergy is no more friendly to a happy, an ordered, an efficient church, than is the divine right of a king conducive to a free and progressive State. To make the kingship the constitutive factor of a State, and the clergy or the episcopate the constitutive factor in the church, is to degrade equally the ideas of Church and State. And it is here justified by assigning to the clergy a place and a function quite unknown to the New Testament. " There is a most exact correspondence between the ministerial office and the nature of the religion, or the offices of the church and its essential character. Sacerdotalism means that an office is conceived to be so sacrosanct, and so necessary to man's worship of God, and God's access to man, that without it there can be no perfect worship on the one side, and no adequate or regular communication of life on the other. It means that the priest, as a priest, and not as a person, and his instruments as his, or as used by him, are the only authorized and divinely constituted media through which God reaches man and man God, or through which the recognized and approved intercourse of the creature with the Creator can proceed. Now, in the New Testament no such ideas are associated with the ministry, or with any person appointed to it. No man bears the priest's name, or professes his functions ; the studious avoidance of the name by men who were steeped in the associations of sacerdotal worship is most significant ; and so is the care with which they translate sacerdotal customs and ideas into their spiritual antitypes. The priesthood ceases to be official by being made universal." The Christian society is a priesthood,[1] and the sacrifices it offers are spiritual,[2] the living man,[3] the gifts and beneficences which are acceptable to God,[4] and the praise which He loves.[5] The temple is no longer the building where the priest officiates, conducts his processions, and indulges in his ceremonial, but it is the Man[6] and the Society.[7] The virtues enjoined are not of the old sacerdotal sort, but ethical, inner, human—faith, hope, love, the obedience that is so pleasing to God because so helpful to man. " The life of the communities is not bound by any priestly rules or observances,[8] but by the new laws of love. The Church and its ministry, therefore, correspond throughout ; the ministry is one of persuasion, that seeks to

---

[1] Apoc. i. 6 ; v. 10 ; xx. 6.   [2] 1 Pet. ii. 5.
[3] Rom. xii. 1 ; Phil. ii. 17.   [4] Phil. iv. 18 ; Heb. xiii. 16.
[5] Heb. xiii. 15.   [6] 1 Cor. vi. 19.   [7] 1 Cor. iii. 16, 17.
[8] Gal. iv. 9, 10 ; Col. ii. 16–23.

move the will through the conscience, and both through the reason and heart; that cares in the new and gracious way of brotherhood for the poor, the sick, the ignorant, the suffering, the sinful, and attempts to help, to love, to win by sweet reasonableness; while the Church is a society which seeks to realize the beautiful ideal of a family of God, or a household of faith, or a brotherhood of man.   There is no place for the priest or his office; his sensuous sanctities are unknown, and, instead, there is the kingdom of God, and the endeavour to do His will.   The rise of the sacerdotal Orders is a question for later history; it marks a long descent from the Apostolic age, but is certainly no thing of Apostolic descent." [1]

Many questions remain which we dare not here and now attempt to touch.   The Church lives, and moves, and has its being in Christ; but the churches have as conditions of their being what used to be called the pure Word of God and the Sacraments.   We are strictly within the lines of historical truth when we say that without the Word no church can come into being, and without it none can continue.   Every Apostolic Church was created by the preaching of the Word, and lived only as the creative became the preservative agency.   As to the Sacraments, we shall only say, once they became the acts and instruments of a priest they lost their original sense, and were changed from the possessions and seals and symbols

---

[1] *The Place of Christ in Modern Theology*, pp. 533, 534.

of the community into the appendices and articles of an office. The most inveterate schismatic is the person or the party that draws round himself or itself a circle, and says, "within this is the sphere of God's 'covenanted mercies'; all without is the region of the uncovenanted. We are the Catholic Church; all beyond is the province of the Sectaries and the Sects." There is nothing in all history so intensely schismatic as this pseudo-Catholicism; it is the vanity of the Sectary in its worst possible form. And those who believe that the Church of God is as broad and as free as the Mercy of God, may well be forgiven if they speak plainly and frankly about any and every attempt to bind it to a provincial polity, and to make it seem less large and less gracious than the action of God in history has proved it to be.

March, 1890.
February, 1891.

VIII

"THE FOUNDATIONS OF BELIEF"[1]

THE appearance of the statesman as a theologian is a matter of interest not only to theologians, but also to the State. It speaks of interests which have all the greater significance for this world that they embrace another and larger, and of ideals which are potent in making character and governing both private conduct and public policy. What indeed distinguishes the statesman from the man of affairs is not skill in the expediencies of the moment, but the possession of a lofty idealism. Plato has told us that only the statesman under the inspiration of the kingly Muse can implant in the souls he governs the Idea, which is a divine principle, of the noble, and the just, and the good ; while not till philosophers were kings, and political power was wedded to philosophy, could his ideal city live and behold the light of the sun. Aristotle was doubtful whether kings were an advantage to States, but he was clear that they ought to be chosen for their merit, or

---

[1] *The Foundations of Belief: being Notes Introductory to the Study of Theology.* By the Right Hon. Arthur James Balfour. London : Longmans. 1895.

personal life and conduct : while the statesman might be considered as much a lover of virtue as the philosopher, since it was the note alike of the wise State and wise man to regulate life according to the best end. It is well now and then to be recalled to the ancient idea that the State is, alike in basis and aim, essentially an ethical society ; and that virtue and ethical knowledge in the statesman are necessary to order and progress in the State. Our tendency for the moment is to substitute material for moral well-being, to conceive comfort as the highest good and poverty as the last evil. To be poor or to endure hardness is to be thought incapable of being personally happy or of contributing to the common happiness. If Diogenes were to appear among us with his tub, he would be told that before he could be heard or be regarded as other than an object of charity, he must have a more desirable dwelling, exchange his sack for respectable broad-cloth, and demand of Alexander not only that he get out of the sun, but actually dispel the smoke or the fog that was intercepting its beams. If Epictetus were to set up as a teacher of morals, he would be assured that he could not be a philosopher while he continued a slave, or think worthily while his labour was another's. We ought, then, to welcome a book which' shows us that we have a statesman who at least thinks as deeply of ethical as of material well-being, and who spends his quiet days not simply on brown moors or breezy links, but in attempting to lay anew, broad and deep and strong,

"the foundations" of the beliefs on which he conceives society to rest.

§ I. *The Statesman as Divine*

1. It does not indeed always follow that the statesman who studies theology either applies his religion
to the State or serves it by his studies. We all
remember Gibbon's[1] famous aphorism as to "the
various modes of worship which prevailed in the
Roman world" being "considered by the people, as
equally true; by the philosopher, as equally false;
and by the magistrate, as equally useful." But if the
philosopher chanced to be also a magistrate, his use
of the religion he held to be false was more a tribute
to the expediencies of government than to the integrity of philosophy. Cicero, too, as orator and
statesman, praised the popular religion, and played
the *rôle* of sincere believer, fervently recounting the
miracles it had accomplished on behalf of himself and
the Republic; but as a philosopher we find him in
his treatises flouting this same religion with lordly
disdain. Marcus Aurelius appears in his *Medita-
tions* as the typical Roman saint, the ideal man of
the Stoics embodied in breathing flesh and blood; but
he stands in history as one of the chief persecutors of
the Christian Church, leaving to us the hard problem
of reconciling the tolerant philosopher with the intolerant Emperor. In the long roll of English kings
two stand out as eminent and learned theologians,
Henry VIII. and James I. To the former we owe,

---

[1] *Decline and Fall*, chap. ii. 1.

among other things, the famous book against Luther, the *Assertio Septem Sacramentorum*, which procured for its author and his successors the proud title of " Fidei Defensor " ; to the latter, among other things, the *Basilikon Doron*, which declared that he hated " no man more than a proud Puritan "—a being no king could suffer, unless indeed " for trying of his patience, as Socrates did an evil wife "—and the *Apology for the Oath of Allegiance*, which explained his theory of kingcraft in the province of religion. But he would be a bold man who should assert of Henry that he was one of the most just and magnanimous of kings, or of James that he was one of the wisest. Still there is no principle which English history more illustrates than this, that problems, even in passing politics, are best understood when looked at in the light of large ideas and high aims. If we are unable to name Bacon a statesman, yet we cannot forget that he was the most eminent English philosopher of his day,—to say, as some have said, of all time, is to speak foolishly. Clarendon, once chancellor of the kingdom, has given us a history, not unconcerned with church and religion, that will live as long as the English tongue. Last century Bolingbroke discoursed through five prolix volumes on sundry matters, philosophical and theological, including such congenial themes as " the folly and presumption of philosophers, especially in matters of the first philosophy," and " authority in matters of religion ; " and "Alexander Pope, Esquire,"

to whom the essays and letters were addressed, did
the system of his "friend and genius," the "master
of the poet and the song," into the polished measure
and empty optimism of the *Essay on Man*. But,
though Bolingbroke professed deism and upheld the
church, yet we may reckon it among the kind things
of Providence that he had not the opportunity of
realizing his "Idea of a Patriot King," or maintaining as a statesman the church he did not believe
in as a man. In this century, statecraft and theology
have often gone hand in hand. In France, Joseph
de Maistre led the counter-revolution, and evoked
the papacy as the spirit which was to reduce to
order the chaos of loose and lawless wills ; the Duc
de Broglie described the early, that he might inform
and defend the living, church ; Guizot, when relieved
by the Second Empire from the service of the citizen
king, occupied himself with the interpretation of
Evangelical Christianity and the revival of French
Protestantism ; while Jules Simon had edited *Descartes*, and vindicated *La Religion Naturelle*, before
he was known as a politician and minister. Nearer
ourselves stand statesmen who were scholars, and
minded the affairs of the State all the better that
they did not neglect their own studies. We remember that one English Prime Minister of Queen
Victoria translated Homer ; another, the "little great
man" who "knew that he was right"—Earl Russell,
—was almost as active in literature as in politics ;
a third, Lord Beaconsfield was the author of some

of the cleverest, most brilliant, audacious, and malicious novels of the time ; but novels as they were, they were yet full of social, political, and ecclesiastical theory. And to-day the most venerable of English statesmen has also been throughout his long life an eager and prolific theologian. He began his career as a sort of lay divine, claiming for his church a higher place, more independent authority and indefeasible rights, than even her official heads had then either the courage or the faith to affirm. In his maturer manhood classical studies absorbed him, and we had those delightful excursions into the world of Homer and the Homeric poems, which were all the more instructive that they were in character so entirely distinct from the performances of the mere scholar. If he had not what the youngest scholar thought the only, because the newest, scientific method of inquiry into the date, the composition, the authorship, and the mythology of the Homeric poems, he yet showed an unrivalled mastery of the text and a familiarity with the world it described and illustrated, which was all his own. And now in his later days he returns—though one may say from a maturer and higher point of view— to his earlier interests. It is less the political form and idea of religion, and more the metaphysical and ethical contents—*i.e.*, the truth of it—that interest him. There is a certain fitness in the man who began his life as an apologist for a given theory of the church in the State, ending his life as the editor of the greatest of all the apologies of the Christian religion ever written in the English tongue. And now, just as many have been feeling how the withdrawal of a mind accustomed to study the State through the large and luminous atmosphere of religion, had impoverished politics, a younger statesman descends into the arena and boldly challenges attention and criticism by his *Notes Introductory to the Study of Theology.* And what can a theologian do but ask, Whither does this Introduction lead—into theology ? or whither ?

2. Mr. Balfour here repeats and expands his older book,[1] developing and applying its principles. And we may at once say, the old book is the best introduction to the new, and is, indeed, necessary to its complete elucidation. The new work is distinguished by many admirable qualities, is at once lucid and subtle, brilliant and eloquent, always grave, yet often lighted up with flashes of a nimble though ironical humour, with a delicate yet elastic style, excellently suited to the deft and sinuous movement of the thought. If to be well put were to be victoriously argued, this would indeed be a cogent book ; but I must frankly, even at the very outset, confess that to one reader at least it has been a deep disappointment. The early chapters awakened high hope ; their form threw over one a sort of spell ; but the

---

[1] *A Defence of Philosophic Doubt: being an Essay on the Foundations of Belief,* 1879.

spell slowly faded, and pleasure turned to pain, as the underlying philosophy was seen to be shifting sand rather than solid rock, and what could its unstable weakness do but fracture the whole frail superstructure? The farther the reading proceeded, the less satisfactory the argument seemed. The criticism that had appeared so pleasantly potent at the beginning, became sadly impotent at the middle, and mischievously inadequate or irrelevant at the end. This was a conclusion most reluctantly reached; but whether justly reached, it will be for the readers of both the book and this essay to determine.

It is, I hope, not necessary to say how thoroughly I sympathize with Mr, Balfour's purpose, and how entirely I admire the motives of his book and the ability by which it is everywhere distinguished. As one whose work and interests lie altogether in the domain of theology, I would welcome the incursion into it of this brilliant amateur. For so far as it relates to theology, properly so-called, it is an amateur's book, and as such it ought to be judged. It is difficult, for example, to conceive that any one whose knowledge was first-hand, especially if possessed of a philosophic and scientific mind, could have written the note on pp. 278-9 as to the decisions of the early Church relative to the doctrine of the Trinity. The very thing that the creeds were not, was " the negation of explanations." They were framed by men who had elaborated doctrines which were theories concerning the highest mysteries, and their decisions were definitions which were expressly intended to affirm their own and exclude other and opposed doctrines. The symbols both of Nicæa, and Chalcedon are distinguished by terms as strictly technical as any terms in either philosophy or science ; and, indeed, the great struggle at Nicæa, which it needed all the subtlety of Athanasius and all the authority of the Emperor to overcome, was against the introduction into a symbol of terms and phrases which had been coined and used in the schools, but had not hitherto been sanctioned by the Church. In other words, the terms were exactly what Mr. Balfour says they were not—"of the nature of explanations"; they expressed theories, embodied definitions, affirmed one doctrine and denied another, and were for this very reason introduced, and for the same reason strenuously resisted. But if in historical theology he shows the mind and art of the amateur, it must not be understood to mean that his appearance as a philosophical theologian is held to be unwarranted. On the contrary, there is no field of inquiry where a fresh and well-disciplined mind may be of more real service, especially if he be in thought and language neither derivative nor conventional. And there are sections or borders of the field where a man of Mr. Balfour's knowledge and speculative capacity is absolutely in place ; and it is with such a section that his book is mainly concerned. The men who are in this field, as it were, common day labourers, may well feel cheered and exhilarated at the appearance amongst them of an occasional workman so effective in form and so dexterous in the use of his tools as is this last comer, who so happily combines the capacities of the philosopher and the statesman.

Mr. Balfour well defines his initial position, which also implies the function he is best able to fulfil, in the sentence : " The decisive battles of theology are fought beyond its frontiers. It is not over purely religious controversies that the cause of religion is lost or won. The judgments we shall form on its special problems are commonly settled for us by our general mode of looking at the Universe." [1]   This, of course, means that theology is implicit in philosophy, or philosophy explicit in theology. As the late Sir William Hamilton used to say, every question which emerges in theology has before emerged in philosophy. So the philosopher can render no greater service to theology than the discussion in his own free way and province of those principles which determine its problems. But I wonder that Mr. Balfour failed to feel how fatal to his theological purpose is his want of an explicit philosophy. Without a positive philosophy how is a positive theology possible ? The " mode of looking at the universe " which is to determine our attitude to theology, will not be created by a negative criticism of philosophical or scientific ideas ; this is more likely to leave us in an attitude of vacant expectancy, where perception is blind and conception empty, than in one of intelligent receptivity. One may deeply sympathize with Mr.

---

[1] *The Foundations of Belief*, pp. 2, 3.

Balfour's purpose, and be all the more deeply regretful that he has, by his peculiar method, done so much to defeat it. But this is to anticipate a criticism which has still to be made good.

The book, though divided into four parts, really falls into three main divisions, which we may distinguish as the critical, the transitional, and the positive or constructive. In the critical, Mr. Balfour discusses and dismisses as philosophically inadequate both the empirical and the transcendental theories of knowing and being, especially as regards those ideas which are held to be the assured and necessary principles for the interpretation of man and nature. In the transitional he discovers and emphasizes what he holds to be a group of neglected factors in the formation of belief. In the positive, he attempts a provisional justification and unification of beliefs. What is to be here said will deal with these three divisions in succession.

§ II. *The Critical Philosopher as Positive Theologian*

1. The critical discussion, which runs irregularly through the entire book, though it is more systematically dealt with in Parts I. and II., is applied to four provinces—two philosophical, empiricism and transcendental idealism—and two theological, the older rationalism and its corrective yet counterpart, the older apologetic and rationalistic orthodoxy. The latter two need not concern us, though they are perhaps more kindly handled than as tendencies

historically effete they altogether deserved to be. Nor need we concern ourselves with the discussion on Transcendental Idealism. It is not very serious and in no respect thorough, nor is it marked by the author's usual subtlety and grasp; while it really stands outside the argument, which has not been "arranged" "with overt or tacit reference to that system" (p. 6). Only two things need be said: (1) Mr. Balfour fails to recognize the conspicuous services this Idealism has rendered to the cause he champions; and the recognition might very well have been associated with the name of the late Professor T. H. Green, whose position is mainly here criticized. To see what these services have been, we have only to remember the controversies of from twenty to twenty-five years ago, when, under the impulse given to pamphysicism by evolution, agnosticism became belligerent and constructive; and the doctrine that "matter had the promise and potency of every form and quality of life," was preached with eloquent assurance from the chair of the British Association— and then compare that most electrical atmosphere with the very different "psychological climate" we now enjoy. If to-day our empirics cultivate a modesty which was then unknown, if they are more conscious of the limitations and impotence of their physico-metaphysical theories, it is largely due to the criticism of the Idealism which is here so cavalierly dismissed. (2) This Idealism is not to be understood from the subjective point of view emphasized by Mr.

Balfour. He fails to apprehend its objective significance, its ability to explain those problems in the
history of mind which remain in his hands the most
hopeless of puzzles. The one philosophy which has
done even approximate justice to the religions of man
and the nature by which they are, certainly deserved
juster treatment in a book concerned with the
"foundations of belief." It reveals, at least, an imperfect sense of the gravity and range of the most
serious attempt yet made to solve these problems.

2. But the author's serious and perfectly tireless
criticism is concentrated on what he terms "Naturalism."[1] His dexterity in dealing with it is marvellous; he argues against it, he examines its psychological data, analyzes its logical principles and
processes, tests it by man, measures it by nature, and
finds it, in all its fundamental doctrines, either impossible, or unveracious, or self-contradictory. Its creed
is composed of two elements: "The one *positive*,
consisting, broadly speaking, of the teaching contained in the general body of the natural sciences;
the other *negative*, expressed in the doctrine that
beyond these limits, wherever they may happen to lie,
nothing is, and nothing can be, known."[2] One would
have expected him to be rather more careful in his
definition. What is here described as the positive
element does not belong to Naturalism in any special
or even in any tolerable sense at all; and what is
termed the negative is really the only positive

---

[1] p. 6.   [2] p. 92.

element.   For what constitutes " Naturalism " but the
affirmation that beyond the limits of nature, as it
exists to sense, " nothing is, and nothing can be,
known "?   The " Natural Sciences " have nothing to
do with it; it existed before they were as they
are now; they exist now where it is denied; it
exists to-day where they are known only in
part.[1]   Nobody knows better than Mr. Balfour
that the most distinguished names in Natural Science
are those of men as averse to " Naturalism " as he
himself is.   And this double definition was an argumentative as well as an historical blunder; it forces
him to become, as it were, a scientific agnostic, in
order that he may the better refute metaphysical
agnosticism; and to become a fictitious character is
certainly not the most effectual way of ending fiction.
Nor is he a happy warrior who in battle strikes at
friends as well as foes; in the result he may slay
what he most of all wishes to save alive.

The Naturalism he thus defines he discusses from
two points of view: the personal and practical, and
the psychological and speculative.   Under the first
aspect, he shows its insufficiency to man as an ethical,
æsthetic, and rational being.   This is, to my thinking,
his far most satisfactory piece of work; for it I have
nothing but praise.   In Part I., which deals with it,
his dialectical and literary qualities are seen at their

---

[1] That Mr. Balfour is perfectly well aware of the distinction
is obvious (see p. 134); but in his reasoning he often allows it
to seem as if he forgot it.

best. Under the second aspect he shows that Naturalism is psychologically unjustified and speculatively incoherent; its theory of knowing contradicts its theory of being. His arguments are not new; they are the commonplaces of transcendental criticism; but they are vigorously put and strikingly illustrated and applied. The experience which supplies Naturalism with its premisses, is not a thing of nature;[1] nor are these premisses in the strict sense true to nature. "The most immediate experiences carry with them no inherent guarantee of their veracity." "Habitual inaccuracy" attends "the cognitive leap through perception to object." "Our perceptions, regarded as psychological results," are, "regarded as sources of information, not merely occasionally inaccurate, but habitually mendacious."[2] As a consequence, "science owes its being to an erroneous view as to what kind of information it is that our experiences directly convey to us."[3] Nay, more, "Out of a succession of individual experiences, such a fundamental scientific principle as causation cannot be "reasonably extracted."[4] The conclusion therefore is—"A philosophy which depends for its premisses in the last resort upon the particulars revealed

---

[1] p. 108. [2] p. 111.

[3] p. 118. Cf. *Philosophic Doubt*, p. 287. "Science is a system of belief which, for anything we can allege to the contrary, is wholly without proof. The inferences by which it is arrived at are erroneous; the premisses on which it rests are unproved." [4] p. 119.

to us in perceptive experience alone, is one that
cannot rationally be accepted." [1]

Now, why this elaborate analysis and refutation of
empiricism? It serves various ends, negative and
positive. It is only by "an effectual criticism of
empiricism" that Naturalism can be effectually destroyed,[2] and the admission compelled that we are
"as yet without a satisfactory philosophy." [3] Doubts
are started "as to the theoretic validity of certain uni-
versally accepted beliefs," [4] in order that a scientific
standard may cease to be used as "sole test of truth." [5]
Beliefs that are so open to doubt cannot be logically
held to make other beliefs doubtful; the weapon
sceptical criticism has blunted, has lost its power to
kill or even to wound. The result is that our ethical
and religious ideas have nothing to fear at the hands
of those termed scientific; their provinces differ, and,
as regards the right to be, the one class has no advantage over the other. They are in many respects
parallel, yet, in a sense, inter-independent. "Philosophic Doubt" as to "an independent outer world" is
possible; but "for all practical purposes" the belief in
it "should be accepted with a credence which is immediate and unwavering." [6] Similarly doubt may be
possible as to theological and ethical beliefs; yet they
ought to be accepted as necessary to the satisfaction
of human needs and the regulation of conduct. Both

---

[1] p. 133.   [2] p. 134.   [3] pp. 246, 247.   [4] p. 246.
[5] p. 235.   [6] p. 238.

classes of belief are alike "symbolic"; "the world as represented to us by science, can no more be perceived or imagined than the Deity as represented by theology."[1] Our idea of Deity is no more anthropomorphic than our idea of the external world.[2] Our knowledge of matter is no more direct than our knowledge of Deity.[3] So ideas that are alike symbolic and alike open to sceptical criticism agree in a kind of unity ; neither can claim pre-eminence or be used to discredit or disprove the other.

3. The cogency of the criticism is undeniable ; its usefulness, within limits and properly balanced and qualified, may be undoubted ; but what precisely does it accomplish in Mr. Balfour's hands, and how does it serve his purpose in regard to the "foundations of belief"? He himself recognizes its thoroughly sceptical character, not only so far as empirical theory but even so far as fundamental scientific ideas are concerned.[4] His two books are indeed models of mordant scepticism. He has said of his earlier book that "the title has attracted more interest than the contents,"[5] but the title is hardly just to the contents or their interest. It is not so much a "defence of philosophic doubt" as critical doubt of all the philosophies. These two are not only different, but almost opposite things ; "philosophic doubt" is more posi-

---

[1] *Philosophic Doubt*, p. 245.   [2] *Ib.*, p. 246.   [3] *Ib.*, p. 258.
[4] *F. B.*, pp. 245, 246 ; cf. *Philosophic Doubt*, pp. 287, 293.
[5] *Essays and Addresses*, p. 284.

tive in character than doubt of philosophy. Hume is
the typical exponent of "philosophic doubt," but he
is in some respects much more positive and even
constructive than Mr. Balfour. He accepted the
current philosophical doctrine of his day: Locke's
"ideas of sensation," Berkeley's "ideas of sense," were
his "impressions"; while, we may add in passing, the
familiar "phenomena" of our contemporary thought,
and Mr. Herbert Spencer's "vivid manifestations of
the unknown," may be regarded as their living representatives, if not strict equivalents. Locke's "ideas
of reflection," Berkeley's "ideas of imagination," were
Hume's "ideas," which were echoes or reminiscences
of the impression, true in the measure that they repeated it, false in the degree they omitted any feature
of their original. Now, Hume did not trouble himself with Descartes' speculative deduction of being
from thought, with his innate ideas and occasional
causes; nor with Spinoza's substance with its two
attributes of extension and thought; nor with Leibnitz's monads and pre-established harmony, or his
pregnant hint that the intellect was needed to interpret
the impressions which the senses conveyed in from
without. On the contrary, he resolutely left philosophical criticism alone ; and, assuming the premises of
the home or native philosophy, turned to the problem
they set him. He saw quite as clearly as our author
sees, that if "impressions" were ultimate, the origin
of all knowledge and its only authentic elements,
then those fundamental beliefs by which we inter-

preted both man and nature had no warrant in reason. Every "impression" was of a single or individual thing, a subjective experience which could tell nothing of the reality or nature of the objective world, its system or coherence, its causation or continuity, or of the continued personal being of the subjective. What caused and what experienced the "impressions" were alike unknown: nor were we endowed by nature with any faculty or instrument sufficient for their discovery. But Hume was at once too subtle and too speculative to remain satisfied with so purely negative a conclusion; and so he boldly essayed to explain how beliefs that had no warrant from nature yet naturally came to be. His problem was twofold: How did a fleeting succession of subjective "impressions" come to suggest and to seem a permanent and ordered outer world? And how could a stream of ideas in perpetual flux, and succeeding each other with inconceivable rapidity, come to bear the appearance of a continuous personal and conscious self? The solution lay in the mystic words "association" and "custom"; association was personal, individual, the tendency to join together in thought things perceived together in sense, to conceive as inseparable, objects invariably associated in perception; but custom was collective — association worked into a habit at once common and personal. Now, Hume's scepticism, so construed, cannot, whatever we may think of its intellectual or philosophical validity, be denied a positive character. His formation of ideas or beliefs by association or custom, whether arbitrary, illicit, or accidental, was a philosophic theory of knowledge adapted to a special, though current and common, psychology.   His speculative sincerity may be doubted, even when his speculative genius is admired;[1] but his philosophy was a theory intended to account for beliefs which, however unreal, had all the appearance and served all the purposes of realities.   But Mr. Balfour, while more critical, is less positive than Hume.   He may not be sceptical in his results; but he is so much so in his argumentative process as to leave us without any premisses that can justify his conclusions.   His book is the work of a man who has "always found it easier to satisfy himself of the insufficiency of Naturalism than of the absolute sufficiency of any" other system of thought;[2] and what he gives is cogent destructive criticism, unredressed by any equally cogent constructive argument.   In other words, he vindicates his own principles by invalidating those of other people; but he does not explicate or justify the principles on which he builds his superstructure, or discover the basis on which they ultimately rest.   Hume was sceptical both in his premisses and in his conclusion, though positive in his method; but Mr. Balfour, though positive in his conclusion, is negative in his method, and uncritical as to his premisses.   He dismisses, by a

---

[1] *Foundations of Belief,* p. 96.   Cf. *Philosophic Doubt,* pp. 85, 86.   [2] *Foundations of Belief,* p. 92.

searching critical process, our current philosophies, empirical and transcendental; then confesses he has no effectual substitute to offer·; and finally offers a provisional theory for the unification of beliefs which throws into the most startling relief all the sceptical elements in his own criticism.

4. This criticism need not perhaps be further elaborated, but it is necessary that its precise point and purpose be not missed. There is no complaint that Mr. Balfour's criticism of empiricism is destructive; the more thorough he can make it in this respect the more wholesome will it be. The objection is to its purely sceptical character; it creates doubt, it does nothing more. It does not make the formation of belief more intelligible, the process of knowledge more conceivable, its results more real, or its conclusions more trustworthy. It involves all these things in deeper doubt; it turns the relation of mind to nature and of nature to mind into a hopeless maze, and creates suspicion as to the truth and reality of knowledge. And this cannot be done at one point of our intellectual being without affecting every other. Scepticism is a double-edged weapon, and very dangerous in audacious hands. If faith in one class of beliefs is broken down, the result is more likely to be that all classes will suffer than that any one class will specially benefit. Doubt of the veracity of mind in its simplest operations, has a subtle way of becoming doubt all round. Certainly faith is not made more possible by the processes and products of mind being

24

made less intelligible and real. The want of a
constructive philosophy, an architectonic idea and
method, is a fatal want in a book which aims at the
conservation of belief. Descartes' universal doubt
was not doubt, and was not universal; it was a process of digging down to what the thinker believed to
be solid rock, in order that he might build upon
thought a system which thought could clearly conceive : *i.e.*, the critical process was necessary to the
architectural purpose—was, indeed, the first stage in
its realization. So, too, the Transcendental Idealism,
which is here so episodically criticized, may handle
Empiricism quite as caustically as our author ; but it
does so that it may discover the real factors or positive conditions of knowledge. Its aim is to make the
universe more intelligible to man, and man more intelligible to himself; to show the subjective reason
and the objective rationality in such reciprocal action
and correspondence as to make the process of knowledge a solution of the problem of being. The theory
may be true or it may be false, but, at least, it is
positive : for it so uses the transcendental factor in
knowledge, viz., the interpreting reason, as to discover
and determine the real ultimate of being, viz., the interpreted reason, and to make the thought which unites
these a veracious and rational process. But Mr.
Balfour's method is purely sceptical; he leaves mind
bewildered in the face of nature, unable to trust its
perceptions, unable to determine what is truth, unable
to feel any reality in knowledge. By this means he

may have made the fundamental ideas of science too doubtful to be used against faith ; but what is the only logical deduction possible from the principles which he has used his sceptical method to obtain? Why, this :—Since error creeps into all our thought, and uncertainty surrounds all our knowledge of nature, how can we know that there is any truth anywhere, in any premiss or in any argument, any certainty in any knowledge, any reality in any belief? If such be the result of his sceptical criticism, where is the advantage to faith ? For what does it represent in thought save the method of the blind Samson, who sacrificed himself in order that he might the more effectually bury the Philistines under the ruins of their own temple ?

§ III. *The Philosophy of Theology*

So far we have been concerned with what may be termed fundamental philosophical theory ; we have now to proceed to its application to religious or theological belief.

1. And here I may say, Mr. Balfour seems to me to have no adequate sense of the range and complexity of the problem he has set for himself ; *that* is nothing less than to find a positive philosophy of religious beliefs. And this he is all the more bound to find, that his destructive criticism has been so merciless and so complete. But this problem cannot be discussed simply as if it were a matter of individual experience, or a question of con-

temporary thought. There is nothing at once so universal and so particular, so uniform and so varied, as religion. Man everywhere possesses and professes it, yet it is never in any two countries, with any two peoples, or even any two persons, exactly the same thing. There are, therefore, two distinct yet cognate questions : Why are religious beliefs at once so invariable and so varied ? Why do they everywhere emerge, and yet everywhere assume some specific local form ? It is evident that the special function of the philosophy of religion is to explain at once why religious belief is so universal and uniform, and . religious beliefs so multiform and varied. The causes that produce it must be common and continuous in their action ; but the conditions that produce variation, local and occasional. The creative factor can never cease to operate, otherwise the belief would cease to live ; and were the modifying conditions to become inactive, all beliefs would tend to a monotony of character or sameness of form. The one question is wholly philosophical, the other is partly philosophical and partly historical ; and taken .together they signify that the only scientific and satisfactory method of enquiry and discussion is the constant correlation of the permanent factor of belief with its varying forms, in order to the discovery of the reason at once of its continuous life and constant change. Now, what one most of all misses in this book is the sense that there is such a problem, that it is initial to all philosophical theology, that

till it be discussed neither the bed nor the material
for any foundation for belief has been found. One
is surprised to find Mr. Balfour distinguishing as
he does between "causes" and "reasons" of belief;
in the only sense tolerable in such a discussion,
"causes" are "reasons," and reason is cause. In a
scientific theory of the genesis of knowledge we find
its justification; in a philosophical explanation of
the origin of belief we have its vindication. The
very process which, consciously and analytically pursued by the individual, justifies his theism, produces,
when spontaneously and synthetically pursued by
the race, the beliefs which have organized and built
up its religions.

But we must take Mr. Balfour on his own terms;
we have no right to demand his acceptance of ours.
Well, then, let us grant that his sceptical criticism
has been completely victorious; empiricism is vanquished, and its scientific ideas so paralyzed that
they can no longer be used as tests or standards to
determine the credibility or incredibility of theological beliefs. What then? The beliefs are *there*.
What are they? How did they come to be? How
are they to be justified? He has proved scientific
ideas to be so incapable of proof as to be without
normative value or force in the ethical and religious
realm, but he has not proved theological beliefs to
be true; on the contrary, he has pursued a method
which compels us to approach them in an attitude
of doubt or even negation. The radical scepticism

which has created doubt of one class of beliefs, has
created a presumption against the truth of the other
class. But what do we find here? A sudden re-
versal of the method before pursued, and no attempt
made to compel the beliefs to give an account of
themselves, to justify their being, or to examine their
form and contents in the light of their source. The
whilom sceptic becomes curiously credulous, while
he skilfully does not see the questions which he can
neither discuss nor answer frankly and explicitly;
but he offers an instructive substitute for a discussion. There is a titular inquiry into the " Causes
of Experience."[1] What are these "causes"? The
most diligent search through the book has left me
still with the question, but without any answer.
This, of course, may be purely my fault, but the fruits
of the search are worth recording. " Naturalism " is
dismissed; what, then, is to be our system? Not
dualism, "a natural world immediately subject to
causation, and a spiritual world immediately subject
to God." This is "a patchwork scheme of belief,"
" a rough and ready expedient" for escaping from
"the rigid limits of a too narrow system," excellent
in a measure, and not to be hastily condemned, but
clearly a system in which many find it "difficult or
impossible to acquiesce."[2] To those who " ask for
a philosophy which shall give rational unity to an
adequate creed " he answers, " I have it not to give."[3]

---

[1] Part III. chap. i.   [2] pp. 186, 187.   [3] pp. 187, 188.

Instead, "provisionally restricting himself to the scientific point of view," he forbears "to consider beliefs from the side of proof," and "surveys them for a season from the side of origin only, and in relation to the causes which gave them birth."[1] This is excellent; the best philosophy of belief is an adequate theory of its origin, though we note that the forbearance from proof is here logical, or rather inevitable; the sceptical criticism had made any other course simply impossible, especially any course involving rational proof. What, then, is the cause or origin of "the apparatus of belief" (a most significant phrase) "which we find actually connected with the higher scientific, social, and spiritual life of the race"?[2] The causes are many, "presuppose the beliefs of perception" (the very perception which had been proved so habitually inaccurate and mendacious), "memory, and expectation in their elementary shape," and "an organism fitted for their hospitable reception by ages of ancestral preparation." We may note, in passing, how empirical and scientific this mode of speech is; but "these conditions" (not *causes*, it will be seen), "are clearly not enough"; there must be "an appropriate environment," and within this is "a group of causes" (not conditions), "so important in their collective operation" as to demand "detailed notice." The name of this group is "authority," and our immediate concern is with it as "a non-rational cause of belief."

[1] p. 188.　　[2] p. 193.

2. Now, our first question here is, What does Mr. Balfour mean by "Authority"? It is a large word, denotes varied things, connotes many ideas. It has one sense in literature, another in science, another in law, still another in religion; in the realm of opinion it denotes the right to define and the power to enforce belief; in the sphere of action, the right to prescribe conduct and to exact obedience. It has been conceived as both personal and impersonal, vested in the one case in a society like the church, or in a body of beliefs like tradition, or a written word like the Sacred Scriptures; or, in the other case, in either an invisible Head like our Lord, or in a visible head like the Pope. Now, in what sense does Mr. Balfour use the term? He says it is "a word which transports us into a stormy tract of speculation nearly adjacent to theology";[1] it may be too much to say it "has been for three centuries the main battlefield of new thoughts and old," but we can contrast it with reason, its "rival and oppo-nent."[2] "We are acted upon by authority," but when "we reason" we act, we produce.[3] When it is so described we seem to be dealing with authority in its special religious sense, as legislative over opinion, and judicial as regards conduct; but this soon turns out to be a mistake. For under one aspect it is the *Zeitgeist*, the spirit of the age; then it appears as a "psychological atmosphere," or

---

[1] p. 194.   [2] pp. 195, 219.   [3] p. 203.

"climate," favourable to some, unfavourable to other beliefs ;[1] then it assumes the shape of "custom, education, public opinion, family, party, or Church " ;[2] in a, for Mr. Balfour, curious antithesis, "the equities of reason " are opposed to " the expediencies of authority " ;[3] and finally, it is said to "stand for that group of non-rational causes, moral, social, and educational, which produces its results by psychic processes other than reasoning,"[4] and in this sense it is contrasted with " Papal infallibility."[5] What, then, does he mean by "authority"? Why, exactly what Hume meant by "custom"; what Mr. Spencer might describe as the accumulated and transmitted experience of the race, of the State, or of the family. It is an explanation of belief by means of a "non-rational cause";[6] in Hume's phrase, it is "belief engendered upon custom," which custom he would, in turn, have termed the creation of " a certain kind of accident"—*i.e.*, a result which was " non-rational," or for which he could give no reason. We may understand why Hume should tell us that the "ultimate cause of the impression is perfectly inexplicable by human reason," that reason itself is only

---

[1] p. 206.　[2] p. 213.　[3] p. 215.　[4] p. 219　[5] pp. 223 ff.

[6] In *Philosophic Doubt* Mr. Balfour seemed prepared to apply his theory to theological as well as to other beliefs : " The progress of knowledge has led us rather to diminish our estimate of the part which reasons as opposed to other causes have played in the formation of creeds ; for it has shown that these reasons are themselves the results of non-rational antecedents," pp. 200, 201.

"an unintelligible instinct," that "belief is an act of
the mind arising from custom," which is "the foundation of all our judgments "—for *that* was scepticism
logically applied to all classes of beliefs. But what
we do not understand is how custom, though transmuted into "authority," should be able to save one
class of beliefs, while criticism is free to inflict upon
another the sentence of intellectual death. What
seems plain is that Mr. Balfour has, by emptying
the reason, or normal nature of man, of all constructive ideas, emptied it also of all the higher beliefs,
and so has to invent a special agency or method for
their introduction.   In other words, the sceptical
criticism has evoked its inevitable Nemesis—*i.e.*, has
divorced thought as completely from God as perception from the realities of nature ; and so has made,
in Mr. Balfour's own words, "certitude the child of
custom,"[1] only custom has undergone baptism and
appears as "authority," the demure mother of Christian beliefs.

3. Now, on this very curious theory, which is also
most instructive, especially so far as it illustrates
Mr. Balfour's own mind and attitude to theology, I
have some criticisms to offer.

i. What is the "reason" to which "authority" is
here opposed ?   It seems to be not so much
"reason," as ratiocination. The use and interchange
of terms in this chapter is indeed a perplexing, but

---

[1] p 164.

highly educative study. We have "reason," "we
reason"; "reasoning," gliding out and in of sentences
and taking each other's places as if they were strict
synonyms. Now ratiocination may denote an activity
or exercise or process of the reason, but it is not
reason; and is in no sense the antithesis of authority,
under which, as scholasticism shows, it may live and
operate with quite preternatural acuteness and success. If these opposed terms had been carefully
discriminated and defined, we should have been
spared this chapter.

ii. It is curious that the author, in dealing with a
matter so fundamental to his argument, should never
raise the question, how this authority, or custom, or
group of causes "of psychic processes," acting within
our psychological environment, came to be. To
what kind or class of factors or agencies does it owe
its existence? He describes it as "a non-rational
cause of belief": but what is it itself—a creation of
reason, a result of purpose, or a non-rational effect of
a non-rational cause? If reason made it, how can it
be truly described as "a non-rational cause of belief"?
If reason did not make it, what did? Accident or
chance? But these terms denote the worst sort of
Agnosticism; they are the kind of words which a
moment of puzzled incompetence surprised out of
sceptic Hume, and so they are alien to the mind
which comes to lead us into the inner court of theology. The question as to the source or cause of the
authority is determinative of its nature and character.

One would think that if it be a "rational effect," it could not be a "non-rational cause" of a thing so rational as ethical and religious belief. And the greater the function authority has in history and in the formation of mind, the less can we conceive it as a non-rational factor of rational things ; otherwise the forces which govern man will cease to be either theistic or ethical. And the puzzlement is increased by some of Mr. Balfour's own phrases. His "authority" assumes various most rational forms ; "the spirit of the age," which is just the intellectual atmosphere created by its living thought ; parental discipline, which is surely the action of rational will upon rational will ; education, which is the more mature acting by means of rational instruments on the less mature mind ; custom, which is a mode of intelligent action become habitual and common.[1] What acts under these forms and conditions is surely incorrectly described as "a non-rational cause of belief." The phrase seems, therefore, to me either insignificant or absurd. If what is here termed authority, viz., our organized ethical ideals, intellectual habits, and social instincts in their organizing action, have a rational cause—and unless this be granted we depose Providence for accident—then it must be rational when it becomes a cause of beliefs. And, whatever their cause, what are beliefs? Non-

---

[1] Mr. Balfour in one place explains "authority" by "the non-rational action of mind on mind" (p. 238). Sentences of this order cause one's ideas to get a little mixed.

rational effects? If so, what are the things whose being Mr. Balfour would justify, but blind creations of a blind cause, which man must with his growth in reason get progressively rid of?

iii. It is also curious that Mr. Balfour did not raise the question as to the relation of the individual to these beliefs of non-rational origin. Man is ever modifying his environment by his action on it; which means that this so-called authority is ever in process of change, being, as it were, ever called to account and compelled to adapt itself to the new mind and its new forms of belief or modes of thought; and this further means that the person whom the authority forms, in turn reforms the authority. For the life of the belief is quite as significant as its origin. If its origin is non-rational, it lives its life in a rational medium, and has to accept the conditions under which life there is possible. And surely it is more philosophical to bring the causes of the origin and the conditions of the maintenance of life into harmony, than to set them at war with each other. We must also remember that the life of the belief within the reason ever acts as a modifying force on the environment. Mr. Balfour knows the distinction which the Roman jurists drew between *jus naturale* and *jus civile*, and the use they made of the former to affect the latter. The *jus civile* was statutory, established and fixed law—so to speak, the actual legal environment; the *jus naturale* was ideal, the principle of justice and equity immanent in the man,

yet, with the progress of his ethical culture, growing
ever more articulate.   And the great jurists of the
second and third centuries, who were also for the
most part Stoics, so applied the ideal of law within,
to the actual law without, as to compel the actual to
embody the ideal, at least in as perfect a degree as
we are ever likely to see in time.   And precisely the
same action is ever going on in the region of belief.
Whatever may be its origin, thought is a potent
factor in its modification ; and on its harmony with
thought its continued life depends.   A "non-rational
cause" is no explanation of the being of a rational
thing ; and we may be certain that in the last
analysis the real source can never be different in
kind from the cause which secures continuance.

iv. The most curious point of all is this : Mr.
Balfour never raises the question as to whether the
authority which causes the belief justifies the belief it
causes.   This surely was for his purpose the most
vital point in his problem ; apart from it, his cause
was without character or logical function.   The real
question he set himself to answer was this : What
are we to think of Christian theology and the principles on which it is built?   It is not any or every
religious belief that he seeks to justify ; it is our
specifically Christian beliefs.   He has made his
appeal to authority, which is "the spirit of the age,"
our "psychological climate," public opinion, custom,
family, party, Church ; but these are all the most
variable of things.   Our "psychological climates" are

more numerous, varied, and changeable than our
geographical ; the extremes are greater, the grada-
tions steeper, and the variations more sudden. Mr.
Balfour is a statesman as well as a philosopher, and
he will not think me impertinent if the point be
illustrated by his own position and experience. He
is by descent and family a Scotchman, but by education and political place an Englishman ; the "psychological climate" in Scotland is Presbyterian ; in
England, Episcopalian : does his double nationality
duplicate his beliefs? Does it justify his being a
Calvinist and Presbyterian north of the Tweed, an
Arminian and an Anglican south of it? Are the
proper beliefs of a man those of his "psychological
climate?" or is this "climate" a justification for the
beliefs? or has it no significance for their character?
But this is an innocent comparison, involving what
may be thought no very radical difference. Well,
then, Mr. Balfour, as a statesman, has helped to
govern India ; and he may one day be at home the
responsible minister for it, or even go out there to be
the representative of his Sovereign. Its "psychological climate," customs, education, public opinion—
in a word, "authority"—is very unlike ours : what of
the beliefs it causes? What is their truth, their
validity, their value and warrant? The question is
not simply curious ; it is vital. If authority is invoked to explain belief, how do the beliefs it explains
stand related to theology and theological truth? Is
religion to become a theory of "climate?" And is

all idea of a religion true for all places, all times, and all men, to be allowed to fall to the ground? This would be indeed a strange result to follow from a philosophically conservative attempt to lay " the foundations of belief." Yet it recalls the attempt of another conservative and sceptical philosopher to make the " psychological " coincide with the civil or national, if not with the geographical, climate ; it exactly repeats the theory of Hobbes, with impersonal authority substituted for the personal king. We were not surprised at it in his case, for he had a frankness which was so blunt as to leave no room for surprise ; but we do wonder at finding it in so acute a critic of " Naturalism," and so strenuous an upholder of theology, as Mr. Arthur Balfour.

§ IV. *The Theology of the Philosopher*

But it is more than time we passed to the constructive part of the work, if constructive it can be called. Here it is more difficult to criticize, for the points of agreement and difference are in these later chapters so intricately intermixed. His argument has about it the waywardness of genius ; it halts in unexpected places, turns back upon itself, breaks into felicitous asides, diverges into delightsome by-paths The book indeed is redeemed by its digressions ; without them it would have seemed a mere exercise in cunning sword-play, but with them it has all the appearance of an army of victorious arguments marching into the battle. Were battles won by gallant bearing, gay banners, and martial music, our author would deserve to be saluted as a victor indeed.

What, then, is the method and principle of the constructive argument? It starts with the provisional scheme for the unification of beliefs; and here the definition of faith is significant. "Faith or assurance, which, if not in excess of reason, is at least independent of it, seems to be a necessity in every great department of knowledge which touches on action."[1] In this sense it belongs in an equal degree, at once to science and theology, to ethics and religion; and while the belief in an outer world is more universal and inevitable than any single religious belief, yet "these peculiarities have no import. They exist, but they are irrelevant." For man is a being of needs as well as of sense-perceptions; and his needs require ethical ideals and religious beliefs for their satisfaction. And just as in every belief which has its origin in perception, we assume some kind of harmony between ourselves and the outer universe; so a like harmony ought to be assumed between "that universe and our higher needs."[2] What strikes one in this rather rudimentary equation of beliefs, is its unreasoned character, indeed the utterly illogical and unphilosophical procedure by which it has been accomplished. Nothing could be more different than the measure which is meted out to the two orders of beliefs respectively. The one class has been analyzed, criticized, satirized,

---

[1] p. 240.   [2] p. 247.

beaten and buffeted in every possible way; the other class is allowed to enter without any kind of question, or any attempt to examine either its subjective warrant or objective validity. But this difference is a serious confession, either of the incompetence of the philosophy to justify the beliefs, or of the incapability of the beliefs to be justified. It is an acknowledgment that they cannot bear to be reasoned about, but live in a region of emotion or instinct, of feeling and impulse. This is of all positions the most intellectually dangerous, especially when the basis for it has been laid in philosophical scepticism. For feeling is an individual thing, living an unstable and dependent life, noble only as it is penetrated by the intellect and governed by the conscience. A distinguished German thinker, whose philosophy was even as Mr. Balfour's, described himself as a heathen according to the intellect, but a Christian according to the heart. And where such a schism has been introduced into the nature, the old heathen is certain to prove himself subtler and stronger than the young Christian.

Mr. Balfour, indeed, maintains that the relation between our "needs" and their satisfaction is not as "purely subjective in character" as that between "a desire and its fulfilment." The correspondence is that between "the immutable verities of the unseen world," and "these characteristics of our nature, which we recognize as that in us which, though not necessarily the strongest, is the highest."[1] But what are

----

[1] p. 248.

these "characteristics"? What faculty in us corresponds to verity in the universe? Is it not reason or thought, the faculty by which we know rather than feel? He had everything to gain by as free a use of the critical method on the source, the form, and the matter of religious beliefs, as on the basis and truth of scientific ideas; by his failure to use it he leaves to the beliefs an unjustified existence, introduces a hopeless schism between knowledge and faith, and tends to reduce religion to a mere consuetudinary and institutional system. Indeed, the notion that religion—though not religious ideas—is the creature of custom, the thing of "psychological atmosphere" or political "climate," is the historical correlative of his fundamental philosophy; and, though incompletely developed, it lurks in all the constructive parts of the book, notably in his theories of "authority" and of "beliefs and formulas."

But I would not part from the book and its author without expressing anew my admiration of its spirit, and of his purpose and endeavour. It is a remarkable achievement for a statesman; and gives to the State the happy assurance that a mind which may yet control its destinies, has visions of higher and more enduring things than the strife of parties, the collision of interests, or the jealousies of classes. We live by faith; and this faith is here often fitly and finely expressed. To his belief in a God capable of "preferential action"; in an inspiration "limited to no age, to no country, to no people"; in an incarnation which may transcend science, but is "the abiding place of the highest reality"; in Christianity, as a religion so "effectually fitted to minister to our ethical needs" as to be made even more credible by the mystery of evil, which it so forcibly recognizes that it may the more victoriously overcome—I entirely and heartily subscribe. My criticism has concerned not so much the end he has reached, as his mode of reaching it. The way of faith is in these days hard enough; it need not be made more difficult; and it becomes those who believe that the highest truth of reason is one with the highest object of faith, to make it clear that, in their view at least, a true theology can never be built on a sceptical philosophy, and that only the thought which trusts the reason can truly vindicate faith in the God who gave it.

April, 1895.

IX

SOME RECENT ENGLISH THEOLOGIANS

THE heaviest loss which theology has sustained within the past decade seems to me, even after the lapse of more than seven softening years, to have been the sudden and premature death of Edwin Hatch. Within his own communion more eminent churchmen, and scholars of equal or even higher name, have died ; but each, in a sense that was not at all true of Hatch, either had finished his work or was more a loss to his church than to theology. Lightfoot, a son of the same school, though of another university, only a month later followed him to the grave ; and he had by his learned labours built himself an enduring monument, worthy, alike as regards magnitude and quality, of the most heroic age of English scholarship. In the following year two distinguished churchmen died : Canon Liddon, whose fine piety and noble eloquence made him while he lived a potent influence both within and beyond the Anglican communion ; and Dean Church, who preferred to remain a dean when he might have been an archbishop, and who was perhaps more a

man of letters than a theologian, with the keen
literary temper, and a tense nature which the love
of the old humanities rather cultivated than subdued.
Two years later Hort died, leaving behind work
much less in quantity than Lightfoot's, but marked
by rarer and more stimulating qualities, and a band
of eager disciples, quickened to activity by regret at
the stores of knowledge and the energy of constructive thought which had perished with the master.
In 1893, about a year after Hort, death claimed
another victim, Benjamin Jowett, though he indeed
" came to the grave in a full age, like as a shock of
corn cometh in his season." He had made his name
in theology, but had for years forsaken what he had
found to be its unquiet ways for the serener atmosphere of classical scholarship and philosophy, and
had in consequence become, though in a narrower
region, an intenser and less resistible power, because
a power more intangible. He was the most distinguished figure in the Oxford of his day, the one name
that created a new mythology and attracted to itself
the most picturesque elements in the old, affecting
belief the more potently that his public silence and
his sphinx-like utterances in private compelled, in
order to the interpretation of his mind, a free use
of the young academic imagination. There was
indeed a peculiar pathos about his closing days ;
though he was a most social man, loving society and
loved by it, yet he was one of the loneliest of men.
He was the last Broad Churchman of the old school,

i.e., he was a Christian whose Church was the State, whose beliefs were more akin to humanism than to dogma and the creeds, œcumenical or particular, whose love was for civil society and sanctity ; while he feared priestly claims and despised the show and the make-believe of sacerdotal religion.   He was one of the rare characters who could be cynical without being bitter, who could be audacious in speech while he seemed most innocent and bland ; and, though he looked with a wonder, not untouched with pain, at the ancient comrades who had risen in the church by falling in the faith, he was yet able to retain affection even where he had ceased to feel intellectual respect. When he died, Oxford and England were the poorer for the loss of one who had served the church by being true to himself.

The two men we have described as " distinguished churchmen" lie outside the scope of this paper. Neither was, in the strict sense of the term, a theologian.   Canon Liddon was a man of strong religious convictions and eloquent speech ; he believed intensely, thought earnestly, and reasoned concerning his beliefs with a sort of impassioned logic that was very impressive when it had a large and strenuously sincere personality behind it.   But neither as thinker nor as critic and scholar did he make to the theology of his age any contribution that will outlast his personal influence.   And even before he died, his influence had, just because of his intellectual limitations, suffered, even within his own party in his own

church, what may be alternatively described as re-
striction or eclipse. He had built on tradition, and
when tradition manifestly failed as a basis of doctrine
and was forsaken by the more clear-sighted of his
pupils, he felt as if the whole structure of faith had
broken up beneath him. What we may term his
farewell to the pulpit was fitly spoken in St. Mary's,
Oxford, and was little else than a forlorn apology for
an impossible position. Dean Church, again, had
a keen and sympathetic intellect, a quick and assimilative mind, which came of his literary instincts and
made him the very converse of Liddon ; one capable
of appreciating new points of view, adopting and
adapting them to older forms of thought, and of
securing for them, by vigour and grace of exposition,
acceptance and recognition. He was by nature and
capacity a *Vermittler*, and he did his work with most
excellent discrimination. He understood Darwin
and appreciated evolution ; he had a critical intellect,
knew that criticism was inevitable, and saw how its
sting could be drawn by some of its results being
appropriated. And he wrote with the strength and
moderation of one who stood fast in the conviction,
that the old could best be preserved by taking to
itself as much of the new as it could absorb without
danger to its distinctive character and claims. But
most of his work was provisional and occasional, and
had a sort of periodical character about it ; as it was
done to meet an emergency, its significance passed
away with the emergency it satisfied. His essay on

Dante is perhaps the most perfect thing he ever did ; while his book on Anselm shows how he could write on a great theologian and find his theology—which, after all, was his great claim to name and fame—the least attractive or significant thing about him. What he achieved instead was a most genial appreciation of one churchman by another.

§ I. *The Cambridge Scholars and Divines*

We turn then to the four scholars who were theologians as distinguished from churchmen : and of them, two were typical of Cambridge, and two no less typical of Oxford. This is not a study in academic types ; but the difference in these universities is a basis for a classification which is not altogether unjust to character. It will be most convenient to begin with the Cambridge men. But we can hardly think of the two who have died, without thinking of a third, who, happily, still lives, though in a sphere which, unhappily, forbids the expectation of much further theological work from his hand.

1. Lightfoot, Westcott, and Hort represent the nearest thing to a triumvirate in learning any English university has known, at least in our century ; possibly too, the nearest approach to a distinct tendency or school, since the days of the Cambridge Platonists, Whichcote, Cudworth, and More. Each in his own way was a genuine son of his university, enhancing its reputation by embodying its historical

character and distinctive genius. Lightfoot was a
scholar whose learning recalled that of his illustrious
namesake of the seventeenth century; while his
energy in controversy and mastery of his weapons
reminded one now of Whitgift and now of Bentley.
He was, indeed, altogether too massive and sincere
to stoop to the arts and language of Elizabeth's
famous archbishop, though, in explanation, it ought
to be remembered that in these respects the distance
between the sixteenth and the nineteenth century
is simply immeasurable; and his manhood was too
large and sane and kindly to allow him to flay an
opponent in the merciless manner of *Phileleutherus
Lipsiensis*. He had, as his criticism of *Supernatural
Religion* showed, all Bentley's power to hit an opponent hard and straight, though, happily, without his
marvellous ingenuity in quarrelling with his friends
and provoking quarrels where he need have none. He
had, too, if not all his fine scholarship, yet his rare
critical genius, and, again happily, without the
eccentricity of mind that made the greatest English
scholar of his century the worst judge of English
literature.

Dr. Westcott we here think of as the Cambridge
professor with a very distinct message to his age, and
not as the Bishop of Durham. We now know that
he combines in a rare degree the natures of the
speculative and the practical man, the dreamer and
the realist, the intellect that can see visions and the
will that can realize the visions he has seen. But,

meanwhile, we forget the administrator and think only of the scholar, who seemed almost like a Cambridge Neo-Platonist strayed out of the seventeenth century into our own; yet with most characteristic differences. These we may indicate rather than define thus : He was a Neo-Platonist of the ecclesiastical rather than of the classical *Renaissance.* He did not so much seek to find the Church in philosophy as philosophy in the Church; he came to his Platonism through Clement and Origen, not through Plotinus and Numenius; and so it tended to be sacramental more than symbolical, to be allegorical in thought and expression, in art and history; which means that he was in intellect less rational than emotional and intuitive. His system, which is only another name for the attitude of his mind, was more Biblical than classical, deduced from John and the Hebrews, not from Plato and the Academy. But though the form was changed, yet it held the old spirit. The idealism was not the less real that it found its material in the Gospels and Epistles, instead of in philosophical treatises; and that it was developed in commentaries on the books of the New Testament, and not on all the mythologies.

Hort, again, was more the pure scholar and critic than either of the other two. And so he was too conscious of the possibilities of error and the limitations of knowledge, to reach the clear-cut and assured conclusions of Lightfoot; too much alive to the complexities of thought and the inadequacies of human speech, to be as prolific and facile a writer as Westcott. We know Hort, indeed, only from his works, and especially from his *Life and Letters*; but in this we are far from singular ; for it may be said of the men who knew him in the flesh and were thought to be his friends, that only one, his twin soul, or it may be two, knew him in any other way. Before fame had idealized him, and turned his very peculiarities into notes of distinction, he was to swift and obvious academic wit, but *Hortus siccus.* He has been described by the most competent of living hands, and a hand made competent no less by love and reverence for his memory than by knowledge of his work, as "our greatest English theologian of the century," yet as "a man of humble mind" and "inexorable sincerity." [1] If unable to accept without qualification all that is implied in the first statement, yet, as one who knew him only from afar, I may be allowed brief space for a few sentences of appreciation and regret. For his character and history appeal in a signal degree to a man whose main interests lie in theology. Academic distinction came earlier to the other two than to him ; and they had in due season the highest ecclesiastical preferment, which was, of course, in

---

[1] The Rev. Dr. Sanday, in the *American Journal of Theology*, pp. 95-117.

both cases unsolicited, and certainly not beyond their deserts; while Hort was never more than a humble parish priest, though no man appreciated more than he the dignity of his office. But he so used his quiet and comparative seclusion as to qualify himself for the very highest work—nay, to do work of the very highest order. There is safety for some men in an early escape from the university, especially if it be an escape to the obscurity where independence can be cultivated, congenial work undertaken, and the problems of the time wrestled with in a spirit and with a labour becoming their gravity. For my own part, I never know whether to congratulate or condole with a young scholar who gains a fellowship or holds a tutorship which keeps him up at the university. It may deprive him of the opportunity he needs to develop the best that is within him. The atmosphere of the common room may be stimulating, but it is not always bracing; and it may tend to the creation of that most impotent of tempers and most depressing of habits, academic conventionalism. It was thus a real gain to Hort that he for so long escaped not only promotion in the church but even office in the university. But in due season there came to him what may be described as an honour and an office which was all his own. He became the ideal of a band of younger scholars, a sort of unconscious mentor, a literary conscience which exacted independence, accuracy, and the patient

search for truth. We do not know any modern
English scholar who was so much a hero to scholars,
so progressively loved and admired and trusted. On
his immense resources the obscurest could draw, and
could be certain of meeting no repulse. His silence
was at once a cause of perplexity and a source of
power, for men wished that he would speak so as
to solve their problems, or to help them to a solution ; yet they felt that before the silence of one
who had inquired so long, who knew and had
thought so much, they could only cultivate the
reverence and the spirit he had so splendidly
exemplified. And so the young scholars he influenced are keeping his memory green by attempting
to become even such as he was, or such as he would
have approved.

2. What distinguished these men and made them
amid all their differences a unity, members of the
same family, or varieties of a single type, was the
formal attitude of their minds, or, in other words,
their apprehension of theology as a problem in
literature rather than in history. Of course their
attitude was not in all respects or at all points
uniform, but this was its general character. Lightfoot settled the Ignatian controversy for, at least,
our generation. That was his great achievement,
where his really great qualities showed themselves
in their most perfect form. His Clement and Polycarp are not unworthy to stand alongside his
Ignatius, though his work, especially as regards

Clement, was not so finished as he himself could have wished it to be. But as his distinguished successor has justly and soberly said—his edition of the *Apostolic Fathers* is "a monument of learning, sagacity, and judgment unsurpassed in the present age." [1] His *Pauline Epistles* are not nearly so successful ; there is often a curious hardness in his tone, his exegesis is not seldom marked by imperfect sympathy and defective insight. The man who was both by friendship and knowledge most capable of judging him, said of these Commentaries : " The prevailing characteristic is masculine good sense unaccompanied by either the insight or the delusion of subtlety." [2] In matters of thought he had what seems a very curious, but is a very common combination of qualities, a real love of positive dogma with little interest in the history of doctrine, or much real comprehension of its inner meaning. But it is in dealing with literary and critical questions, as distinguished from questions historical and exegetical, that his true power appears. He does not so much construe history, as compel us to find room in any future attempt at construction for documents he has proved to be authentic, and for the facts they describe. This, of course, must be taken as a general statement which admits of being variously qualified, as by the ability for historical criticism

---

[1] *The Apostolic Fathers*, pt. i.   Prefatory note, p. vi.
[2] Hort in *Dict. of National Biography*.

so clearly exhibited in his dissertation on *The
Christian Ministry*, and his remarkable and illuminative discussion of the martyrdom of Ignatius;
but in the broad sense it is, if not quite adequate,
yet true.

I have found it no easy thing to write these sentences concerning a man whose memory is so revered
and whose work is so pre-eminent in its own order;
but unless the limitations of the workman be recognized, his work is certain to be falsely valued. Dr.
Sanday, writing under the sense of recent loss, confessed that Lightfoot's mind was not naturally
"metaphysical," that he was without the "metaphysical fervour, the delight in the contemplation of
mysteries" combined "with strong, clear, logical
thinking," which distinguished Cyril of Alexandria.
"But few Englishmen have this; and Bishop Lightfoot was English to the backbone."[1] And with this
judgment Hort agreed. "Lightfoot," he said, "is
not speculative enough or eager enough to be a
leader of thought."[2] His "mental interests lay
almost exclusively in concrete facts or written words.
He never seemed to care for any generalization. No
one can with advantage be everything; and he
gained much by what was surely a limitation."[3]
Indeed, Lightfoot's mind was severe and rigorous,
and had a certain vigorous native belligerency, which

---

[1] *English Historical Review*, vol. v. p. 214.
[2] *Life and Letters of F. J. A. Hort*, vol. ii. p. 89.   [3] *Ibid.*, 410.

Hort described as "its correspondence to the prevalent English habit of mind, by which he gained enormously in ready access to English people of all sorts."[1] And these are the very qualities and limitations which stamped with its formal character all his work.

Westcott, on the other hand, has more of a mystical nature than Lightfoot, though it would be incorrect to say that he was more metaphysical. His mind has more affinity with literature and criticism than with philosophy and history. He is a contemplative rather than a speculative thinker. He is an idealist who loves the sources where he finds the lights that give him life; he is not a dialectician who loves to discover and follow and weave together the sequences of thought. It was real affinity that attracted him to " John "; a similar, though a less complete, affinity that drew him to " Hebrews." To his peculiar idealism Alexandria is more congenial than Athens, and the personal equation limits the insight and the range of his interpretative power. His mind can hardly be described as pellucid ; he loves the twilight which subdues the stronger colours and softens the harsher or more rigid outlines. In his discussions in literary or historical criticism he manages often to leave a sort of unsatisfied feeling, as if the mind had not got fairly face to face with the facts, but had instead

---

[1] *Life and Letters of F. J. A. Hort*, vol. ii. p. 411.

looked at them through a haze, which flooded the scene with more harmonizing effects than would have come from the pitiless light of day. But while as a thinker he appeals to a comparatively restricted class, as a textual critic, *i.e.*, in the region where he deals with the most formal and exact of all literary studies, he has as his audience the whole of the learned world. He can speak as a man of science, and classify and marshal his authorities, and where they are in conflict decide between them for reasons the competent can understand and will either approve or condemn. And so his great contribution, though it is not his alone, to the theology of the age—as pre-eminent in its own order as Lightfoot's great work was in its—is a Greek text of the New Testament. And the name which stands on the title-page indissolubly associated with his is Hort's. They were indeed *par nobile fratrum*, and the text which bears their joint names is the fit monument of their brotherhood. But the precedency in name and in honour will only be fully known and determined when the letters which passed between the two, while the work was in progress, have seen the light.

What has been said as to Westcott applies, *mutatis mutandis*, partially to Hort ; but it needs to be qualified by being enlarged. He was a man of rarer, in some respects of higher qualities than either of his compeers. His nature was more complex, and, in obedience to something wiser than instinct, he had given his varied faculties a no less varied discipline. He was long remembered at Cambridge as the Man of four Triposes—mathematical, classical, the natural and the moral sciences. This was a dangerous beginning, and might well have signified a fatal facility for drudgery, but no capacity for better things. In Hort's case, however, it expressed a real demand of nature. It did not tempt him either to sacrifice his life to his academic reputation, or to try to become an expert in all or any of his tripos subjects : but it saved him from the limitations of the mere scholar, the sectionalism of the mere man of science, the abstract idealism of the mere metaphysician, while it drilled him into the habits of accuracy and methods of research which were the factors of his later efficiency. His regard for facts, however trivial, his love of research, his faculty of delicate discrimination and classification, his sympathy with the spirit of discovery, his mental hospitality, the welcome he was ever ready to offer to a theory which promised to shed new light on old things, his eagerness to discover causes and conditions of variation or of relations between old and new forms, different or cognate, in nature or in history, in morphology or in MSS., sprang out of a discipline which had been at once philological, scientific, and philosophical. The mental attitude which is thought to be typical of the apologetic divine—the attitude which looks upon every new discovery or theory in science as a masked danger to faith, and deals with it as such—was utterly alien to him. He was always on the outlook for fresh truth, for new ways of viewing and interpreting men and things. On the morrow of its appearance he hailed *The Origin of Species* as, " in spite of its difficulties," an " unanswerable " book. But, while the university drilled him, his intellectual quickening came from personal teachers, notably Newman Coleridge, and Maurice. They made the ideal elements of his mind, the regulative principles of his thought; yet their application, the realm in which he moved as a thinker, was specifically his own. It was the history of primitive Christianity, construed not simply for its own sake or in its more phenomenal being, but rather as the parable of the universe, the mystery in whose interpretation all time was interpreted.

In a quite exceptional degree Hort's own intellectual problems were those of the early Church; and in him the great thoughts of the second and third centuries seemed to be re-incarnated. To him the doctrine of the Logos was no mere orthodox dogma, but a living belief, a whole philosophy of being. In its light he read the texts, the early Church, its literature and its creeds. But while the thought that lived in him was ancient, the man it lived in was modern, looking upon the problem of the universe through eyes that science had trained and that philosophy had opened, yet with a mind which faith had illumined. It was this which created the atmosphere that surrounded both the man and his work, which filled with the enthusiasm of hope the disciples who got near enough to catch some glimpse of the things he saw in the light he saw them under. And yet it helps to explain why he found speech so hard as to be well-nigh impossible. There is something singularly pathetic in the volumes which have been so lovingly edited and published since his death. They are, indeed, but shadowy fragments of a once vivid mind, as it were half articulate words from lips which seemed silent for ever. When these posthumous volumes are read through the *Life and Letters* we see this; that Hort's inability to write what would satisfy himself sprang from the conflict of two tendencies within him—the scientific and the speculative; and the conflict was the more acute that the speculative stood at the end, and the scientific was the way which led up to it. Of all rare combinations, that of the scholar and the thinker is the rarest; and, curiously, it is often a paralyzing combination, especially when each of the two so retains its integrity that the scholar insists on all his facts being reckoned with, and the thinker that every several fact must have its place and reason. And we see in Hort's *Hulsean Lectures*— long brooded over, printed in part, carried about for years, revised, re-revised, growing to him ever less adequate—the thinker struggling after this immense co-ordination. His son says " he viewed all the movements of the time in connection with theology." He

did more than this; he construed through theology
all nature and history. In his system he wanted to
find a place for the documents and institutions and
persons of the Church ; but also for the religions and
civilizations of the world, as well as for the discoveries of science. Without physics theology was
incomplete; without theology all the speculations
and discoveries of man had no unity. And the
unification was to be carried out by a process of
verification. The experience of man was at once to
authenticate and justify the truth of God. And so
he believed that freedom was as necessary to theology
as authority to religion.

§ II. *The Oxford Scholars and Divines*
i. *Benjamin Jowett*

1. Of the two Oxford scholars named above,
neither may seem comparable as theologians to these
three eminent members of the sister university. But
we must distinguish. As to the late Master of Balliol two things have to be remembered—he forsook
theology early, and he occupied, first as tutor and
then as head of his college, positions that were little
friendly to the vocation of the scholar or the cultivation of the higher learning. But it is easy to be here
unjust. The very force of his personality and his
success as an administrator and educator helped to
obscure Jowett's higher qualities and achievements.
And the clouds that did so much to hide his real
character were not always lined with silver ; they

were often very dark and earth-born indeed, whether due to the undergraduate imagination, which dearly loves the mythical, or to the ecclesiastical, which has the art of invoking unconscious invention to justify dislike. The Oxford of his early manhood was a stormy place, not kindly to the golden mean, or what is fabled as the academic calm of philosophic mind ; and too narrow to allow the hostile forces free play, it compelled the men who embodied them so to jostle each other, or even so to collide, as to transform intellectual difference into personal heat. The history of what is known as "the Oxford movement" has still to be written ; of books dealing with it, more than one has earned a name which once fell from the late Master, "a reservoir of posthumous spites." The worship of fictitious heroes is an easy and common cult, but is not noble or elevating ; and it has had free scope and full exercise among the Tractarian men. In no circle of men in modern days have there been more extravagant loyalties or violent hates ; and the hates were not always allowed to perish with their occasion—they survived among the men who became "Catholics" and did not altogether die among the men who remained "Anglicans." And exaggerated praise or immoderate admiration is as little just as extravagant blame. John Henry Newman has been made to live before the imagination of the multitude as the most typical Oxford man of the century. As a matter of fact, he is typical, not of Oxford, but of a school that has now and then attempted to find there a home. The men typical of Oxford, as a home of learning and knowledge, are Roger Bacon, the interpreter of nature; Duns Scotus and William of Ockham, the one the most critical, the other the most speculative, of Schoolmen; Cardinal Wolsey, statesman and munificent patron of letters; Dean Colet, student of Scripture and founder of a great school, selecting for his trustees, as Erasmus says, "married laymen of honest reputation," because he had observed generally "that such persons were more conscientious and honest than priests"; Richard Hooker, stateliest of English prose writers as well as most judicious of divines; John Hales, "the ever memorable," who loved breadth and hated the ecclesiastical tyranny which created schism; William Chillingworth, who tried Catholicism only to return into a larger and thorougher Protestantism; John Selden, jurist, scholar, and historian; John Hampden and John Pym, English statesmen; Edward Pococke, Orientalist, the last representative of an illustrious race of scholars who made the English name famous in Europe; Joseph Butler, philosopher and divine; John Wesley, preacher and organizer; Charles Wesley, preacher and poet; Adam Smith, moral philosopher and economist — founder, indeed, of the modern science of economics; William Hamilton, metaphysician and man of learning; Thomas Arnold, schoolmaster, historian, and man of affairs—these are the men most typical of Oxford, representing all that is finest in her culture and truest in her handiwork, and most beneficent in the contributions she has made to the common weal. But under the spell and passion of Newman she renounced the serenity in which she loved to walk and to meditate, and turned her home into a sort of fiery furnace, glowing with sevenfold heat; and the youth that were then cast therein had to be made of good stuff, if they were to walk in the midst of it unsinged and undismayed. And there were men, though they were few and elect, who stood the fiery trial, and came out of the furnace without so much as the smell of fire upon their garments. It was, indeed, a brave thing to keep a quiet soul in those days of quick speech, which yet was not quick enough for the feeling it would fain express. But the young academic Liberals were gallant men, the very chivalry of their time—Arthur Stanley, Benjamin Jowett, Arthur Hugh Clough Matthew Arnold, and we may name other two, though their course was more troubled and less straight, Mark Pattison and James Anthony Froude. These men have not been made saints or heroes of; their party is too critical to be apt at canonization, while, to speak the blunt truth, one, or possibly two, were of too mixed material to be built after the heroic model or made into a heroic form. But Jowett was certainly compacted of the finest stuff; struggle did not fret him, nor, what is a far rarer thing, did petty persecution sour. He had to suffer the martyrdom of silence, but he bore it like a man ; and when he found speech, he spoke like one who did not know or feel that his lips had been sealed.

2. We have to remember these things if we would understand what Jowett did in theology, or the spirit he did it in. The work which he did in this field, the commentary on certain Pauline Epistles, with its incorporated essays, appeared just ten years after the Tractarian movement had culminated in the secession of Newman ; but between it and the *Development of Doctrine*, which marked the event, the distance must be measured by centuries rather than by years. It was a most modern book, puzzling by its very modernity, misunderstood because it was so new and strange a thing in sacred criticism and exegesis. It was subtle, penetrated by intense religious feeling, often distinguished by lucid elegance of form and phrase, yet with the frequent lapses in the sequence of his thought which marked all Jowett's work to the very end. What bewildered the student was its absolute freedom from tradition ; and the curious thing was that the old scholastic tradition had not been argued down, analyzed—an airy nothing—or otherwise forcibly expelled ; it simply was not, and for the author seemed not to have been. Paul appeared to be lifted bodily out of the world in which learned interpretation, held in the leading-strings of theological formulæ, had for ages made him live and move, and placed back in a simpler and roomier world, where thought was more fluid and less fixed. Men did not know what to make of this Paul ; he

was too much of a real man, and too little of the scholastic theologian to whom they had grown accustomed. They thought he had been simplified out of existence and did not see the profound insight of this new presentation, how cunningly he had been unclothed, how deftly re-clothed in his hidden and forgotten raiment. We might describe the commentary as, in one sense classical, in another sense historical, in a third sense secular, understanding that term in its true and literal meaning. It was classical as distinguished from theological; the Epistles read as literature, for themselves and in order to the discovery of their thought, their writer, the forces that made him, the influences that surrounded him, the character that moulded his conduct, and the men whose friendship or hostility affected his opinions and helped to determine his policy. It was historical as distinguished from traditional: the canons of the schools counted for nothing, but the world the man moved in was thoroughly realized; that world Jewish, Hellenistic, Greek, Roman, was made to relive for the interpreter; then the mode which the man had of using the Book he best knew and most used was studied, and the forms of thought which were his rather than ours subtly analyzed and determined. It was secular as opposed to isolated and sectional: Paul and his books were part of the age in which they lived, shared the life and reflected the experience of their own time; his relation to the Twelve and to the Churches were explained and illustrated by the action of kindred personalities in distant times but similar circumstances. Luther and Calvin, Wesley and Whitefield were summoned to show how Paul and Apollos, or Paul and Peter might differ in theology, yet preach in the same church or address the same people. Philo was re-embodied that he might express the ideas which were current in the Judaism that Paul knew. The work was that of a comparatively young man, yet one who had far passed the age of paradox and crude originality, and who lived under conditions where continuous study and concentrated thought are least of all possible; but it deserves to be called a book which marked, if it did not make, a new era. It was a book which owed much to Baur's *Paulus*, though it had an originality of its own; it was English and not German, for it was less ridden by theory and stood more soberly face to face with fact. It showed more creative and constructive power than any of Lightfoot's *Commentaries*; and as it represented only the firstfruits of Jowett's labours in this field—though alas, the firstfruits were destined to be also the last! —one may almost venture the prophecy that if he had not turned from theology to classics he would have done here the work for which England was waiting; and by supplying the Broad Church with a basis at once Biblical and reasonable, he might have saved it from the extinction which he lived to see it experience.[1]

---

[1] Cf. Hort's judgment. " Certainly his (Lightfoot's) doctrinal

ii. *Edwin Hatch*

1. But we turn from Jowett to the younger scholar whose work suggested this paper, Edwin Hatch. Of his hard struggle for a foothold and even a livelihood, of his long unrecognised merit and unrewarded labours, I will not venture to speak. For years, even after he had attained European fame, he was allowed to hold the office of Vice-Principal of St. Mary Hall, which may fitly be described as the least of all the cities of Judah; and even at one time he was forced to undergo the exhausting and depressing drudgery of taking private pupils. When University recognition did come, it was parcelled out in small offices, which in most cases involved the maximum of uncongenial toil. These things are said only that they may indicate the difficulties under which he did his work; but they were difficulties that neither broke his temper nor abated his resolution, though, without doubt, they overtaxed his strength and shortened his life. One thing more of a personal nature I will dare to say.

comments are far from satisfying me. They belong far too much to the mere Protestant version of St. Paul's thoughts, however Christianised and rationalised. One misses the real attempt to fathom St. Paul's own mind and to compare it with the facts of life which one finds in Jowett." And again, "Doctrinal questions are almost entirely avoided, as Lightfoot means to keep them for Romans. However, that is certainly the weakest point of the book; and Jowett's notes and essays, with all their perversities, are still an indispensable supplement."—*Life and Letters of F. J. A. Hort*, vol. ii. pp. 79, 35.

He did not escape the ordinary misjudgment that
falls to the men who take their own line in theological inquiry.   Men who were party leaders did
not love him, and, conscious of his at one time
almost unbefriended loneliness, they did not care
to conceal their dislike.   But, though we had much
intercourse and many confidences, I never heard
him speak one unkind or ungenerous word of any
man among those from whom he had suffered
many things.   I well remember how an old friend
of mine met him at first with some reluctance and
much misgiving, because he had been accustomed
to hear him described by certain ecclesiastical
opponents, one, in particular, whose name occurs
elsewhere in this paper, as a man of "a cold and
hard nature," of "a rationalistic temper," "without
faith in the supernatural" or "feeling for historical
continuity in the Church."   But my friend, being
himself a man of fine character and open eye,
learned in the course of a few days' progressively
intimate companionship how utterly Hatch had
been misconceived and belied.   These are things
I had no intention of saying when I began this
paper, but a man's work can never be really understood unless it be read through his character.

Hatch was not a scholar in the sense and degree
in which Lightfoot was one, though his *Essays
in Biblical Greek* and the *Concordance to the
Septuagint*, which he planned, organized the work
for and did so much to carry through, show how

much he could have accomplished in the field of constructive scholarship. But Hatch was strong where Lightfoot and Westcott are weak, in using literature for the interpretation of history, in analyzing the forces that determine its course, shape its institutions, formulate its beliefs, create its tendencies, regulate its thinking, in a word, govern its development. It is doubtful whether in the delicacy and success with which he handled and explained the most complex phenomena in early ecclesiastical history, he had a superior or even a peer. His method was scientific, at once analytic and comparative, though, in order to its appreciation, it was necessary to see him at work. He was, in the strict sense, as an historical inquirer without dogmatic assumptions. The Church as it lived and moved, took shape, and grew into an organic structure, was something to be explained ; and the only thing which could be regarded as an explanation must come through an analysis of the forces and conditions which had made it. To say that it was, in its political and organized or in its social and secular being, a supernatural creation, was to lift it out of the category of things with which the scientific student of history could deal ; and such supernatural power could be logically invoked only when every normal and intelligible cause had been tried and failed. To postulate a miraculous cause when historical causes were discoverable and sufficient, was a most needless multiplication of hypotheses. In harmony with this principle, he proceeded to examine the structure, and the several forms or stages through which it passed, in relation to the various conditions under which, and forces amid which, it lived and grew; in order that he might discover whether there were any cause or causes which could account for its organization by a normal historical process. He began with the ministry, for it was the most obvious point for him to begin at. He lived face to face with a theory of it on which a most portentous series of claims was based; and he was, as it were, every day of his life challenged to accept or contradict the theory. It was characteristic of him to seize on elements and aspects of the idea and functions of the original Christian society which had been overlooked or neglected by ecclesiastical writers. The Church which history revealed to him was not simply a new organ for worship, equipped with the officials, ritual, and authority needed to establish an appropriate cult; but it was rather a ministry of beneficence, a society charged to create a new social order, where the distinction of bond and free should cease, and to exercise those charities which made the poor share in the abundance of the rich. He examined the guilds and religious associations of the Græco-Roman world; he compared their constitution with the constitution of the Church, and found analogies that made it probable that the new Christian societies were not dissimilar from the old associations. Then he examined the Jewish communities, found special features in their administration, "elders" who formed a "synedrion," or local court, which had many points of similarity with the Roman municipalities, and these, in their union, became transformed into the council of the Church. The process was then analyzed by which the bishop rose to supremacy, the clergy and laity came to be differentiated, and the Church organized on the lines of the empire. It was a study in ecclesiastical biology, the formation of the clerical orders dealt with as a problem in natural history. And its success may be measured by two things— the violence with which it was assailed, on the one side, and the admiration with which the most competent and dispassioned judges received it, on the other. One thing must have been peculiarly gratifying to Hatch—the letter which in the September of 1886 he received from Hort:

"On the question of organisation, I imagine that we agree more than we differ; but some of your language is not such as I should naturally use. I quite go with you in condemning the refusal of fellowship with sister Churches merely because they make no use of some elements of organisation assumed to be *jure divino* essential. But it seems to me that the rejection of theoretical and practical exclusiveness clears the ground for the recognition of at least the possibility that other kinds of (relative) *jus divinum* may be brought to light by history and experience. In organisation, as in other things, all Churches have much, I think, to learn from each other, the Church of England as much as any. It does not follow that organisation ought to be everywhere identical. But it

27

may well turn out that there are some elements or principles of organisation which cannot anywhere be cast aside without injury ; and, at all events, each Church has need to ask how far its peculiarities may be mere gratuitous defects, not right adaptations to its own special circumstances." [1]

What this means is obvious enough ; it showed that Hatch stood no longer alone. The man he regarded as in the region of literary and historical criticism the most capable, detached, and constructive intellect of the English Church, substantially agreed with him. To Hort, as to him, a special organization was not of the *esse*, though it might be of the *bene esse* of the Church ; it did not forbid "fellowship with sister Churches," or justify "theoretical and practical exclusiveness." What Hort desiderated was "practical tolerance and practical brotherliness" ; and he regretted that "Anglican prejudice and exclusive theory" barred the way, but felt that even these "needed tender handling if their power is to be sapped." [2] Reflection and research had effected a revolution in the quondam High Church-man which his son and biographer has not appreci-ated or even perceived.

2 But Hatch did not imagine that to trace the organization of the ministry was to explain the Church. On the contrary, the Church represented to him a most complex growth, and was a highly complicated structure. As he conceived the matter, it was not explained at any point unless it was

---

[1] Hort's *Life and Letters*, ii. p. 357.   [2] *Ibid*, p. 358.

explained at all. The Bampton Lectures were but a small section of a much greater whole ; they did not express his complete view or cover the field within which he had pursued his researches. They were not his solution of the problem, but only a step towards it. The Hibbert .Lectures carried the problem another step forward, but in the mind of their author no more than a single step. Their special question was as to "the influence of Greek ideas and usages upon the Christian Church"; but the question had so many ramifications and raised so many issues that adequate discussion of any one, let alone all, within the limits allowed him, was simply impossible. As it was, the ease and force of his exposition enabled him to perform a task that would have been to any less well-furnished mind simply impossible. He analyzed the medium or soil in which Christianity had to live when it became the religion of the Gentiles. The mind that assimilated also transformed the religion, and the transformation was only explicable through the mind that accomplished it. He sketched the Greek mind as it was in the first and second centuries of our era, how it was educated and exercised, what its interests were, and what sort of life it led ; and he indicated the relation in which the habit of mind created by the vagrant philosophers, who speculated and argued in public and preached so as to gratify curiosity, tickle the fancy, and exercise the understanding, stood to the new system which

came to claim belief in ways so instructively analogous '
to the old. He examined the methods of exegesis
which had been used to extract reason from Greek
mythology and to reconcile Moses and Plato, and
which in due season became in the hands of the
Fathers now a weapon of apology, now a means
of proving doctrine, and now the instrument of
bringing the New Testament out of the Old. He
analyzed the action of philosophy on the Greek
mind, and traced its influence on the tendency to
speculate and define in the region of belief. He
showed the distinction between Greek and Christian
ethics, and indicated how the Greek penetrated,
changed, in some respects superseded, the Christian.
Then he traced how the region of theology proper,
man's intellectual interpretation of God as the
highest and most real Being, was invaded by the
metaphysical Greek mind, with its inherited instincts,
its well-disciplined habits, and its elaborate ter-
minology ; with the result that the faith of the Church
in a living personal God was transmuted into a
series of abstract yet rigorously defined dogmas.
The Greek mysteries, it was further argued, had
affected the Christian sacraments, changing them
from their simple primitive sense and purpose to
acts and ceremonies akin to those associated with
the ancient secret cults. The result of the whole
was the transformation of the original basis of the
Christian society, and a correspondent change in
the whole structure it supported.

Immense and intricate as the problem was, it by no means adequately or fairly represented the question he had put to himself, and the material he had collected for its discussion. He did not imagine that the Church had been explained when, as in the Bampton and Hibbert Lectures, the forces contributing to the formation of its ministry, the formulation of its creed, the rise of its mysteries, and the evolution of its ethics had been analyzed and described. Other and quite as integral elements in its constitution had still to be reckoned with. The action of Roman law, of the civil organization of the empire and its administration, of its religious legislation and institutions, had still to be traced. There was the constitution of the Church, catholic and provincial, national and parochial, the functions and powers of councils and synods as affected by the imperial system, now independent of the emperor, now dependent upon him, and the whole remarkable body of legislation called the Canon Law to be explained. There were also to be traced the changes which the growth and application, the consolidation and codification of this law effected in the discipline, in the internal organization and the external policy, both of provincial Churches and the Roman Church. And in the light thus shed it became more possible to discover the state and influence of the localities where given synodical or conciliar canons had been framed ; to watch the development of the clerical orders and the definition of their authority ; to study the methods of the

Church in dealing with offences, ecclesiastical and moral, lay and clerical, the manners, conduct, vices of special classes, places, and times, the relation and reciprocal action of Church and State, with the increasing emphasis on the monarchical idea in the one, and the changes due to the weakness or the strength of the imperial or regal power in the other; to ascertain the attitude of city to surrounding country, and of province to capital, with its correlative action in the creation of diocesan episcopacy. And he had made large researches and collected considerable material towards a history of these things, though nothing more than the merest hints as to his conclusions and fragments of his work ever saw the light.

3. These are dry records of the streams of fertilizing light which he poured into dark places well known to scholasticism, dead and living, but all too seldom visited by science. In his hands the study of Canon Law, as some of us remember it, was distinguished by vivid reality. He made one see the Church as she lived in the age when the special canons, whether of a council or a synod, which he was at the time studying, were framed, the age she lived in, the difficulties she had to meet, and her mode of meeting them. And the study was always comparative; the new canons were examined in relation to the old, and the action of the whole on the constitution and history of the Church carefully traced. By his method he made us see, as if it were going on under our very eyes, the whole process of organic change, which

transformed the free Christian societies of Syria, Greece, and Italy, into a new empire, ecclesiastical and Roman. He did not describe the process with Harnack as the secularization of the Church or with Sohm as its naturalization [1] ("the natural man is a born Catholic," "Church Law has risen from the overpowering desire of the natural man for a legally constituted, *catholicized* Church"); but the process certainly appeared as one of progressive alienation from the primitive ideal. Nor did Canon Law exhaust his question. Over against it stood two very different classes of phenomena, one in the region of opinion, represented by the Heresies, another in the region of emotion and worship, represented by the Liturgies. The growth of legislation made the Church partake more and more of a political character, and heresy appear more and more as a political crime; and I have no more instructive recollection than a private discussion with Hatch, in which he illustrated the influence which the ideas Augustine had derived from these two sources—the political idea of the Church and the criminal character of heresy—had on his mind and system. His discussions of the Liturgies brought him into a deeper and more sacred region; but he so handled the question as to make the Liturgies illustrate the growth at once of religious

---

[1] *Outlines of Church History*, pp. 35, 36. This position is most elaborately and learnedly worked out in Sohm's great work on *Kirchenrecht*, vol. i.

ideas and of customs, especially as concerned the relations of clergy and people.

The whole of the question he had set himself to solve he was never able to discuss publicly, or even in his university lectures. And so much as he did publicly discuss was in a form that hardly enabled him to do justice to his mind. What I have called the immense and intricate problem of the " Hibbert Lectures" was treated in a book of only 350 pages, originally given as a series of twelve lectures, each being of about an hour's duration. Looked at thus, the attempt might seem to say more for Hatch's courage than for his discretion. But he knew him-self so well, felt so much the brevity and uncertainty of life, believed so thoroughly that truth could best be served by early and frank discussion, that he did not feel as if he had any choice. And the death which came so soon and sadly showed that he was wise. But he felt strongly that his argument de-pended for its cogency on its evidence, that the evidence was cumulative, and that its strength could only be fully appreciated when its lines had all been drawn out and mustered and marshalled in force. It was, therefore, signally unfortunate that his theory and its proof came out, as it were, piece-meal, especially as his style and manner of exposition increased the evil. He threw himself upon his subject, laboured at its elucidation, seemed to think of it alone, and of how best to compel others to think of it as he did. The result was a fine lucidity, a brisk incisiveness and cogency, which made it easy to follow his meaning, though it hid from the polemical or the undiscerning much of his implied but unexpressed mind. As a result, he had more than his share of misconception and irrelevant criticism. His theory of the ministry was criticized from assumptions as to his beliefs which he would not have admitted; and on the basis of a localization of the divine energy and an externalization of the means of grace which he would have vehemently denied. His opponents spoke as if he did not believe in the supernatural character of the Church : while, as a matter of fact, his supernatural was larger than theirs, not limited and defined by external organs, but expressed in the whole of history and in the lives of men. His purpose was as positive as any problem in science ; it was to seek from history an answer to this question : *How* and *why* has the Church, as a whole and in its several parts, become what it is? But his critics— though only so far as they were English, his Continental critics understood him better—assumed his purpose to be polemical or controversial, and not merely historical and scientific ; and they answered him as the person they assumed him to be. He spoke of himself as having " ventured as a pioneer into comparatively unexplored ground," and confessed that he had no doubt " made the mistakes of a pioneer "; but he was handled as if his inquiries were a process of dogmatic affirmation towards a predestined conclusion. It was complained that he

neglected " central and positive evidence in favour of
what is external, suggestive, and subsidiary ": when,
as a simple matter of fact, his evidence was as
"central " as it could be for his own purpose, though
his purpose was not that of his critics. The very
title of his Hibbert Lectures, the " Influence of Greek
Ideas on the Church," was forgotten ; and he was
rebuked as if he had meant that Greek ideas had
created as well as helped in the formulation of
Christian doctrine. His contention that the Nicene
Creed was due to the influence of " Greek metaphysics " was answered by the obvious commonplace,
that " Christianity became metaphysical simply and
only because man was rational."[1]　But so to argue
was to answer what he had never questioned, and
contradict what he had never affirmed. He had said
nothing about metaphysics in general ; but about a
special school or type of metaphysics, to wit, " Greek
metaphysics "—*i.e.*, the school philosophies of the
patristic period, with their elaborate technical termino-
logies and scholastic methods. And his problem was
to inquire how far these had contributed to the becoming of " the metaphysical creed," which stands in
the forefront of the Christianity of the fourth century.
The process of production, with its several factors, the
worth of the product, the value of its form, and the
sufficiency of the form to the ineffable beliefs it would
express, are all distinct questions. Dr. Hatch under-

---

[1] Gore, *Bampton Lectures*, p. 21.

took to deal with only one of these, and it was no very
relevant reply to deal with him as if he had denied
one of the most flagrant facts of human nature.

It lies outside my purpose to examine the criticisms, relevant and irrelevant, made upon his method
or his argument ; but as I have said so much, I may
as well say one word more. Canon Gore complains
that Hatch, in his book on the *Influence of Greek
Ideas*, left out of consideration the theology of the
Apostolic writers.[1]   It is so very obvious a criticism
that one would have expected an acute critic like
Canon Gore to have jealously questioned himself
before making it. Surely, if Dr. Hatch's purpose
had been, as Dr. Gore supposed, a polemic against
doctrine, and not simply, as it was, an historical
inquiry into "the influence of Greek Ideas and
Usages on the Christian Church," he could not have
made a more extraordinary blunder than the omission for which he is censured. It would have been
a sort of unconditional surrender of himself into the
hands of the enemy. But for his purpose such an
inquiry was not necessary, though it seems to me
that it would, if it had been prosecuted, have enormously strengthened his contention. He did not
analyze the Sermon on the Mount, though he introduced his subject by an allusion to it. He did
not attempt an exhibition of the theology of Jesus,
though from Dr. Gore's point of view this ought to

---

[1] Gore, *Bampton Lectures*, pp. 99, 100.

have been a much more serious omission than even his neglect of "the theology of the Apostolic writers." His work, in reality, begins outside and after the New Testament, though he is never forgetful of its being. It is a matter the student of the primitive Church can hardly be ignorant of, that the development of doctrine does not begin where the New Testament ends ; it begins, not behind it, but without it ; though, perhaps, after it, yet on a lower level, amid influences less strong and less noble than those of the Apostolic circle. It starts with tradition, with confused memories, with blind and stumbling endeavours to comprehend what was said and believed among the multitude, not what had been written and explained by the Apostles. The New Testament might be written at the end of the Apostolic age, but its material had not been assimilated by such Christian mind as then was, had not been fused in the fire of experience, refined by the labour of the intellect or stamped by the hands of thought. Hort would have taught Dr. Gore that a written revelation without "discipular experience" is but a virgin mine rich in unwrought wealth. To deal, therefore, with the sub-Apostolic age as if it had, or had used, the New Testament, as we have it, or as we use it ; or to speak as if the Pauline or the Johannine theology had worked itself into the collective consciousness and become intelligible as a reasonable system or even as an oral tradition—is not to exhibit the historical or scientific spirit, or to show critical comprehension of the man who has followed it. The age when "Greek ideas and usages" began to exercise their influence on Christian thought, was an age when for that thought the theology of the New Testament, as we understand the term, could not be said to be. And when it did begin to be, the mind that came to the New Testament was one penetrated by those very Greek ideas whose influence it was the function of the historian to trace. Hence the "leaving out of consideration the theology of the Apostolic writers" seems to us to have been due to a scientific appreciation of the problem ; the criticism of the omission to be due to the absence in the critic of a like scientific appreciation and critical sense. In Hatch's own words, he was concerned, not ,with the "spiritual revelation" which the Apostolical communities had "accepted," but with "the influences" which enabled them to translate what had been thus "accepted" into "an intellectual conviction."

§ III. *Comparison as regards Mind and Methods of Drs. Hort and Hatch*

1. It is not my purpose to attempt any comparative estimate of the men whose work has been here passed in hurried review. Indeed, only two of them can be fairly compared—Hort and Hatch. They had many points of resemblance, but possibly more of difference ; and the differences were the more characteristic. Hort was the more courageous thinker, Hatch the more adventurous inquirer. Hort

suffered permanently from the inability to give exact
or adequate expression to his mind ; Hatch had
much of the passion of the explorer, who rejoices in
the double delight of making discoveries and telling
of the discoveries he has made.   Hort was fastidious
to the last degree ; he feared lest he might err, for
to his scrupulous intellect the possibilities of error
were infinite ; he feared to affirm a position lest he
should fail to prove it, or lest, on further research,
his proofs should turn out false.   But Hatch was too
much a master at once of historical analysis and
constructive synthesis to be deterred by the inadequacy of the tools he must employ, or even by any
defect of skill on his own part in handling them.
He was as much alive as Hort to the possibilities of
error, but believed that it was better to run the risk
of erring than to leave great questions undiscussed ;
for the way to success lay through failure.   He saw
as much as Hort the value of good texts, but he also
saw that it was the duty of science to work with the
materials it had at hand ; to wait till its materials
were better was the very way to postpone their im-
provement, was to allow religious inquiry to stagnate,
and to cause the methods of research into the past
of theology and the Church to fall out of relation to
the whole living body of the historical sciences.   As
a result, little as Hatch accomplished compared with
the work he had designed, his published work bears
a fairer proportion to his mind as a whole than what
Hort has left behind.   Hatch did nothing that was

in its order so satisfactory and thorough as Hort's work on the text of the New Testament; on the other hand, Hort has not started so many questions or done so much as Hatch to suggest new problems and new methods to the workers in the field of ecclesiastical history.

2. But we shall better see the significance and the difference of the two men if we try to seize what we may term their fundamental and regulative ideas. The passion of Hort, we may say, was to conceive Christianity from within, to discover its intrinsic quality and capability, the power by which it penetrated man and worked out its idea or purpose. We must here speak with caution and reserve, especially as the material for the interpretation of his mind is scanty; and it has the double disadvantage of being as a whole incomplete, almost chaotic, while single parts have been elaborated with often repeated toil. As he said, " Beliefs worth calling beliefs must be purchased with the sweat of the brow." His idea is embodied, or, let us say, has suffered a sort of incarnation, in the evangelical history. That history is a parable which sets out the mysteries of being; in it the inmost truths as to God and the universe have so become flesh and dwelt among us, that we may even in its visible things behold the glory of the invisible idea. The centre of the system is Jesus Christ; in Him the whole mystery of God and nature is epitomized, interpreted, realized. His significance for man is

measured by man's experience of Him ; the larger
and deeper the experience the richer the significance.
In the early Church there was a difference between
the disciples being present with the Master and the
Master being present with the disciples. The record
of the former state is in the Synoptists ; the record
of the latter is in John. In the Synoptists we see
the disciples learning from association with the
Master; in John we see the disciple, all the more
a disciple that he is an apostle, enriched in thought
because richer in experience, teaching what he has
learned through the Master having taken him into
association with Himself. The Fourth Gospel is,
therefore, neither a supplement nor a correction to
the other three ; it is their interpretation, nay, it is
the interpretation of the universe, not in the abstract
unities of philosophy—which represents "a corpse
god, not a living God"—but in the concrete personalities of religion. All its terms are vivid with
reality, " spirit," " light," " love," " way," " truth,"
"life." In these terms God is conceived, and they
are the terms which articulate Christ. " He is not
a supplement to belief in God, but the only sure
foundation of it." " Impersonal names are dilutions
of the truth meeting the weakness of human faculties "; even of God " the personal mode of expression alone is strictly true." God read through Christ
ceases to be a silent mystery, the darksome background of our collective insolubilities, and appears
as light, and life, and love. These things were

realized for time in Christ; through Him they are realized in us; as they are realized in us we are united to God, the living point of unity being the Person who creatively embodied what we are to realize.

This is not a speculative dream, it is a process of experience verified in the life of the disciples, of the Church, and of the individual. These three ex· periences repeat and complete each other; that of the disciples is reflected in the Church, that of the Church in the man. The more inchoate the experience, individual or collective, the more confused and the less adequate our apprehension of the divine. " There is a truth within us, to use the language of Scripture, a perfect inward ordering, as of a transparent crystal, by which alone the perfect faithful image of truth without us is brought within our ken." The pure in heart see God ; and to create this vision is the function of all we co-ordinate under the term Church. To the eye that can see it, there is here a large philosophy both of religion and of history. The end of all things is the inward vision, but it is late in being reached, and to it many things are necessary that are yet not of it. Outward forms, tradition, systems may be methods of discipline to be used and valued as such, with seasons and functions of their own ; but in character they are provisional and transitional. The natural expression of this mood was a large catholicity, to which a political Catholicism grew less and less congenial. As his thoughts deepened they widened, and out-

ward matters he had emphasized in earlier life became much less prominent in his later life. " There
is," said he, " no ' Christianity as it is,' but a multitude of Christianities, each of which covers but a
small part of what is believed in the nineteenth century ; while this as a whole excludes much that has
been believed in past centuries, and the sum of the
whole covers but a part of the contents of the Bible."

" Christianity consists of the most central and
significant truth concerning the universe, intelligible
only in connection with other truth not obviously
Christian, and accepted by many not Christians."
" The history of the Church, if it could ever be truly
written, would be the most composite of all histories,
since it would have to set forth the progress of every
element of humanity since its invisible Head was
revealed." These broad principles followed from his
fundamental conception of the place and function of
Christ, and the " discipular experience " by which
alone He could be interpreted ; and they show how
far he had travelled from the days when he " could
almost worship Newman " and imagined himself a
High Churchman somewhat in Newman's sense.

3. Hatch, on the other hand, had a more purely
intellectual conception, one more distinctly interpretable, whether by himself or others. He was not
a mystic. Nature was not to him a parable, nor was
history an allegory which could be read back into its
divine realities by the eye which had learned the
secret. But he was indeed a very positive thinker,

and was for this reason inclined to regard with something severer than impatience those who took accidents of time and place for the very essence of eternal things. God was to him the Spirit who manifested Himself in history through the spirits of men. Character was His creation; ethical distinctions were the most real of things, moral qualities the most sacred. God, as He conceived Him, was too catholic in character, too varied in His activities, too rich in grace to be confined to one society, or to be represented as making certain artificially created orders of men the covenanted channels of His mercies. The charities and simple beneficences of the early Church seemed to him worthier of the divine than the priestly claims of Cyprian or the offices of the Roman priesthood. To use political distinctions to circumscribe the society of God, was opposed as an unjustifiable interference with His modes of action. But he was scrupulously anxious to avoid the speculative determination of history. He would not and did not determine beforehand what the Church was, but he conceived his function to be one of strict historical inquiry. Hence his real contribution to theology was his problem and his method. His problem was: How had the Church—understanding under that term all the institutions, usages, and beliefs which the Christian society had created as at once an expression of its life and the means of its maintenance—come to be? And his method was by an exhaustive historical and comparative analysis to discover how far the home in which it lived, the conditions under which it thought, the forces which worked for or worked against it, were responsible for the formation and development of its peculiar organization. In other words, it was the application of a rigorously scientific method to a field which science had seldom been allowed to explore. He was permitted to state his problem and illustrate his method only in part, and to reach conclusions which were so far tentative as they were due to a process which was incomplete. But he fell as the "pioneer" falls, who has opened the way to disciples that have learned his secret and are eager to follow in his footsteps.

But here our study of these English theologians must end. They have shown us that the race of the great scholars who were great divines, has not yet ceased in England. They were men who were loyal sons of their country and their Church; they have enriched the English mind, adorned the English universities, enhanced the reputation of English scholars, and made even the Christian religion more honourable and more credible, by the consecration of all their powers to the investigation of her history, the study and elucidation of her literature, and the exposition of her beliefs. May not the men of whom these things can be said assure us that the race of the noble and the godly has not yet perished from the earth?

March, 1897.

X

OXFORD AND JOWETT

WHILE the Life of the late Master of Balliol [1] is the work of two minds, it has throughout the unity of one spirit, and shows everywhere the hand of a filial affection, fine yet discriminative. It is well and even gracefully written, with a reserve he would have approved, a moderation and an accuracy he would have commended. It is tender and appreciative without being blind, judicial without being censorious, reverent without adulation or idolatry. Its errors are but trivial, and mainly in matters of personal detail ; its omissions are inconsiderable, and its chief defect a too uniform smoothness which has tempted its authors to mask some ancient fires, which are not yet extinguished, and touch lightly characteristics that ought to have been clearly filled in. There are no "blazing indiscretions," which makes it, indeed, all the truer a mirror of the man ; for though Jowett was audacious, he was never indiscreet. If he did a bold thing—and he did many—it was not by impulse or by accident, but of set purpose ; and he was too wise ever

---

[1] *The Life and Letters of Benjamin Jowett, M.A., Master of Balliol College, Oxford.* By Evelyn Abbott and Lewis Campbell. Two Volumes. London : John Murray, 1897.

to explain it or to apologize for it, being well content to leave it to be justified or condemned by the results. His correspondence and memoranda are peculiarly instructive, and open up unexpected glimpses into the beliefs and ideals that were the springs of his action. The mind revealed in his letters and note-books is so pure, the aims so high and generous, the life so unselfish, the spirit so silent as to its own sorrows, while so tender and sympathetic to those of others, that even the men who are most alien from his creed and his policy may well feel compelled to respect the man. Still the biography is, if we may say so, too biographical, and lacks background. We are not made to see the world the man lived in, or to measure the forces he resisted and overcame. Much of his most characteristic work was indeed imperceptible and incalculable. The qualities and acts which made him to so many a loved and revered memory stand written in the lives of men. He was great as the head of a college, because he was quick at discovering and apt at educing what was most excellent in its sons. Only those who can read this biography in the light of the living background they form, will be able to see the central figure in its real proportions, adjusted, as it were, to scale.

Jowett was certainly a man who deserved to have his biography written. He contributed more to form the mind and character of his age than many men who occupied more conspicuous positions. He fought a battle that was the more splendidly successful that

it was so long without the outward signs and spoils
of victory. It was not that he had transcendent gifts
in any one direction; nay, in most respects he could
be easily surpassed. As a scholar he had superiors
both in his own and in the sister university; as a
philosophical thinker he was eclipsed by some even
of his own disciples; as a theologian he early fell out
of the race, and though to the last wistfully anxious
to take up the running, grew progressively unfit to do
it; as an administrator of the university he had the
defects of a man whose ends and means were too
much his own to be easily adjusted to the temper and
ways of an assembly which can only be deliberative
by being critical. But when every deduction has
been made, it will still remain true that the late
Master of Balliol was the most potent academic personality which Oxford, at least, has known in this
century. To have been this, was to be a person
whose memory, especially as regards the elements
and secrets of power, ought not to be willingly let die.

§ I. *Oxford University and Colleges*

Jowett is not a man that can be studied apart from
the Oxford of his day: and as that is an Oxford
which is of large and varied significance, we may be
forgiven if we preface our criticism of the man by
some remarks as to his university.

1. When he entered Oxford it was less a university
than a city of colleges, which had the differences,
jealousies, antagonisms of societies that were at once

neighbours and rivals, rather than the homogeneity
and harmony of a corporate body whose several
parts are members' one of another.   Oxford has, to
the outside imagination, a remarkable unity of
character; but, to inside experience, a remarkable
variety of temper and tendencies.   Each college has
its own traditions, methods, capabilities, ambitions,
develops distinctive qualities in its men, and appeals
to its special constituency; with the result that it
affects the university more than it is affected by it.
The college is a small and exclusive society, with a
completer and more direct control over its men than
is possible to the university; it deals with them more
as boys and less as men, interprets the *status pupil-
laris* more rigorously, enforces discipline more easily,
is less open to new ideas, and is more concerned with
the practical function or use of knowledge than with
its expansion.   The college tutor has more the
charge of men, and exercises in a very real sense the
cure of souls; but the university professor has more
the care of a subject, a field or a province of knowledge which it is his duty to cultivate and enlarge.
The more a tutor feels the men he has in charge, the
less will he have of the scholar's mind; the more the
professor tills his field, the less can he charge himself
with the care of men.   But the very difference of
college and university makes each essential to the
other.   Their combined functions may be described
as the cultivation of learning and the formation of
men, or the communication of knowledge and the

culture of character. And these functions are, while distinct, yet not separate or even separable. It is by the communication of knowledge that men are formed and character cultivated. Men live the more nobly that they have been trained to think the thoughts of the great masters of mind and morals in the language they themselves used. And they feel the more humble, teachable, and reverent before the mysteries of being, that they have learned to love and obey nature in order that they might discover her secret. It is in this that the difference lies between a university and a learned society—the one cultivates knowledge that it may discipline men, the other prosecutes discovery that it may enlarge science. The society seeks knowledge for its own sake, but the university seeks it for the purpose of evolving the humanity latent in man. Each may equally pursue learning and encourage research, but it must always be with this fundamental difference of end. And it is here where college and university so well supplement each other ; the college, by its culture of men, keeping the university from sinking into a mere learned society ; the university, by its cultivation of learning, giving to the college a larger atmosphere and more liberal mind.

The ideal academic state, then, would be one where the forces represented by the university and the college existed in a condition of equilibrium and constant interaction. And Oxford, in its twofold character of a university and a city of colleges, stood

in an unrivalled position for realizing the ideal
academic state. But in order to this it was necessary
that neither character should devour or enervate the
other. Of course, it might be possible, were the two
functions separable, to argue that it is better to form
character than to cultivate knowledge. The men
whom the university contributes to Church and
State, to literature and art, to medicine and science,
are a more solid test of academic competence than
the books she directly produces, the discoveries made
within her laboratories, or the ideas and doctrines
stamped with her name. But, as a matter of fact,
these two things go invariably together. Where
intellect is not active, education can never be efficient ; unless knowledge be loved, character will not
be cultivated. In other words, the college can never
do its work unless inspired by the university, nor the
university fulfil its end without the help of the college.

2. It is significant that during the eighteenth century, when the colleges were most exclusive and the
university almost moribund, the sterility of the
studies which Oxford pursued had its fit counterpart
in the sort of men she produced ; for her most illustrious sons then, were either the men who owed her
least, or those she was least inclined to acknowledge.
Of the Oxford men in that century three stand easily
foremost in literary fame—Butler, Gibbon, Johnson ;
but it would be hard to find men for whom the university did less. Butler was no raw schoolboy when
he entered Oriel, but a man who had been formed

under one of the most influential teachers of his age, if we measure the teacher's power by the eminence of his pupils. We know that the problems that were later to occupy Butler's mind had, before his coming to Oxford, greatly exercised his thought; and we also know that he went down, on taking his degree, without either his college or the university in any way recognizing his eminence. It need not surprise us, therefore, that we find so little trace of Oxford in either the *Sermons* or the *Analogy*, or that she did not learn to appreciate or use them until they had been well studied and appreciated elsewhere. He appealed more to the Scottish intellect than to the English understanding; and men so dissimilar as Thomas Reid and David Hume, Adam Smith and Dugald Stewart, Thomas Brown and Thomas Chalmers, united in owning him a master in metaphysics and ethics, and in helping to make his name famous in his own school. Gibbon, again, acknowledged " no obligation to the University of Oxford," which, he said, with less than his usual prescience, would " as cheerfully renounce me for a son as I am willing to disclaim her for a mother." He entered Magdalen " with a stock of erudition that might have puzzled a doctor, and a degree of ignorance of which a schoolboy would have been ashamed "; and he spent there " the fourteen most idle and unprofitable months of his whole life." It is no lovely or attractive picture which he paints of college and university ; in the one, the conversation of the dons " stagnated in a round of college business, Tory politics, personal anecdotes, and private scandal " ; in the other, " the public professors have for these many years given up altogether even the pretence of teaching." Yet so deeply rooted were this state and these abuses in " law and prejudice, that even the omnipotence of Parliament would shrink from an inquiry into" them. Samuel Johnson, after two years' residence, went down without a degree: and though later, as became an exuberant Jacobite, he idealized the place, its memories, and its idolatries, no man knew better than he how little it had done for him, or how it would have spoiled him had he been absorbed in its dreary routine. And so he was angry that, on the very eve of its publication, the Master of his own college would not order a copy of the *Dictionary*, or speak about it, or even invite its author to dinner ; and he said in his wrath : " There lives a man who lives by the revenues of literature, and he will not move a finger to support it." And when he met his old friend and rival, Meeke, whose " superiority" he used to feel unable to bear, Johnson could not help lamenting that a man " of such excellent parts " had been

"Lost in a convent's solitary gloom."

And if the sons who achieved most eminence in literature were those who owed her least, the men she most harassed and despised were those who accomplished most for religion. The story of the Methodists at Oxford is too familiar a tale to bear repeating, but I may add, as one of its less

recognized incidents, that the evil system and associations of the old servitorship left for life their ignoble
stamp on the soul of Whitefield.

Of course, it must not be inferred that we conceive
college or university to have been as black as, say,
Gibbon or Whitefield painted it. On the contrary,
we do not forget either the learning of Bingham,
though it is only just to remember that he was
compelled to resign his fellowship and leave Oxford ;
or "the classic elegance" of Lowth, what he did
for Hebrew poetry, or his fine vindication of the
university against the insults of Warburton ; or the
genial insight and healthy piety of Horne, who not
only commented on the Psalms, but broke into verse
to describe "weeping London's crowded streets"
and "grand parade of woe as Garrick's funeral
passed," and who, in the *Olla Podrida*, gave this
characteristic apology for Johnson : "To reject
wisdom, because the person of him who communi-
cates it is uncouth, and his manners are inelegant
—what is it but to throw away a pine-apple, and
assign for a reason the roughness of its coat ?" And
we ought also to remember that in one region of
thought Oxford even then showed her old intellectual
activity, producing several eminent jurists, like Black-
stone and the two Scotts, who later became respectively Lords Stowell and Eldon. But when every
possible deduction has been made, we may certainly
say, during the eighteenth century the poverty of
Oxford in learning was truly reflected in her poverty

in men. The supremacy of the colleges was fatal to both scholarship and culture.

§ II. *Oxford and its Sons in Two Centuries*

1. The Oxford of the nineteenth century stands out in striking contrast to the Oxford of the eighteenth. The attempt which from the middle of the century onwards was so strenuously made to resuscitate the university without depressing the colleges, has had its counterpart in the activity which each has displayed in its most characteristic field. In the region of thought Oxford has, on the whole, produced no work of such relative eminence as Butler's; in history, nothing that can be compared to Gibbon's; in literature, no man that lives in the imagination like Johnson. But there has been, on the whole, a much more uniform and disciplined mental activity. The university has not, indeed, been without creative thinkers in philosophy, and writers in history who have a fair title to the term "classical." Nor has it been deficient in learning, both of the older and newer order. Yet what is remarkable is that its performances on the arena of the intellect have been surpassed by its productivity in the field of character and life. Into the causes of this double change we need not inquire, though certain of them are obvious enough. For one thing, Oxford has lived much more in the life of the nation, has been a sort of epitome or centre in which all the forces that have moved the day have

been intensified by being concentrated. It has not, like the Oxford of the eighteenth century, cultivated treason in its heart, and been proudly disloyal to the reigning House through loyalty to a House that could not govern ; nor has it, because it could not continue Jacobite, sullenly turned Tory, as the most agreeable form in which it could maintain its aloofness from the outside world. On the contrary, no place agrees less with Matthew Arnold's description of Oxford than Oxford herself. It is only to the poet's fancy that she can seem "the home of lost causes, forsaken beliefs, unpopular names, and impossible loyalties." She has been no "adorable dreamer," but, on the whole, a matron of excellent worldliness, who, naturally indeed, retains her "ineffable charm" to the reminiscent imagination or the mind that sees her from afar. There has been no spot less serene, or more scorched by fierce intellectual fires. Where mind is young, thought must be active : the place where youth is perennial can never grow old. And Oxford has for our generation such infinite significance, because within her borders so much of the unending conflict of the new mind with the old has been fought. And the conflict has been prolific in heroes, whose monuments, in the shape of their biographies, stand thick upon the field. They are a multitude even more significant for their quality than for their number. In the first quarter of the century the change begins. Coplestone feels in a dim way the dawn of the new era, and attempts by manipulation of terms, by the use of an ingenious but not very profound philosophy, to awaken the young mind to it and create room for it within the old forms. His pupil and admirer, Richard Whately, continues and perfects the process, acting, as Newman said later, on his younger contempories "like a bright June sun tempered by a March north-easter." Into the Oriel which Coplestone had quickened there came, in Thomas Arnold, a larger and humaner nature, with an outlook into history that promised to do for ancient Rome what Gibbon had done for "the Decline and Fall." Another sign of the coming change was the rise of learned philosophers like Hamilton, men of letters like Gibson Lockhart, and exuberant and imaginative athletes like John Wilson. Then into the rather exhausted ecclesiastical traditions of the university came Blanco White, with his practical experience of Romanism, vivified by the moral passion and the sceptical intellect which had made continuance within it an impossibility to him.

2. But with the second quarter of the century, what is regarded as the most characteristic Oxford movement of the century began. Its causes were many and complex. One cause was the fear lest political change should do for the Church in this century what it had done for the Monarchy in the last; and spare the divine right of the clergy as little as it had spared the divine right of the king.

Another was the association of political liberalism on the Continent with a negative rationalism which threatened death to the higher ideals of man and the State. A third was romanticism, which idealized a past it did not know, in order to find its realization in a present to which it was alien. But deeper than these, the factor that moved and unified it all, was the splendid sincerity of a few men and the transcendent genius of one man. Now that we stand at a distance sufficient to enable us to see the men in true perspective, we are impressed both by their extraordinary intellectual limitations and the elevation of their moral and religious aims. The late Dean Church is right in regarding the motive of the men as "the love of holiness"; but in religious conflicts the ways and the words of the men are seldom as holy as their motives or their ends. We may thus say that the interest of the Oxford Movement lay in its men. If knowledge or if intellectual veracity had been the conditions of success, they could not have succeeded; but the instinct which made its great leader issue in his early days R. H. Froude's *Remains* as a sort of impersonated programme, and in his later the *Apologia pro Vita Sua*, was an instinct which came of the insight of genius.

And here, if we may digress for a moment into a question which is not so irrelevant as it may seem, we may say that, in one sense, Newman's great contribution to the age is—the interpretation of Newman. He is the greatest subjective writer of

29

our age ; his power over it is but the fascination
exercised by his revelation of himself. In his more
scholastic treatises—in his dogmatic works, in his
attempts at historical writing—his strained subtleties,
his violent prejudices, his wilfulness, and his often
startling pettiness, make him one of the authors a
dispassionate student finds it hardest to read. But
the moment his own experience is distilled into a
sermon, or tract, or book, his peculiar and often
almost irresistible fascination appears. His *Present
Position of Catholics in England* is a sort of earlier
Apologia ; in it speaks the proud consciousness of
a man who knew the English feeling to Catholics,
and met it and rebuked it with lofty irony. His
Letter to the Duke of Norfolk may be described as
a later *Apologia*, written by a man who could not
but stay in a system he must believe infallible ; yet
stayed because he was able so to conceive what he
must believe, that he could, when convenient, qualify
out of existence the infallibility which guaranteed
his belief, or at least prevent it becoming too intru-
sive and troublesome. In his *Idea of a University*,
ideals and experiences which he owed to his loved,
lost, Oxford are embalmed. In his *Grammar of
Assent*, in a greater degree than in the *Apologia*,
his own mental history is analyzed and described.
The hymn which for the multitude most preserves
his name, owes its exquisite beauty and charm to
its being so perfect an expression of a mood that
was the man. But it is the *Apologia* that conquered

for Newman the reverence of the younger generation, and left them no choice but to believe in his sincerity and do honour to his motives. It is doubtful if there is anything in literature to compare with it. Here is a man who has practically determined the judgment of an age concerning himself, who has so interpreted himself as he was to himself as to compel his own day and his own people to accept the interpretation. Yet the man was a poet, and the poet's autobiography can never have *Wahrheit* without *Dichtung*, were it only because what has passed through the imagination is transfigured in the passage. The unconscious or the undesigned is ever the truest autobiography ; and even more than in any *Apologia*, the true Newman may be discovered in the books that come, as it were, unbidden out of his spirit, and seem still to throb as if they had within them the very breath of life.

It has not been the fortune of the other men of that time to be so splendidly transfigured and, as it were, embalmed for posterity in fragrant spices. But they have received all that loving hands, uncommanded by genius, could give them. John Keble has, perhaps, been happy in the brevity of his biographers ; but his name may remain all the more loved that it lives as an ideal rather than a being clothed in the coldest black and white. The voluminous *Life of Pusey* is all too pathetically faithful to his morbid nature, so curiously compounded of mystic emotion and pugnacious obstinacy. The two brothers-in-law,

Samuel Wilberforce and Henry Manning, have issued from the hands of their biographers as rather wounded and wingless seraphs ; while Ward, even in the hands of skilful and filial affection, appears as one who took himself more seriously than a sober and critical world will ever be persuaded to take him. But when all possible deductions have been made, it will remain true, that the University which produced these men did a greater thing for England and the Church than either the Church or England has as yet been able to conceive.

3. But over against the Tractarians stands another and no less imposing army of Oxford men. Tait, sober, cautious, essentially Presbyterian in temper, doubtful of new things, yet most wishful to find a *modus vivendi* for old and new, is a good type of a man who keeps the middle path and seeks safety in moderation. Next to him comes Stanley, who may be described as in a way a Broad Church Newman, without his self-consciousness, his subtle and corrosive scepticism in thought, his passionate imagination and mystic feeling, whose ideal is a mixed and organized State, as distinct from a graded and governed and obedient Church. Stanley was an ideal biographer, as Newman was a master of idealized autobiography ; and the *Life of Thomas Arnold* by the one may well challenge in the eyes of posterity comparison with the apologetic " Life " of the other by himself. One thing Arnold, as Stanley represented him, and Stanley himself, did in a quite singular and intense

degree—viz., reconciled minds that would otherwise have remained radically alien from the' English Church. Justice in this respect has never been done to either of the two men. The Anglican Revival has been ungrateful to its most distinguished and effectual friends. Their idea of a Church as comprehensive as the State, tolerant of differences, zealous for a liberal education, which the clergy might share but must not control; devoted to religion, yet aiming at the secular weal of all men and the reconciliation of all classes to each other and to God—made its way into the hearts of multitudes who had lived alienated from the Church in thought and feeling, and supplied an ideal which they believed could be realized in modern England. This idea made many gentle to the Church of Arnold and Stanley, who would have contended to the bitter end against the Church of Newman and Pusey. The Anglican Revival has, because of this idea and the men who were its sponsors, managed to penetrate where it could never have gone by itself; and these distinguished fathers of the Broad Church ought never to be forgotten by those who have so largely entered into their labours.

But it is not simply ecclesiastical men that Oxford has produced. I have but to raise my eyes to certain shelves in my library, and there stand names distinguished in literature, in politics and in the service of the State. There are the *Memoirs of Mark Pattison*, who would have been a kindly and loved man if he had only permitted himself to follow

nature ; and beside him is Conington, whom he did
not love, and Henry Nettleship, who loved him, edited
him, and cultivated in kindred spirit the old *Literæ
Humaniores*. Near him stands T. H. Green, with his
works edited and his life written by another Nettleship, who also all too soon was lost to philosophy and
learning. And beside them is a book which speaks
of Arnold Toynbee—the *Industrial Revolution*. In
the domain of purer letters, A. H. Clough sings a
song of yearning and of a hope that is close akin to
despair ; Matthew Arnold girds at imaginary Philistines in the most Philistinian manner and mood,
attempts to interpret a literature whose charm he
feels, but whose mysteries and problems he has failed
to master, while he allows his better self to escape
in polished and graceful verse. John Addington
Symonds discourses of Greek poetry and of the Italian
Renaissance ; and affords us glimpses into a singularly brave and hopeful spirit, defying disease to
arrest his work. And beside him stands William
Morris, who began as " the idle singer of an empty
day," and ended as the seeker and seer of a new and
higher social order. John Nichol, too, is there, a man
whom all men loved and all believed equal to greater
things than any he ever managed to do. And of
these we cannot think, without recalling the names of
men who had it in them to achieve as great things as
they did, but who fell before they had achieved. As
distinguished in their own order stand the statesmen,
even more numerous than the men of letters, exhibit-

ing that beautiful compound, so distinctive of our English public life, of the statesmen who have not ceased to be students ; and who have known how to beguile the tedium of the Senate or the Civil Service or the Bench by the cultivation of literature, preventing deterioration of mind in administrative work or in party strife by maintaining the studies which had been delightsomely pursued in the Oxford of their youth.

§ III. *Jowett as Reformer in University and College*

1. Into this Oxford, then, just when the Tractarian turmoil was at its fiercest, and the consequent cycle of academic change was about to begin, came Benjamin Jowett. What we have now to understand is the reciprocal action of Oxford on him and his on Oxford during his almost sixty years of residence. To it he devoted his life. He regretted that so many of her most capable sons forsook the university for the wider world ; he deplored, in particular, that Stanley preferred the Deanery of Westminster to his Oxford Professorship, for he believed that higher opportunities and a finer field could be found in the university than even in the Abbey where England has loved to bury her most honoured dead. He himself did not feel the fret and the worry and the distraction that make continued residence to so many impossible. Indeed, his own social tastes, his love of varied society, his desire to have it influence the university and the university to influence it, made him the man who has perhaps done more than any other

to make life in Oxford harder to the student and less kindly to study than even it was before. However that may be, it is clear that he rightly appreciated the value of Oxford as a sphere of influence, certain to repay lifelong service ; and no man who studies his life can deny that he was right.

His residence, I have said, began at a time when it was becoming obvious that reform must lay its compelling hand on Oxford. One of her most eminent sons had subjected the studies of the English universities to a most merciless criticism. Ecclesiastical strife, and its mischievous effects upon both the mind and work of the university, had showed that the terms of life within it must be changed. Universal subscription had proved positively disastrous ; the abuses which it had created, the opportunities it gave, when ecclesiastical passions ran high, to rankest injustice, had been proved in the experience of all reasonable men. Then increased knowledge of the Continental, and especially of the German universities, had created the most wholesome feeling of envy and of self-criticism. The work done by poorly paid German professors, their enthusiasm for science, the success with which they had cultivated the higher scholarship, their philosophical activity and industrious erudition, had made those who had come to know them feel how much Oxford had to learn, and how far she was behind in the work of science and research. In this work, men like Dr. Pusey, and still more his brother Philip, had been forerunners. But in Tait and Stanley it took practical shape ; and an agitation began in Oxford which meant that the university must be resuscitated and a new order of things instituted, or rather an old order restored. This seemed at first a simpler thing than it was soon found to be. The colleges had practically eaten up the university ; and it was no easy matter to find how they could be got to disgorge, or how the *disjecta membra* could be built into a homogeneous structure. It was thought that the system of professorships might be revived and extended, that new branches of knowledge might be added to its studies, new schools created, the university more adequately equipped for learning and research. And it was hoped that thus Oxford might be adapted to modern conditions and needs. Then there were multitudes outside the university seeking admission ; and there was within a corresponding desire to find terms which would make the entrance of fresher minds possible and their assimilation real.

Now Jowett sympathized with these views only in part. While from the first an advocate of university reform, he could hardly be called an efficient university reformer ; on the contrary, his policy was in many respects unwise and his action mischievous. He served Oxford by what he did for Balliol. He showed not what a university ought to be, but what a college could do for the university. His policy and ideals were not so much those that become a university as those proper to a college ; his qualities, intellectual, moral, and administrative, were of a kind that acted with intense force within the restricted area of the college, but would have wasted and spent themselves fruitlessly in the larger arena of the university. He had what may be described as the tutorial character, but not the professorial mind. His character was more powerful to influence than to please ; his prelections pleased more than they influenced. And so, true to his nature, he had more faith in the college than belief in the university ; he believed more in examinations than in lectures. Personal superintendence seemed to him a more vital matter than the dubious learning of the class-room, or the inchoate erudition of a not always coherent or lucid lecturer. But what probably weighed with him still more was the practical difficulty of shaping the policy of a university whose ultimate authority was a Convocation composed of members who could be summoned from the uttermost parts of the kingdom, and who in many cases were not qualified to discuss the question on which they were convened to vote. Reason governs as little in academic as in parliamentary politics. And in a body which was not educated by experience or even frequent discussion, but only came together on special occasions to do a special thing, great questions could never be seriously considered ; and were more likely to be settled by gusts of passion than by deliberative reason, or by arguments more whimsically subtle than morally and intellectually cogent. In such a case unreason is surer to reign than reasonableness. And Jowett had known Convocation summoned to do the most high-handed things, and had seen it do them. And so he came to doubt its competence and to expect no reform in a body over which Convocation remained in a sense legislatively supreme. In this he was by no means singular, for even in Stanley's " Life " we find an ironical account of its proceedings illustrated by a letter to the *Times*, with the characteristic signature, " An M.A. who abhors Convocation."

2. But while to Jowett the university was an intractable body, the college was, if not a manageable society, yet a society where it was possible for a potent individual to accomplish something. And it was characteristic of Jowett to refuse to lessen his personal influence by forcing it to attempt what it could not perform. And so his energies and ambitions concentrated themselves upon his college. Balliol was to him wife and child, home and family. He lived for it, gave himself up to it. It used to be said that whatever uncertainty there was as to the Master's faith, there was none as to his belief in Balliol. He watched its undergraduates with the keenest and most jealous eyes; he followed their later careers with the solicitude of a parent, appreciative of every act and achievement which reflected honour on the college. He laboured unweariedly to make it famous; replenished its ranks from the capable among all sorts and conditions of men; carried out his dream of university extension, which

was to secure to poorer students the advantages of
tuition without the expenses of in-college residence,
and rigorously enforced his method of personal
discipline and superintendence. He gave generously
from his own resources, and persuaded his friends to
give generously from theirs. While no lover of
æstheticism, he pressed music into the service of the
college, and made the Sunday evening concert a new
educative agency. While no devotee of athleticism,
he supplied the college with a field where its young
barbarians could play. On the one side, he dealt
with Balliol as if it were a school; on the other, as if
it were a university; with the result that, though he
stepped into a great inheritance when he became
Master, he yet left to his successor the inheritance
vastly enlarged and enhanced. It was indeed a high
achievement to make and to keep, in a period when
new studies meant new expenditure, one of the
poorer colleges in the university the college whose
scholarships were "the blue ribbon" for which
English public schools eagerly competed, and on
whose books the men most ambitious of academic
distinction were eager to enrol their names.

§ IV. *Jowett as Scholar and Thinker*

But we must look beyond the Master of Balliol, and
consider other sides of his picturesque personality.

1. I have already said that his chief claim to remembrance will not rest on his scholarship. He had,
indeed, many fine intellectual qualities, but they were

literary rather than scientific, critical and discursive rather than philosophical. He thought by intuition, rather than by any process of ratiocination. In scholarship, properly so called, he had only a remote interest ; for its severer methods he had a positive distaste ; for its history he had little appreciation, and few of its great names appealed either to his admiration or respect. This rather curious defect comes out in the biography in a very characteristic way— the paucity of letters to scholars, or concerned with scholarship. There are many letters to scholarly pupils and friends, but few on questions of purely scientific or philosophical interest. He writes to many distinguished people, both men and women. His letters are full of wisdom, whether secular or spiritual, of fine feeling, of delicate insight, of a high sense both of his own duty and of theirs. They express a large conception of the significance of life and its possibilities, and the obligation common to himself and his correspondents to make the most out of it. These letters cannot do other than raise the general idea of the man. He was often suspected of paying too assiduous court to the great, and of loving to surround himself with persons of name. He would, in a sense, have pleaded guilty to the charge, for he had a keen perception of the immense possibilities associated with station. He felt that an aristocracy of rank which was also an aristocracy of intellect and character had opportunities such as were granted to no other class ; and he frankly cultivated the society that he held to promise most for the culture and character of the State. But certainly no man ever lay less open to the charge of toadying to the great. If their advisers had always been as honest, yet delicate and sensitive, in advice, their lives would have accomplished more for the common good. We are, therefore, not at all surprised at the number of letters to women in high places ; and I confess that if his circle had been larger, and his letters always as charming and simple and sincere, it would have been the better for those who seem destined to become ever more potent forces in our public life. But what does surprise one is that he seems to care so little for learning ; that his correspondence has so little to do with it or with the learned. It is remarkable that the man who was the head of Balliol, a representative Oxford scholar, should yet have had so small intercourse with the scholars either of Great Britain or the Continent, and have been so little concerned in the discussions, the investigations, the discoveries, the controversies, that during his long and active life agitated the world of letters.

I have called this want of interest in learning and the learned characteristic of the man, and so it was. Though a student of Plato, yet Platonic scholarship did not interest him, and for its history he had something that may almost be described as aversion. It never seemed to him like a real chapter in the history of the human mind, significant both of its growth and of the influence of the great master on whose interpretation he himself so long and so genially laboured. He was impatient with the older scholarship, because its methods were so unlike his own, and seemed to him violent and subjective. Yet subjectivity was the very note of his own work, and made his Platonic studies and dissertations so largely a reflection of himself. He disliked systematic thinking in whatever field. He feared metaphysics, deplored their fascination for the young mind, regretted their reign within his own college, even under a man he so much admired and loved as T. H. Green. He warned so distinguished a philosopher as his successor in the mastership against a too devoted cultivation of metaphysics. He dreaded their effect on literature and on knowledge, which he somehow persuaded himself to regard as injuriously affected by constructive and systematic thinking, The continuity which was so alien to his own habits of thought, he suspected when it was incorporated in men who loved thought all the more that it was concatenated and could be expressed in a progressive dialectic.

2. The same defect is seen in his relation, or rather want of relation, to the more speculative spirits and tendencies of his own time. This is most apparent in regard to one with whose aims he had much in common, Frederick Maurice. They were contemporaries, and engaged, though not always for the same reasons, in the controversies which made for freedom and comprehension ; but so far as Jowett is

concerned Maurice might as well never have been. The mysticism, the neo-Platonic idealism, the passion for the universal and positive, of the latter, provoked something more than impatience in the former; the more that, though both were alike English, they were divided by almost racial antipathies. Even where their aims agreed, their methods and means differed. Maurice influenced men on their spiritual and ethical side, but Jowett on the intellectual. The one developed moral enthusiasm, but the other tended to repress it. The socialism of Maurice was a generous endeavour to save those wronged or neglected by society, and to ameliorate their lot; but the work among the masses which Jowett commended to his young men was more as an agency for their own education. It is no less curious that Mansel and Mill are unknown both to his correspondence and his table-talk; though the former was once a potent person alike in the thought, the politics, and the society of the university, more justly celebrated for his *jeux d'esprit* than for his learning or his philosophy; and the latter was a great authority in its schools. Hegel indeed he had studied, and had "gained more from him than from any other philosopher"; but it was from his historical rather than speculative side. And to Comte he had a positive aversion.

It was this very quality of mind that attracted him to Plato; and it was also the secret of his imperfect sympathy with Aristotle. He disliked the logical rigour, the intellectual formalism, the ency-

clopædic and systematic temper, in a word, the
scholasticism of the one; he delighted in the imaginative freedom, the variety, the inconclusiveness, the
habit which discussed rather than solved problems,
which he found in the other. The spirit in Plato
which shed light on all things without finally adju-
dicating on any, was the very spirit that Jowett
loved. The impersonated and suggestive discussion
suited him; it exercised mind and cultivated the
mind by its exercise. It supplied views of life, of
society, and the State, that interested, illumined,
educated. It enabled him to turn Plato into an
English and modern classic, and to make him a
centre round which thought could freely play. What
he gave us was indeed Jowett's Plato rather than
the Plato of history, of philosophy, or of classical
scholarship.

3. We may better illustrate at once the action
and effect of Jowett's mental characteristics by comparing him with a contemporary with whom he had
much in common, but still more in difference—Mark
Pattison. Both were academic Liberals, but with
such radical differences as expressed fundamental
unlikeness. The academic ideal of Pattison was a
university consecrated to research; but Jowett's was
a college devoted to the discipline and the culture
of mind. Pattison had a horror of the mental habits,
the formal drill, and shallow omniscience created
by examinations; but Jowett had immense faith in
their educational function and efficiency. Both were

theological Liberals, but Pattison's Liberalism was historical and critical, Jowett's was personal and intuitive. Both passed through the Tractarian storm, and its fires scorched Pattison, while they hardly warmed the atmosphere about the soul of Jowett. It added to the pessimistic nature of the one a deeper element of disappointment, but it left the sunny optimism of the other unshadowed and undisturbed. Both were successful tutors, and were disappointed in their first expectation of the headship of their respective colleges. The disappointment, added to the loss of his earlier faith, permanently embittered Pattison ; but it only made Jowett a more potent because a more self-contained and silent man. Yet these external coincidences are significant only in so far as they indicate internal differences, which had their more characteristic expression in the region of their studies and the style of their work. Pattison had more the mind and temper of the scholar, Jowett of the man of letters. The history of scholarship was a matter of extraordinary interest to Pattison ; he loved to see the action of intellectual forces in any given time, to analyze the ideas and expound the method of other ages than his own ; to trace the behaviour of societies which embodied systems, of tendencies which expressed prevailing habits of mind. But neither the history nor the archæology of thought had any real or living interest for Jowett. Mind was to him too individual a thing to have a collective history or to make its antecedents worthy of scientific investigation and construction. Pattison loved the great scholars of the past. The labours, the struggles, the poverty, the wanderings of Casaubon directly appealed to him ; the Stephenses and the Scaligers were names he loved ; the parts they had played in the revival of letters, in the development of printing, in editing the classics and advancing classical scholarship, made them, as it were, men of flesh and blood to his imagination. The Patristic labours of the Benedictines, the classical erudition of the Jesuits, their use of it for their revolutionary and reactionary purposes, their mode of assailing scholars that were not of their Order, and discrediting by invented scandal the work of men they could not pervert ; the apostasy of Lipsius, the pomposity of Salmasius, and the ferocity of Milton, all interested him, and were pressed into the illustration of the history and the growth of European scholarship. But Jowett had no feeling for the heroes of humanism ; their method was not his ; their implements were less perfect than his own ; their interpretations were often grotesque ; and he was too conscious of the difference of mind and times, and too much interested in classical literature for its own sake, to care much for the men who had contributed to the making of it intelligible. Even in his own country and in his own subject this was true. The Cambridge Platonists lay almost altogether outside the region of his sympathies. Bentley, as Professor

Campbell says, seemed to Jowett "wanting in judgment, which is the first element in criticism"; he
was only an example "of the baneful influence which
a great philologer, like a great philosopher, may
have on whole generations of his followers." He
was, "upon the whole, a man who kept bad company
in literature."[1]   Selden, indeed, he greatly admired.
But it was not the Selden of the *De Jure Naturali
et Gentium*, nor the Selden of the *De Diis Syris*;
rather it was the Selden of the "Table Talk," who
supplied him with such aphorisms as, doctrine in
theology is "rhetoric turned into logic," and the
Authorized Version of the Bible is "the best translation in the world."   And so, too, he loved Samuel
Johnson, whose criticism of life and of men, of
books and of manners, made him a man after
Jowett's own heart.

§ V. *Jowett as Theologian and Churchman*

1. The mental qualities which regulated his judgments and achievements in the field of scholarship
determined also his attitude to religious and theological questions.   He had an intensely religious
nature.   He was a man capable of doing his duty
with almost stoic severity; but his duty was apt
to be conceived under rather peculiar and personal
forms.   There is no truer thing said by Professor
Lewis Campbell than this: "What Jowett said of

[1] "Life," ii. 186.

Greek literature became more and more applicable to himself: ' Under the marble exterior was concealed a soul thrilling with spiritual emotion.' "[1] He progressively realized the truth of Aristotle's words, " Pure thought alone is ineffectual." But the feelings and imagination in him had to contend against a singularly shy and yet emotional temper ; there was nothing he could so little do as unbosom himself, even to his dearest friends, as to what was deepest in his heart. Very early he says to Dr. Greenhill: " Why I don't write to you oftener is that I do not like writing about religion ; and it seems so cold and prosy to write to an intimate friend about anything else." [2] This difficulty increased rather than lessened with the progress of the years. But several incidents narrated in the " Life " show his simple and tender piety, such as his going to Sir Henry Acland when he was ill and reading to him " in that small voice, which once heard was never forgot," the fourteenth chapter of St. John ; or the scene, pathetic in its sacred simplicity, at the deathbed of Archbishop Tait. But I may be allowed to tell, because it is so significant of both men, one little incident which is not told in the " Life." [3] When Robert Browning was staying with him on, I think, his very last visit, he learned, when it was too late to attend, that the Master had

---

[1] i. 388.   [2] i. 109.

[3] It is told, somewhat imperfectly, in Hon. Lionel A. Tollemache's *Benjamin Jowett*, p. 21.

conducted, as he greatly loved to do, a religious
service for the college servants. Browning was met
by a friend walking in the Garden Quadrangle
greatly agitated, and he said to him, " The Master
is the very soul of goodness; yet he makes me
quite indignant. He is hospitality itself; he will
eat with me, talk with me, walk with me, read with
me, take me into his very bosom; but one thing
he will not do, he will not *pray* with me." But
this inability, which Browning so much regretted,
came from a native shyness which much intercourse
with men had deepened, and which the fear of being
irreligious even in religion, or of seeming to mean
more than he actually said, had intensified. But
just because intimate speech on the mysteries and
higher experiences of religion was so difficult to
himself, he was a hard critic of those who found
it easy. Thus he says : " I never hear a sermon of
which it is possible to conceive that the writer has
a serious belief about things ; if you could but cross-
examine him, he would perjure himself every other
sentence."[1] He was anxious to be veracious in
what he himself said, and dreaded very early in his
career the too great stress which "the ordinary
divinity of the day" "laid on words," creating "a
sort of theological slang," which was held to be of
"the fundamentals of the Christian faith." He
quotes, with approval, in a letter to Stanley, the

---

[1] i. 153.

words of a lady who had said to him : "We Liberals should not talk about freedom, but about truth— that is the flag under which we fight." [1]

2. It is easy to misunderstand Jowett's attitude towards Subscription, and to be unjust to him on the ground of it. In order to a proper appreciation of his attitude two things have to be remembered —the mental habit which we have already described, and his own personal experiences. The long enforcement of Subscription at the universities had a most injurious effect upon the mental integrity of the subscribers. The mischief began at a very early date. Boys who could not possibly know the meaning of the act had to subscribe; they must in almost every case have done it as a simple matter of academic form; but the doing of it at all was an initial vice accentuated at every stage in the academic career. Many of the men who subscribed as a condition of holding a fellowship did it intending to do with the articles of belief very much as they meant to do with the statutes of the college—adapt them as far as they legally could to existing conditions. There was thus begotten in the minds of the more thoughtful the worst of all attitudes to religious belief—that of giving a formal assent to what was understood not to represent internal conviction. This mischief was immensely aggravated by the miserable partisan politics which governed

---

[1] i. 299.

the university during the major part of Jowett's career, and which had, by means of tests, instituted an "abominable system of terrorism." He had seen Subscription used by the aggressive Tractarians to damage Hampden. He had seen men who had resisted Hampden's elevation to the bishopric solacing their souls with the idea that his act of Subscription cancelled their obligation to further resistance. He had seen the same weapon of Subscription turned against the very Tractarian party which had made it so powerful an instrument of offence, and he had witnessed this misuse culminate in the comic tragedy of the degradation of Ward. He had seen "all Balliol, as usual, furious"[1] over the giving of an honorary degree to the then American Minister, because he had been a Socinian clergyman. And later in his own experience it was turned into the means of inflicting cruel humiliation on a proud and sensitive spirit; for he was compelled to re-subscribe before being allowed to enter on his Professorship. And this was done at the instance of men who were in certain respects as faithless to the Articles as he was himself, and as little scrupulous in their interpretation of their obligations when the literal sense seemed contrary to their convictions. The subtleties of " Tract XC." show how fast and loose the ultra-orthodox, when their own views were at stake, could play with the

---

[1] Church, *Life and Letters*, 43.

very formula which they could not allow their opponents any latitude in interpreting. The slicing,
as it were, of the Articles, which is not uncommon
even now, was then a fully perfected art ; with the
aggravation that the men who did it most effectually
in their own interests, were the least tolerant to the
men who attempted the same thing, but because
of another conscience. The whole attitude was,
therefore, that of the legalist rather than of the
moralist ; formulæ which were meant to express
high truths were construed as effete statutes to which
conscientious acquiescence could not be expected.

3. This is said, of course, in explanation of Jowett's
attitude, not in justification of it. He and his opponents were alike latitudinarian—he in one direction,
they in another. Nor did his attitude imply indifference to theology, for in it he had from the first very
great interest. He early wished to see a theological
school founded in the university, though, by a curious
Nemesis, when it was founded, he was excluded from
the theological board. His reason was that he wished
to see the clergy trained in the university rather than
in diocesan colleges. And he held that the more
liberal the education, the more liberal would be the
clerical thought : for the highest theory of the office
was held by the men who had the least fitness for it.
For the clerical order, as such, he had no admiration ;
he rather thought that "loyalty to the clergy was
treachery to the Church." He was, if one may say
so, a rigorous individualist in religion ; he loved to

elaborate his own belief, to let his mind play upon history and dogmas, and to translate them into the ideals which could regulate his life. In a letter he describes "the true basis of religion as the life and death of Christ"; but what that means he straight-way proceeds to explain thus: "The life and death of Christ in the soul, the imitation of Christ; the inspiration of Christ; the sacrifice of self; the being in the world, but not of it; the union with God and the will of God such as Christ had."[1] He con-ceived the ideal as the essential element in religion. Christ was to him an ideal rather than a reality: a name that denoted an object of reverence and thought, rather than any historical person. This is perhaps putting it more sharply than he himself would have done, though he has stated his position with almost equal precision. He wanted to see the personal Christ become an ideal Christ, and this pass into the idea of Goodness.[2] But he was not a man that inconsistencies terrified. He had moods that needed only the ideal, and moods that craved for the historical; but he loved to find himself in the Gospels, just as he liked to make Plato the vehicle and medium of his own thought. It is one of the points where the action of a loved author may be subtly seen in similar manifestations in the most opposite of minds. Jowett had too sane an intellect to allegorize; but Plato taught him to idealize. He

---

[1] ii. 273.   [2] ii. 15.

learned a mysticism that made him independent of history, but dependent on the ideas which were the ultimate realities of his life.

4. As Pattison exhibited a contrast to Jowett's attitude to scholarship, so we may find in Dean Stanley a contrast to his attitude to theology. The affinities with Stanley, both in thought and aim, were far more intimate than those he had with Pattison. They formed, indeed, as near a parallel to Jonathan and David as modern conditions permit of. They had almost everything in common—they thought together, planned together, travelled together, worked together. They were in constant consultation about the most intimate matters of private belief and public conduct. Their friendship, indeed, was almost ideal: but in its unity it represented characteristic and fundamental differences. Stanley's was a picturesque mind; he had, as it were, a sensuous imagination; its images came through the senses, and were clothed in the raiment the senses supplied. Where allegory and analogy stood to Newman, history and geography stood to Stanley. But he did not use them as the true romanticist did. He loved to people a place with the figures of the past; but the more unlike these figures were, the more picturesque the contrast they offered to each other, the more attractive did they seem to Stanley. If we may so distinguish, we may say that he was a cosmopolitical rather than a mediæval romanticist. For him romance lay not in the imagined chivalry of a time behind us, though it was

a time that had never been ; but rather in the dissimilarities of the persons, the times, and the causes
he could bring together and combine or contrast in
the strong light and shade of his pictorial pages.

But the creations of the sensuous imagination did
not appeal to Jowett.   Pictorial history was to him a
weariness—almost, indeed, a childishness.   While he
had no love for the sensuous image, he had an intense
love for the ideal.   He delighted to translate a cruder
into a riper conception, an inchoate into a simple and
classic thought.   But this was not the most fundamental distinction between the two friends.   Stanley
was a born warrior ; he was a man with a mission,
and the mission was one which could be carried out
only by an aggressive policy.   He had inherited
Arnold's great idea, and wanted the Church to be
co-extensive with the State, as varied, as rich in the
elements and persons it comprehended.   All the fine
figures which he loved in the past he rejoiced to co-
ordinate in an ideal unity, which he would fain have
translated in the present into the practical unity of
an organized religious society.   So he laboured to
modify Subscription, that it might cease to be a
barrier to the conscientious Dissenter ; and he strove
to make Westminster Abbey not simply the tomb of
English heroes and saints, but the home of English
religion, where the representatives of its varied sections and societies could meet in worship and participate in the common sacraments of their religion.
But Jowett had no mission to be progressive or

polemical in behalf of those who stood outside the society to which he belonged. He could hardly understand why a man should make difficulties about Subscription, when it had become too conventional a thing to be taken seriously. It seemed to him more than a trifle foolish—indeed, only a sort of illiberal scrupulosity — to stand aloof from the National Church because you did not agree with its creed. As a matter of fact, nobody did agree with that creed. Time and use had modified Subscription sufficiently to ease the tender conscience of its pain.

This, indeed, is putting it more sharply than is quite just, if it be understood to apply to academic as well as ecclesiastical tests. He looked at things as they were, found men possessed of differences, and in order to make the university national, which tests prevented it being, he came to urge their abolition. But in the ecclesiastical sphere his attitude was rather " use your liberty," than " make liberty a constitutional and legal thing." It would hardly be too much to say that Jowett never understood either the Dissenter or Dissent, though nothing could exceed his personal kindness and consideration to the Dissenters he knew, or anything be stronger than his determination that men, whether in the university or in the college, should have their due, irrespective of creed. He was perhaps, in the heart of him, inclined to think that to be scrupulous about Conformity was to make much ado about nothing. The pathos of the Dissenter's position did not appeal to him. He had difficulty in conceiving that a man might have an absorbing desire to be a member of a great university, and yet feel under an imperious obligation to refuse membership on the only terms that were then possible. He had in his secret mind the suspicion that Dissent was a sort of obstinacy, an illiberal rigour and vigour of mind that education would soften and finally eliminate. We are often less patient with those who agree with us in part than with those who wholly differ from us. Social toleration of a Dissenter is probably a rarer thing than social toleration of an infidel or an agnostic. The one is a vulgar middle-class form of religion ; the other implies some intellectual distinction and independence. This attitude was not without a parallel in Jowett's own experience. When he was most suspected and persecuted, a friend called to tell him that the orthodox felt more kindly to Congreve and the thoroughgoing Positivists than to him. But in nothing did he so show himself the philosopher, as in the equanimity with which he bore suspicion and isolation.

These sentences must not be construed to mean any lack of appreciation of Jowett's services to the cause of freedom, whether in the college or the university. These services were varied, distinguished, and effectual. It is, indeed, one thing to be opposed to tests, and quite another either to understand or to appreciate the action of a man who will endure serious civil or social or academic loss rather than submit his conscience to their yoke. But Jowett's merit lies not so

much in the region of theory as of practice ; he was
much more than an advocate of abolition ; he honestly
tried to act justly towards the idea of an open college
and a free university. This is by no means so easy a
thing as it may look : and it is especially hard in the
case of one who is head of a college, which is by its
very history, constitution, and traditions a closer and
more rigid society than the university of which it is a
component part. The repeal of tests may be a simple
legislative process, but the enforcement, even of the
repealed tests, may be regarded by men of a certain
order of conscientiousness as an administrative expedient, which they feel bound in some form to follow.
One of the last things that the head, or even in certain cases the tutor, of a college with the history and
antecedents of the Oxford colleges, may be able to
realize, is that his college has ceased to be an ecclesiastical institution, and has become a place of education open to men of all churches and all creeds.
Jowett was far too honourable a man ever so to abuse
his academic position as to use it for the purpose of
winning ingenuous minds from their ancestral faith.
On this point illustration would be easy and grateful,
but it must suffice simply to say that he seems to me
to have been an academic statesman and administrator who knew how and

> " when to take
> Occasion by the hand, and make
> The bounds of freedom wider yet."

5. But the contrast to Stanley suggests another

and most distinctive characteristic. Jowett was one
of the most persistent of men, though one of the least
polemical. If he found his way barred, or if to sur-
mount the bar threatened to be too toilsome a process, he turned aside to seek a passage by some other
way. He had such a feeling for the conditions of
moral influence, that he would not dissipate it by
allowing it to break against obstacles that were for
the moment irremovable. He preferred to go round
the mountain rather than scale the heights. Thus
when the storm was raised, first by his *Epistles of
Paul*, and next by his essay in *Essays and Reviews*,
he simply dropped theology for the time being and
turned to Plato and philosophy. So, too, when he
missed the Mastership and found the college uncongenial, he forsook the Hall and the common-room,
lived much alone, devoted himself to his work and to
his pupils, preparing for the day when he could
emerge from his seclusion and play a more commanding part in the college. So, too, in the matter of his
Professorship, he felt keenly the insults to which he
was exposed both in assuming the Chair and when
refused the salary that was his due ; but he devoted
himself to the duties of his Chair, leaving chivalrous
friends to champion his cause. And his method was
as well suited to his ultimate success as to his immediate peace of mind.

But enough has been said to indicate Jowett's place
and function in the making of modern Oxford. He
was an educator rather than a scholar, a man of

letters rather than a man of learning. He is distinguished at once by the comparative feebleness of his scientific interest and the intensity of his interest in persons. He was an enthusiast for the creation of the best men for the service of the Church and State ; and he believed that there was no place for their creation equal to a well-equipped, well-governed, and well-disciplined college, where the most cultured minds of the present introduced the learners to the classical literatures of the past. And he lived to make the college he ruled what he conceived a college ought to be. It was a noble ambition nobly carried out. And the attitude of his own mind qualified him for the work he elected to do. He educated by suggestion and criticism rather than system and construction, stimulated by questioning rather than informed by instruction. But, whatever may be thought of his educational method or his literary work, one thing is certain—he will be remembered above all his contemporaries as the man who lived for his college, and made it a supreme force in the academic life of the nineteenth century.

June, 1897.

Butler & Tanner, The Selwood Printing Works, Frome, and London

The Person of Christ and the Philosophy of Religion

Demy 8vo, cloth, 12s.

The Place of Christ in Modern Theology

Eighth Edition. 8vo, cloth, 12s.

" In some respects this is a great book. It strikes out a new and generally a fresh line of argument. The story of the development of thought during the Christian ages is a brilliant and vivid historical sketch, and will be a most useful piece of reference to the student."— THE DEAN OF GLOUCESTER, *in the Pall Mall Gazette.*

" His work is, without doubt, one of the most valuable and comprehensive contributions to theology that has been made during this generation."—*Spectator.*

" Dr. Fairbairn starts from the principle that Christian theology must be based on the consciousness of Christ ; and from the fact that the historical Christ is only now, nineteen centuries after IIis appearance on earth, being recovered for human knowledge and faith. . . . A more vivid summary of Church history has never been given. With its swift characterization of schools and politics, with its subtle tracings of the development of various tendencies through the influence of their environment, of reaction, and of polemic ; with its contrasts of different systems, philosophies, and races ; with its portraits of men ; with its sense of progress and revolt—this part of Dr. Fairbairn's book is no mere annal, but drama, vivid and full of emotion, representative of the volume and sweep of Christianity through the centuries."—*Speaker.*

" The volume before us is the most weighty and important which he has yet issued. His treatises entitled ' Studies in the Life of Christ ' and ' A City of God ' contain much of great value, but in a sense they gave promise of better things to come, and this promise has been amply fulfilled . . . in this very able and learned and altogether admirable discussion on ' The Place of Christ in Modern Theology.' . . . The book is evidently one for the times, and doubtless attention will be widely drawn to it on account of the great importance of the subject of which it treats, the honoured name of its author, and the conspicuous ability, the competent learning, and the gracious spirit which it everywhere displays."—*Scotsman.*

LONDON : HODDER & STOUGHTON, 27, PATERNOSTER ROW.

BY THE SAME AUTHOR

Sixth Edition. Price 7s. 6d.

The City of God

A SERIES OF DISCUSSIONS IN RELIGION

CONTENTS :—Faith and Modern Thought.—Theism and Science.—Man and Religion.—God and Israel.—The Problem of Job.—Man and God.—The Jesus of History and the Christ of Faith.—Christ in History.—The Riches of Christ's Poverty.—The Quest of the Chief Good.—Love of Christ.—The City of God.

"We cannot more strongly express our sense of the value of the work than by saying that we have read it through twice ; and that we are meditating to give it a third perusal."—*Contemporary Review.*

" We find in the discourses which form this volume much able statement and much vigorous thought, and an admirable comprehension of the great questions which are being discussed in our day with eagerness and bated breath."—*Scotsman.*

" We have read many of the truly brilliant passages of this volume with thrilling delight. The theology is orthodox, the logic is accurate, and the learning profound."—*Ecclesiastical Gazette.*

" The author approaches the various subjects passed under review in his striking and beautiful book with a poetic depth and refinement of feeling and expression which we greatly appreciate. He frequently waxes into an eloquence that is both thrilling and impressive. The language is nearly always as felicitous as it could well be, and never lacks vigour."—*Literary World.*

" It contains some of the best work he has yet given to the world, and includes many discussions on topics of the profoundest interest to all who take part in the strife between modern Scepticism and Religion."—*Expositor.*

" The object of the author is to satisfy that ' spirit of restless inquiry,' by showing that, so far from there being any antagonism, there is, in fact, the fullest harmony between Christian faith and all that can be known by the highest reason. This position is maintained in the book before us in language as vigorous as the logic is keen, and with all that breadth of culture and of sympathy, that deep philosophic insight which have won for Dr. Fairbairn so high a place amongst the apologists and expounders of the Christian truth. But Dr. Fairbairn is an apologist of the best type ; he defends Christianity by explaining it."—*Leeds Mercury.*

" A book whose every page is replete with matter that invites to thought. There is growth in the volumes as well as in the themes discussed. Respecting Principal Fairbairn's treatment of his varied themes we have to say that it is marked by a keen, strong grasp of his subject, great vigour of thought, and beauty as well as clearness of language. While he handles deftly and well the sword of argument in defence, he is still more intent on the task of reconstructing Christian theology. His tone is high and hopeful. He expects and seeks to further loftier developments of Divine truth and life. Such a book needs no words of commendation."—*Dundee Advertiser.*

" The work as a whole displays deep learning and high eloquence, and is pervaded by the Christian spirit."—*Westminster Review.*

LONDON : HODDER & STOUGHTON, 27, PATERNOSTER ROW.

CPSIA information can be obtained
at www.ICGtesting.com
Printed in the USA
BVHW07*0940220818

525056BV00015BA/1733/P